W9-DET-933

100 of the World's Best BARS

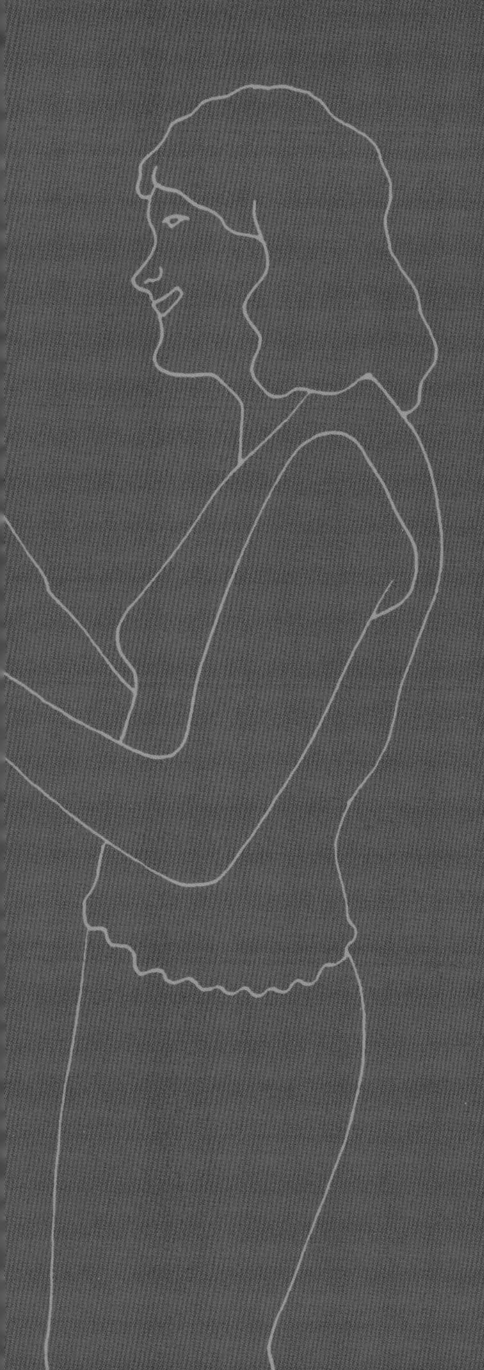

100 of the World's Best

BARS

images
Publishing

Published in Australia in 2005 by
The Images Publishing Group Pty Ltd
ABN 89 059 734 431
6 Bastow Place, Mulgrave, Victoria, 3170, Australia
Telephone: +61 3 9561 5544 Facsimile: +61 3 9561 4860
books@images.com.au
www.imagespublishing.com
The Images Publishing Group Reference Number: 576

National Library of Australia Cataloguing-in-Publication data

100 of the World's Best Bars.

ISBN: 1 920744 50 9
Includes index.

1. Bars (Drinking Establishments) – Pictorial Works. 2. Bars (Drinking Establishments) – Designs and Plans.

725.72

Coordinating Editor: Aisha Hasanovic

Designed by the Graphic Image Studio Pty Ltd, Mulgrave, Australia
www.tgis.com.au

Film by Mission Productions Limited, Hong Kong
Printed by Sing Cheong Printing Co. Ltd. Hong Kong

IMAGES has included on its website a page for special notices in relation to this and our other publications. Please visit:
www.imagespublishing.com

Contents

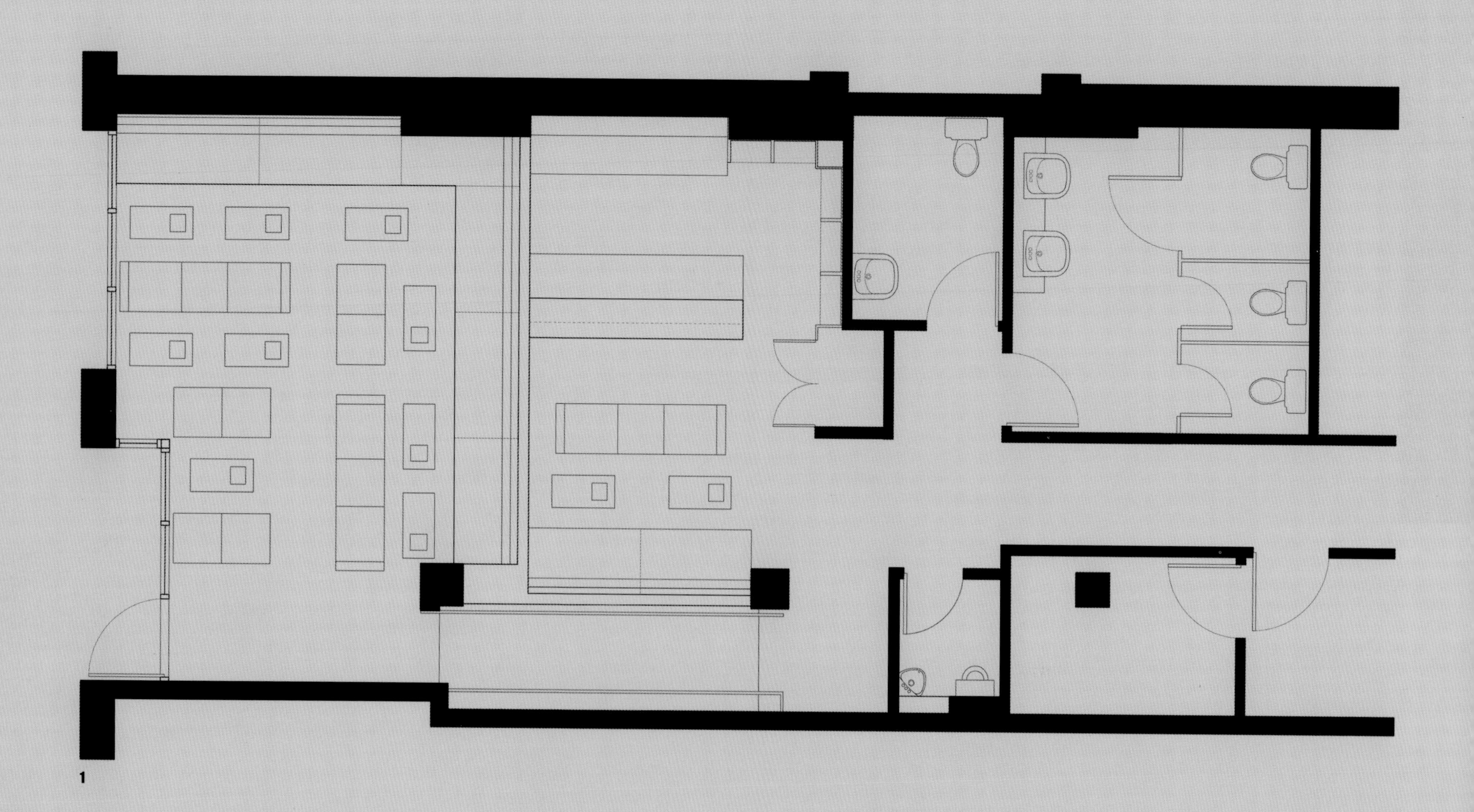

1

1 Floor plan

2 Bar, settees and cocktail table

3 Settees, cocktail table, and interior mural

4 Cushions by Bombast give accents to Afterglow's seating

5 Lounge seating bathed in pink lighting

Photography: Janis Nicolay

VANCOUVER, **BRITISH COLUMBIA, CANADA**

Afterglow **Lounge**

EVOKE INTERNATIONAL DESIGN

2

3

4

5

Usage: Cocktail bar/lounge

Area: 1200 square feet/ 111 square meters

Materials: Epoxy flooring, walnut veneer, white Corian, ultra suede, polyurethane

Afterglow Lounge was conceived as an extension of Glowbal Satay Bar & Grill (a previous Evoke International Design project) and acts as a multifunction space accommodating 30–40 people for cocktails as well as working as an overflow space for the adjoining restaurant.

The street-level windows have been covered with a graphic design to create a sensual interpretation of the Afterglow theme, while also creating a sense of privacy for those inside. Small Corian cocktail tables were custom-designed by Evoke and the couches were designed by Bombast Furniture.

The color scheme is hot pink, red, and chocolate brown. The quality of light was an important element of the design so all of the interior walls were painted white, allowing for the natural glow of the pink lighting to provide a sophisticated and sensual atmosphere.

1

2

DAYLESFORD, VICTORIA, AUSTRALIA

Altar Bar

SIX DEGREES ARCHITECTS

3

1 Sculpted bulkheads

2 Seating

3 Bar

4 Bar detail

Photography: James Legge

4

Client: Tina Banitska

Usage: Bar

Materials: Artifacts, stained glass, concrete, marble, fabrics

The Convent Gallery is perched high on the hill overlooking Daylesford and sits within extensive historic gardens. The heritage buildings are a collection of Victorian styles. The Altar Bar was one component of a larger project that included refurbishment of the conference and function facilities.

The client has worked tirelessly to collect religious and historic pieces that have been layered throughout the buildings by the architects.

In winter the atmosphere is rich, the colors lush, and fabrics comfortable, providing a warmth in which to nestle by the fire and look out over the mist-filled surrounding valleys and township. During summer, the bar opens out to a veranda drenched in western sun.

The detailing is referential and inclusive, allowing new fabrics and materials to blend with collected artifacts. The bar is sculpted from altar paneling and two of the entry screens feature timber tabernacles. The stained glass work by artist Tony Hall of Azez Glass perches prominently upon an in situ concrete bar top, which is separated by a piece of Carrera marble.

The challenge was to create intimate areas within the existing large, open Victorian room. An historic cast iron altar railing is suspended high above the bar and held by new white gloss steel columns. Floating fabric panels and dropped sculpted bulkheads mediate the tall ceilings and create intimate spaces below for nooks and cushioned seating.

1

COLOGNE, **GERMANY**

Apollo Bar

DAVID LING ARCHITECT

2

3

Usage: Bar/comedy club

Area: 2153 square feet/ 200 square meters

Materials: Lead sheet, birch plywood, ebonized fir wood

The German version of the David Letterman Show has found its home in two 1950's movie theaters on the Ring Street in Cologne's medieval inner core. Conceived as a TV production studio with multiple uses, the facilities include the actual theater renovation, an exclusive late-night bar run in conjunction with the show, and a comedy club in the cellar. The Late Night Bar is an exclusivé enclave specifically for Harald Schmidt and his talk show guests, as well as members of the audience to commune in a more intimate setting and enjoy a post-show drink.

A curved wall contains the actual bar. Resembling the inside of a ship's hull, it is a curved and sloped cherry wood surface. Opposite this is a lead-clad folded wall. The forms are juxtaposed in a dialectical relationship of opposites: a gentle fetus-shaped curve versus a lightning bolt, the sensual and warm versus hard edged and metallic.

The bar accommodates up to 100 people and is conceived as a living room of sorts with lounge seating in the form of banquettes and armchairs. The lighting is entirely indirect with the exception of the TV monitors embedded in the walls and niches, and the myriad candles on each table.

1&2 Bar and seating

3 Curved bar detail

Photography: Helmut Stahl

1 Cantilevered walnut stair

2 Double-height atrium

3 Ground-level bar facing piazza

4 Ground-level bar, illuminated glass corner, and café seating

5 Tables at upper level

6 Overlapping illuminated acrylic panels

Photography: courtesy Gabellini Associates

2

1

3

MILAN, ITALY

Armani Café

GABELLINI ASSOCIATES

4

5

6

Usage: Café/restaurant

Area: 3500 square feet/ 325 square meters

Materials: Stainless steel, translucent glass

The Armani Café was developed as part of the 100,000-square-foot Armani Center in Milan and opened in October 2000. Gabellini Associates designed the haute vegetarian cuisine restaurant in close collaboration with Giorgio Armani and the restaurant operator. The café required a casual bar space for coffee service and light lunches, as well as a more formal 80-seat dining area.

The café occupies a two-level space on the corner of Via dei Giardini and Via Croce Rossa on an important public plaza, enjoying high visibility and urban views through a full-height glass storefront. The main entrance to the café from the plaza opens into a double-height atrium space that connects the ground-level bar area to the first-level restaurant suspended above. A long stainless steel bar with a floating curved glass counter extends between the atrium bar space and a more intimate seating area below the suspended floor above. A backlit translucent glass corner invites the customer to a walnut staircase winding discreetly around a soft blue corner element to the restaurant area above.

Three sides of the restaurant seating area are wrapped by sliding blue and white acrylic translucent panels that form a horizontal light band around the space. Transverse light slots in the ceiling accentuate the sleek horizontality of the space, projecting views toward the atrium space and the public plaza beyond. The double-height atrium wall pierces the restaurant level, dematerializing at its edge to allow views into an open kitchen through a suspended clear glass corner. An American walnut bench with flexible cushions provides perimeter seating, while custom-carved Corian café tables with elegantly curving bases appear to spring from the poured concrete flooring.

1

2

3

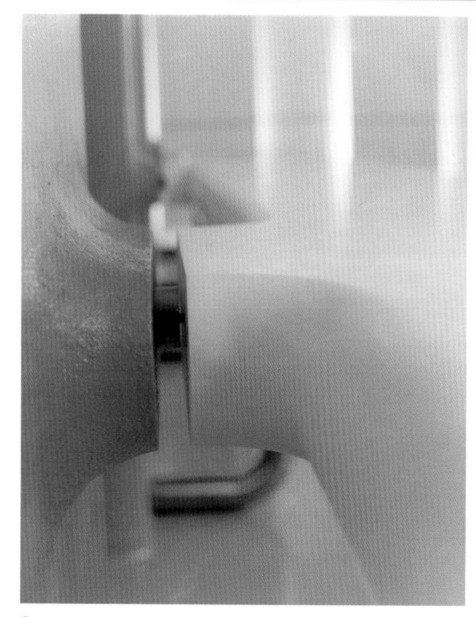

4

REYKJAVIK, ICELAND

Astro Bar

MICHAEL YOUNG STUDIO

5

Usage: Bar/nightclub

Michael Young Studio was asked to refurbish one of Reykjavik's oldest buildings. Battling with a venue that was protected by heritage laws and a lack of straight lines, a well-designed club with four bars and two dance floors was eventually built.

The architect used the concept of a swimming pool crossed with a picnic area to 'bring in a little bit of the outdoors'. With the assistance of a local pool-building company, the final result is an icy-looking interior that suggests Iceland's weather.

1 Barstool detail
2 Overview
3 Corian bar
4 Bar detail
5 'Smartie' pool

7

Opposite Sticklight detail

7 Young chairs

8 VIP room

9 Magazine sofa

Photography: Ari Magg

8

9

1

SAN FRANCISCO, **CALIFORNIA, USA**

Bambuddha Lounge

NOMADIKA DESIGN STUDIO

1 Dining room and lounge

2 Dining nook

3 Bronze Buddhas

Usage: Bar/ restaurant/lounge

Area: 5000 square feet/ 465 square meters

Materials: Epoxy flooring, mother-of-pearl paneling, grass cloth

The 1950's architecture of this pre-existing building added to the sleek geometry of the new interior. Bambuddha Lounge invites the outdoors in with its large sliding windows that open to the outdoor patio, which features an indoor/outdoor stacked-stone fireplace, and Nipa huts situated around the swimming pool for dining and lounging. The rich, cream-colored, glossy epoxy floor and grass-cloth walls juxtaposed against the dark walnut-stained dining furniture, which is lit from below, give the appearance that the room is levitating. The dining nook with its jewel-toned upholstery, chandeliers, and bronze mirror cut into 10-inch-thick planks resembles a cozy but retro-glamour lounge. The 22-foot walnut-stained bar features mother-of-pearl panels and has five single-stream fountains as its backdrop.

3

5

Opposite Restaurant

5 Outdoor seating

Photography: Matthew Hranek (1,2,4,5); Russel Karchner (3)

1

GENEVA, SWITZERLAND

Bar Genf

PLAJER & FRANZ STUDIO

1 Bar

2 Seating area

3 Motorsport bar with red lighting

4 Hanging counter

5 Motorsport bar detail

Photography: diephotodesigner.de

2

4

3

Usage: VIP lounge

Area: 1679 square feet/ 156 square meters

The language and values of the BMW brand were the main influences behind the choice of materials for the walls, floor, and furniture of this sophisticated bar in Geneva. The designers hoped to communicate a sense of comfort and style—concepts synonymous with the dynamic BMW brand. The wood, seat fabric, etched glass, and the use of intelligent materials, like the wall covering featuring marble gravel in resin, subtly moderate this idea.

5

1

2

FRANKFURT, GERMANY

Bar 1AA

PLAJER & FRANZ STUDIO

3

Usage: VIP Bar/lounge

Area: 2110 square feet/ 196 square meters

The primary intention of a bar space at a trade show is to serve VIPs and the media. A clear overview of the cars presented is as important as the opportunity to rest and meet.

The architects had initially aimed to create a bar with a normal ceiling height, but they were able to use the entire 6 meters to maximize the appearance of the venue and create a strong impression. The space that divides the hanging elements above the bar was used to light the counter and the back. The lamps were installed 1 meter through a rectangular opening, creating a sharp beam of light on the bar top.

A metal panel behind the bar features printed images of the car design process, while the bar and the floor were built from walnut, creating a mixture of elegant and technical materials, reflecting the dynamism of the BMW brand.

1 Bar

2&3 Bar and seating

4

5

4 Car design process detail

5 'LEM' barstools

6 Floor plan

Photography: diephotodesigner.de

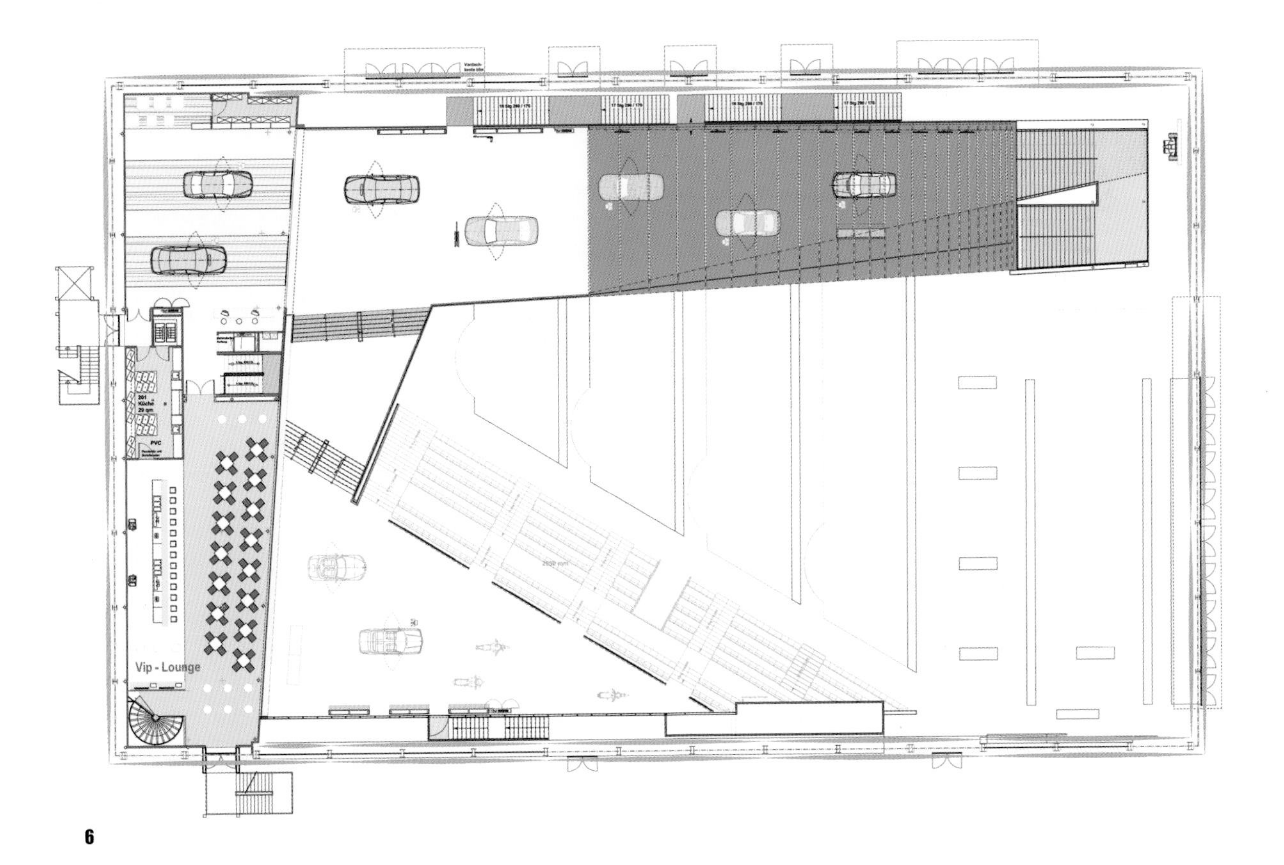

6

1 Mirror, with etched human silhouettes

2 View of mirror from bar

3 Seating area

4 Barcode design entry

5 Bar

Photography: Alberto Ferrero

LODI, ITALY

Bar Lodi

FABIO NOVEMBRE

4

5

Client: Antonio Corsano

Usage: Bar/nightclub

Area: 753 square feet/ 70 square meters

The first space encountered upon entering the bar has rounded corners and floor light-spots, all designed from the barcode of a book written by Fabio Novembre, *A Sud di Memphis,* (Idea Books, Milano 1995). Very few people had read the book, and this was architect's attempt to publicize it.

The bar area was built with the help of a large mirror on the right side. Its shape is a big tunnel, its color brown. The air conditioning system is hidden from view inside this tunnel. The lighting for this area was solved by scratching out the silver from the back of the mirror in the shape of the human silhouettes, taken from Richard Avedon's portrait *Andy Warhol and Members of The Factory*, and by putting some fluorescent lights in the back of it. This had the effect of giving the sense of the presence of people even when the bar was empty. In the shape of a perfect shadow, the mosaic on the floor reflects the silhouettes on the ground.

1

BERLIN, **GERMANY**

barlounge 808

PLAJER & FRANZ STUDIO

2

1 Front bar

2 Bisazza mosaic tables, bar at rear

Usage: Bar/lounge

Area: 2583 square feet/ 240 square meters

The given theme for barlounge 808 was a 1960's American lounge bar. Its design recalls the cool sophistication of a decade in which patrons made an effort to dress up before sipping Martinis.

The venue is divided into two main areas; a café/bar in the front (serving food and drinks), and a cocktail lounge in the back. Design elements like the aquarium, light coves, and costume furniture determine the relaxed atmosphere in the space. Speakers and air conditioning are invisibly integrated in the wooden wall paneling.

The wedge-shaped venue is situated on a corner. Floor-to-ceiling windows, 40 meters long, front two streets and meet in a glass curve at the street corner. The airy drapes serve a double purpose: they allow those inside to watch the action outside, while projecting seductive glimpses of partying silhouettes to passersby. The windows all open to provide a seamless transition to the terrace so that in summer tables and chairs spill out onto the sidewalk in typical European fashion.

3 'Members only' cocktail lounge

4 Furniture designed by plajer & franz studio

Photography: Fritz Busam

3

4

1

2

3

MELBOURNE, **VICTORIA, AUSTRALIA**

Bear Brass

MADDISON ARCHITECTS

1 Entrance from atrium

2 Typical intimate compressed space

3 Raised lounge

4 Dissolving storefront

5 Sit-up bench with view to city

4

5

Usage: Bar

Area: 2798 square feet/ 260 square meters

Materials: Concrete, cork, terra cotta

Bear Brass consists of several unique areas within a small tenancy; its size appears to be bigger than it actually is. Spaces were compressed to emphasize tightness and restriction, such as the area in and around the bar. The hydraulic and mechanical service installations were seen as an opportunity to enrich the experience.

The reconfigured and relocated storefront demonstrates ongoing investigations into ways of dissolving the enclosure. This is particularly important, given the connection this tenancy has with the Yarra River promenade and views to the city.

Changes of level in the built-up timber flooring seamlessly flow inside to out, with sliding bi-folding and gas-strutted glass panels disappearing so that the spaces reach toward the city. This gesture is repeated again with the in situ concrete bar tops that flow through the external glazing system.

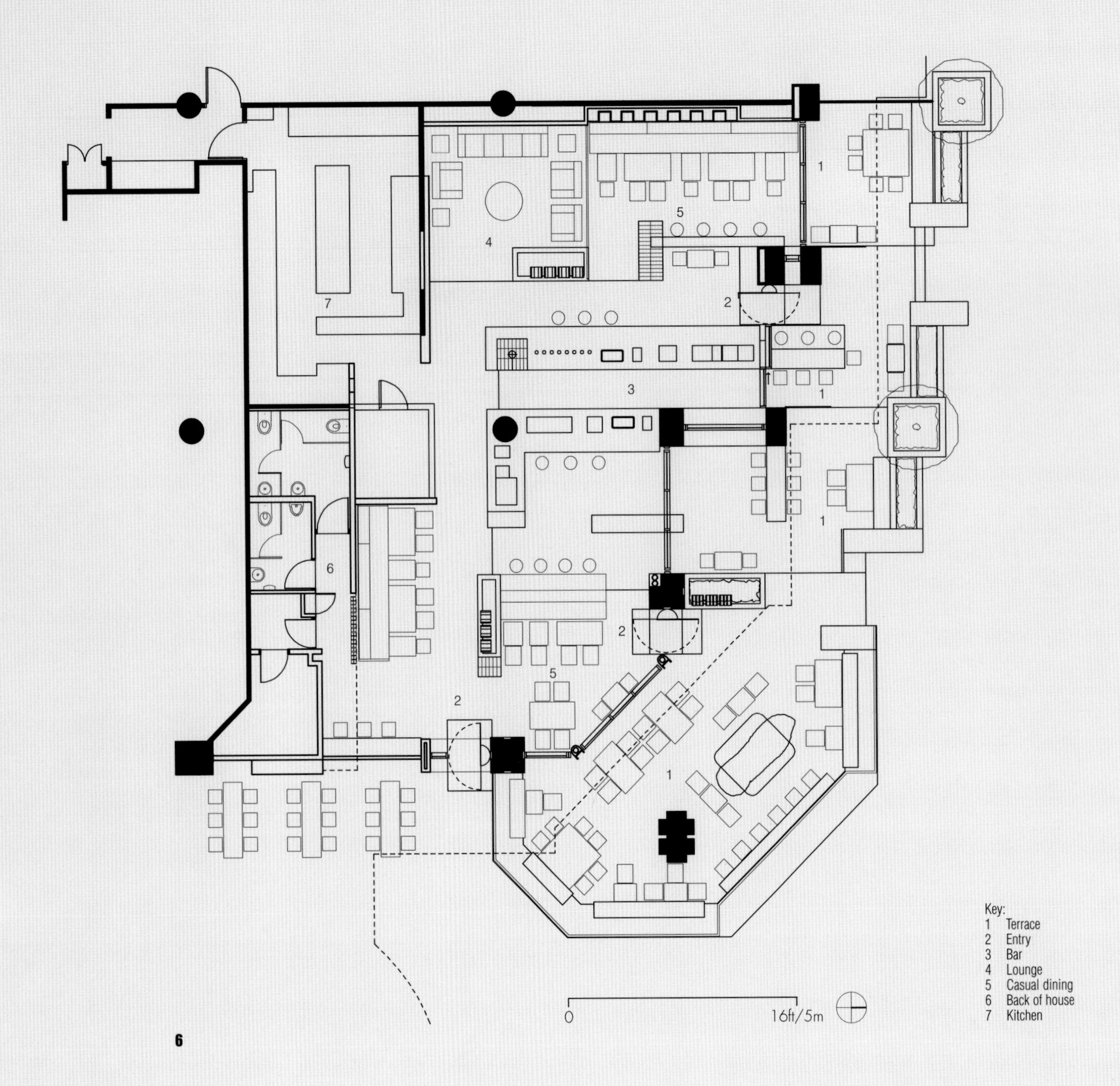

6 Floor plan

7 Bar puncturing façade

8 Bar and glazed pizza oven

9 Outdoor seating

Photography: Trevor Mein

7

8

9

1

2

1 Exterior

2 Interior, different lighting

3 Upstairs seating/beds

4 Main area

Photography: Marcus Gortz

3

BANGKOK, THAILAND

Bed Supperclub

ORBIT DESIGN STUDIO

4

Usage: Bar/restaurant

Materials: Corrugated iron, steel, pre-cast and polished concrete, laminated glass

Designing a custom-made building to house a new concept bar and restaurant was the challenge given to Orbit Design Studio. Most satisfying for the designers was doing the entire job, from architecture and interiors through to the graphic design. This allowed an unprecedented degree of control and integration throughout.

Rising out from the dusty streets of Bangkok, the result is an ethereal, white oval tube that sits bathed with light while colors and shadow play over the frosted glass frontage. A hot red door at the top of a long ramp draws patrons inside.

The distinctive, angled oval façade is now something of an icon in this vibrant city. The tube is entirely made of steel. Inside, the pristine, all-white interior acts as the perfect antidote to the chaos and clutter outside. The smooth clean lines of the furniture and interior match the gentle curve of the building.

Most inviting of all are the beds that line the walls on the ground and mezzanine. Big, soft cushions welcome guests to lounge and dine in style. The open plan nature of the space, and the arrangement of beds and seats allows an uninterrupted view. The blank white canvas of the interior allows a wash of color from the computer-controlled lighting system, so the space can take on many different moods. The bar side is a muted gray, to darken the space and provide a more urban feel. Upstairs there are more beds, and the same curves and shapes are echoed.

1

MELBOURNE, **VICTORIA, AUSTRALIA**

BOND Lounge Bar

PLAYGROUND MELBOURNE PTY LTD.

3

2

1 Club from entry

2 View of dining booths, with 'infinity effect' mirror

3 Bottle display, main bar

Client: Phil Anderson

Usage: Bar/club

Area: 6458 square feet/ 600 square meters

As a visual creation, Bond draws its influences from a combination of Art Deco ideology and minimalism. The simple concept signifies the design affair with repetition, perspective, and unity, while the emphasis on structural integrity accompanied by diverse surfaces creates softness and warmth. Materials such as hard wood, leather, and multi-faceted tiles initiate style and comfort, and reflect the essence of touch and color reminiscent of the Art Deco era. The use of rare veneers stained in classic Tuscan, mixed with plush carpet and stone, further embodies intimacy and elegance.

Entering the space into the reception area, an unpretentious yet inviting mood is set through the use of mixed materials enhanced by a lighting source. Stepping down into the main area, the concaved interior that spans from end to end nestles inside the old office space like a cocoon.

The concave ceiling is functional as well as aesthetically pleasing, and creates a depth and perspective that encompasses a great acoustic presence. Sound installations are predominantly hidden in the walls and the room allows for a small live music ensemble to perform in a low-reverberant atmosphere. Video projector and audio ports placed strategically over the entire area allow for multimedia functionality.

4

5

6

7

4 Make-up room

5 Side lounge and entry from main bar

6 Side dining area and lounge

7 Members' room and bar

8 Bottle display, members' lounge

9 Service bar from dance floor

10 Side lounge and bar

11 Feature wall

Photography: Shania Shegedyn

8

9

10

11

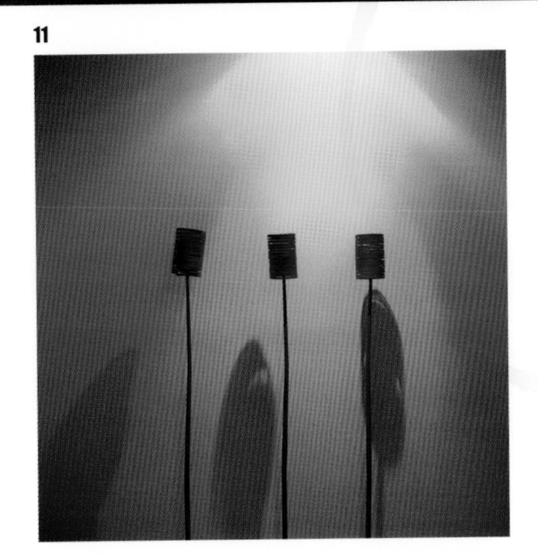

1

2

1 Granite-top bar

2 Timber staircase to bedrooms

3 Lounge bar

EDINBURGH, UK

Borough

BEN KELLY DESIGN

3

Client: Callison Eaton
Usage: Bar/restaurant

A former warehouse was converted into an extensive bar and restaurant with a members' bar and nine bedrooms. The visitor arrives on a black terrazzo floor that forms a 'runway' from the reception, parallel to the main bar, providing a direct route to the restaurant. The main bar consists of a rough-sawn granite front with polished grooves and a clean polished top, while the rear bar consists of a full-height mirror, tiered glass shelves, and dramatic display of backlit bottles. The bar is further defined within the space by a pressed-metal ceiling imported from the US and a row of over-scaled globe light fittings.

A Douglas fir downstand linking the reception area wraps around the lounge bar at a high level, terminating in a dramatic staircase that leads to the upper level members' bar and rooms. The downstand visually contains the lounge, while providing a servicing barrier and allowing the full ceiling height to be used. Exposed structural beams and clusters of smaller globe fittings dramatize this height.

The lounge bar provides seating for 80 on a combination of luxuriously upholstered leather wing chairs, sofas, and banquettes in a range of three complementary colors. Precast tables in matching black terrazzo sit on the dark walnut floor that runs though into the restaurant. The restaurant seats 70 people and features circular booths with backs of varying height, offering intimate tables. Angled mirrors mounted to the perimeter walls provide distorted glimpses of fellow ►►

4

4 Timber reception desk turns into granite bar; terrazzo floor walkway leads to restaurant

5 Restaurant

6 Floor plan

7 Ceiling detail

Photography: Alan Forbes

diners. While being sufficiently removed from the lounge bar, the restaurant area can also be completely closed off by means of a full-height curtain.

The overall impact is of a strong, unique, and elegant environment through the thoughtful blend of modernity and a sense of timelessness. The timeless design will enable Borough to age gracefully and retain its popularity for many years to come.

5

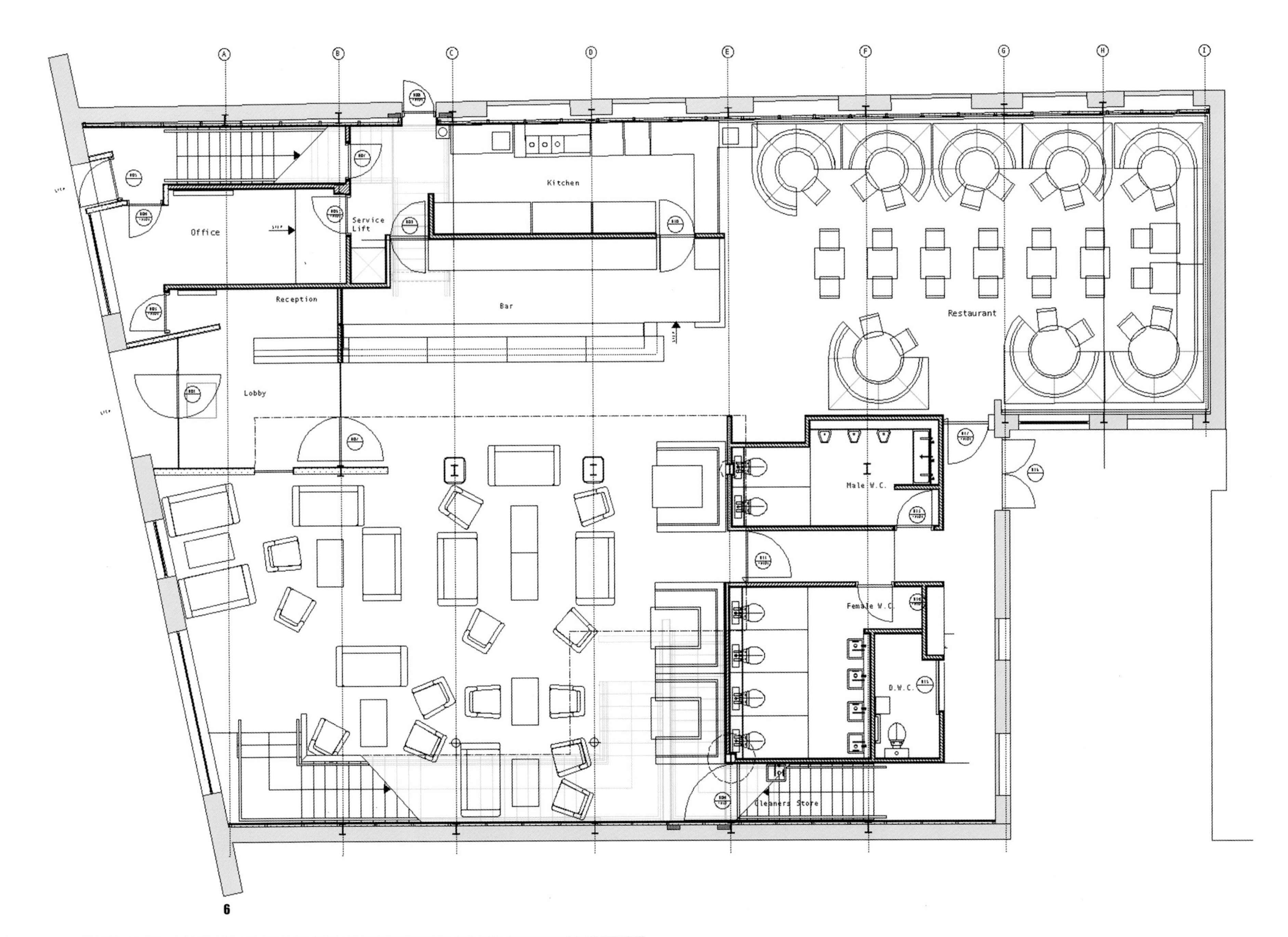
A
B
C
D
E
F
G
H
I
Kitchen
Office
Service Lift
Reception
Bar
Restaurant
Lobby
Male W.C.
Female W.C.
D.W.C.
Cleaners Store

6

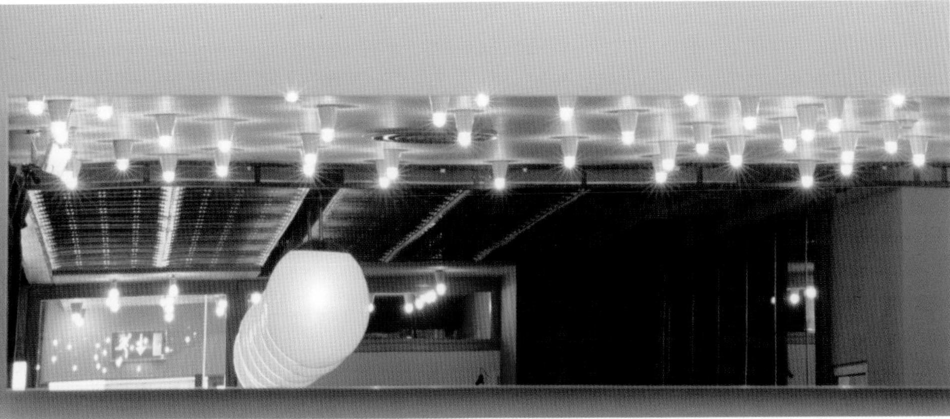

7

1

2

ANTWERP, BELGIUM

Brasserie National

VINCENT VAN DUYSEN ARCHITECTS

1 Entrance
2&3 View into restaurant area
4 Bar

3

4

Usage: Bar/restaurant

Architect Vincent Van Duysen and his team worked on the renovation and decoration of the venue and created a sober but rich interior. The Brasserie National lies at the head of the building where the Fashion Nation is established. The mission of the architect was to create a contemporary restaurant inside the neoclassical character of the existing building, and an authentic brasserie with all its conscious and unconscious connotations. The result is an interpretation of a classic brasserie, with contemporary shapes and modern materials.

The sophisticated materials used in the restaurant are in harmony with the building and its function, and the arrangement of the fixed furniture provides the ambience. The black-brown ceiling is reminiscent of the smoked ceilings of previous times, and creates, with the dark wall, a more intimate atmosphere at the bar. All the brasserie archetypes have been used and reinterpreted: a waiter station with a copper reading lamp, a mirror and illuminated glazed shelves behind the bar, the copper-bronze nameplates, and menu trays.

Although the materials and the overall design are contemporary, the new venue is in complete harmony with the character of the existing building.

5

5 View from rear of restaurant

6–8 Walls are covered with travertine stone

9 Bar stools are an extension of the Vincent Van Duysen Collection for B&B Italia

7

9

6

8

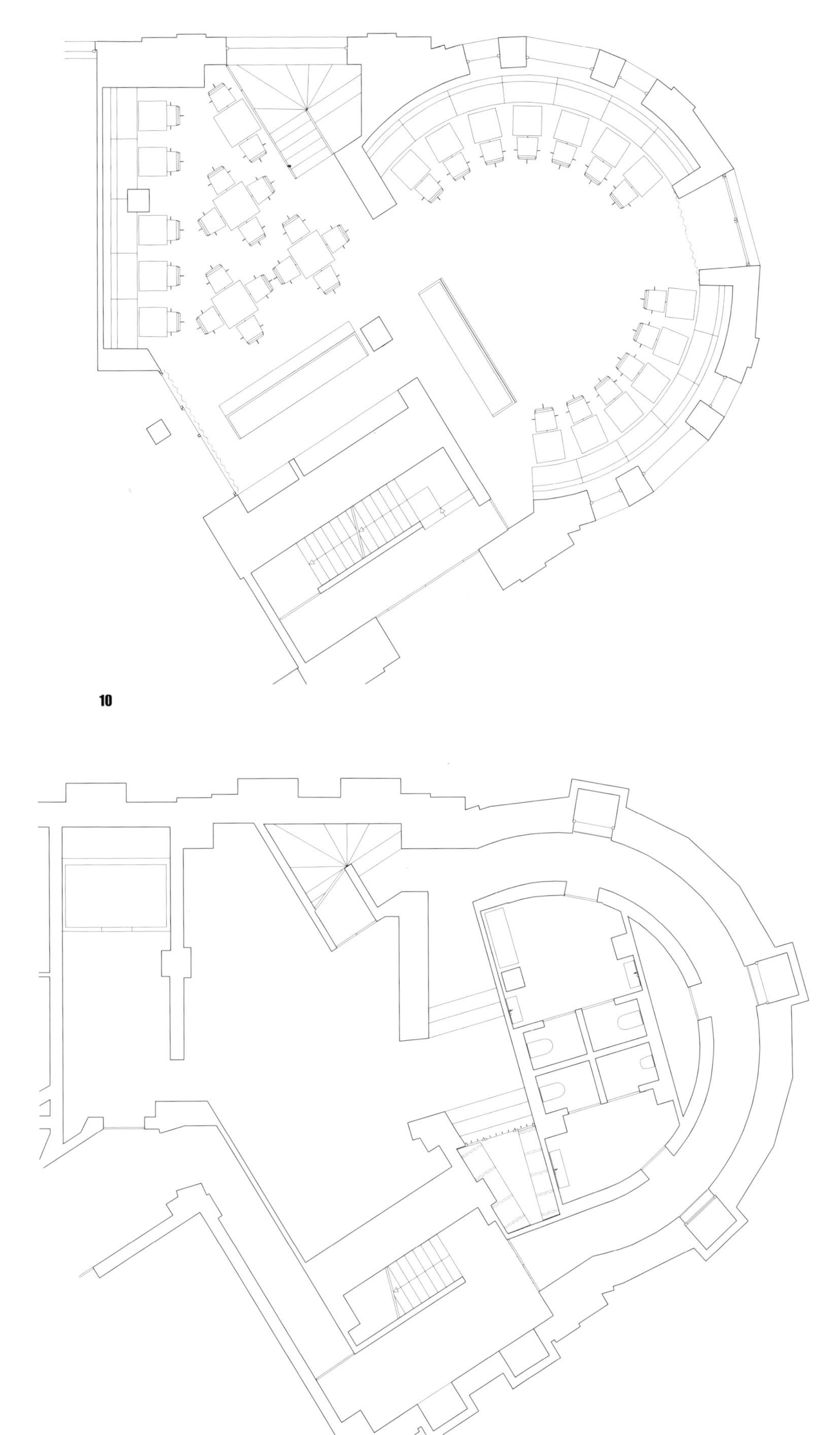

10

11

12

10 Restaurant floor plan

11 Floor plan showing restrooms and technical facilities

12 Waiter station

Photography: Alberto Piovano

1

VENICE, **CALIFORNIA, USA**

The Brig

JOHN FRIEDMAN ALICE KIMM ARCHITECTS

1 Parking lot façade and mural

2 Entrance with sliding table

2

Usage: Bar

Area: 2200 square feet/ 204 square meters

Presented with a run-down, 52-year-old landmark bar with an exterior mural, the architect's aim was to intensify the building's ability to act as a gateway to Venice, maintain the original, ad hoc quality of the bar's interior, and create a public space with a mood that welcomes the diverse spirit of the city. This project is a combination of the raw and refined, the old and new, the highly deliberate and ad hoc. It maintains the edginess of the original bar while adding a new sensuality and fluidity.

The simplicity of the interior plan belies the richness and diversity of materials: colors that simultaneously allow the bar to maintain its original character while appealing to its new patrons. Unifying all elements of the space is the pink and purple terrazzo that forms the ceiling, walls, and floors of the restrooms before it spills out in olive green to cover the floor areas outside. Similarly straddling the crude and the refined is the ceiling of plastic laminate panels suspended over the bar in a standard T-bar ceiling grid. Lit from above, it gives off a sensuous glow that provides much of the bar's mood.

Compressed between the floor and ceiling are a variety of wall surfaces. Of special note is the molded linoleum wallpaper that wraps the freestanding bathroom volumes at the end of the space. Dripping with silver paint, these volumes serve as silent witness to the events unfolding in front of them. Also effective is the 'miniskirt' of glowing sheer white fabric that hangs beneath the bar. Finally, a 14-foot-long steel table with a circular ashtray that moves in and out of one of the bar's two front doors is crucial to the identity of the project.

3

4

5

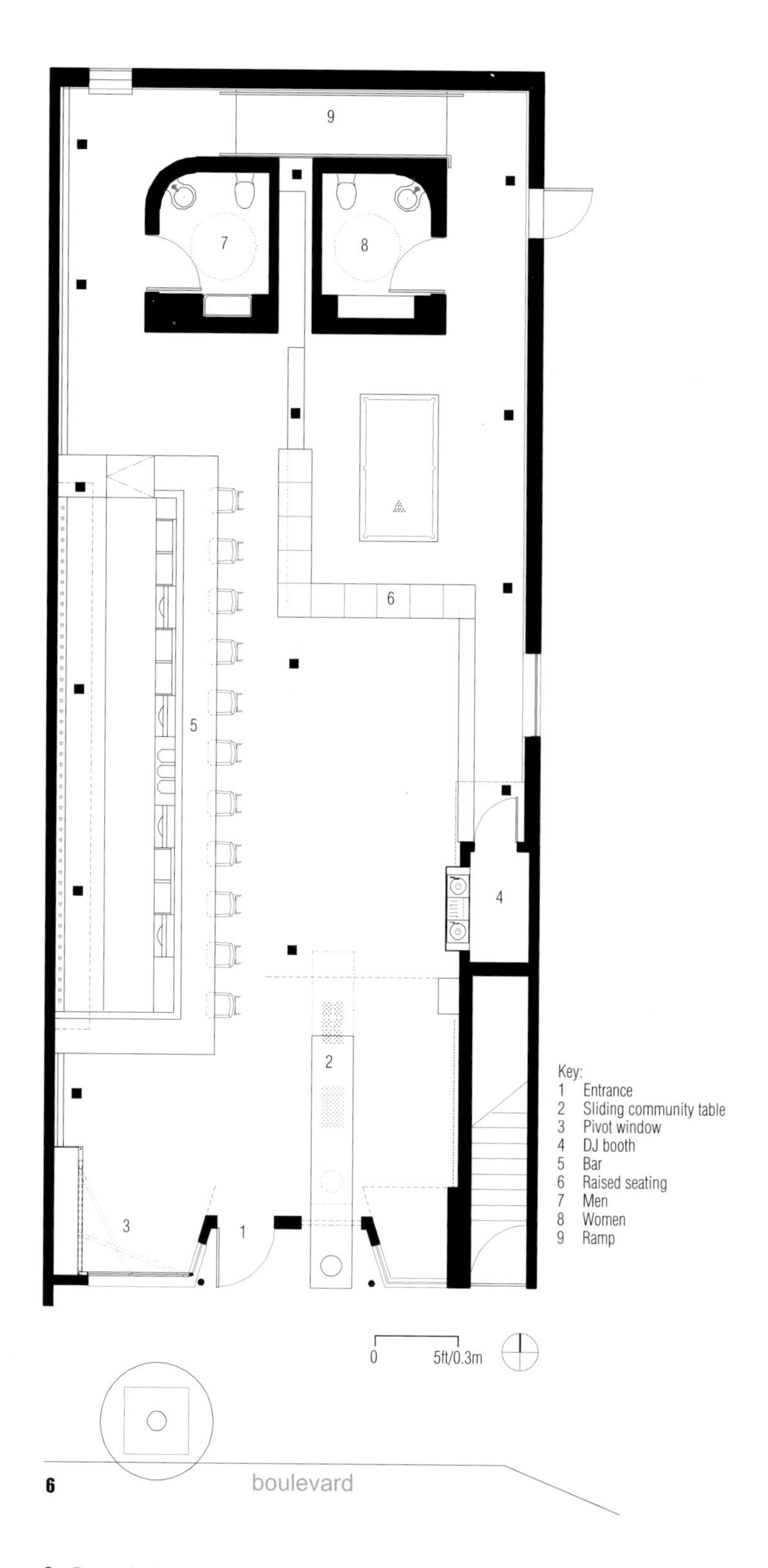

6

7

8

3 Bar and raised seating area from sliding table

4 Entrance and pivot window from DJ booth

5 Restroom volumes from DJ booth

6 Floor plan

7 Bar

8 Raised seating area from sliding table

9

10

11

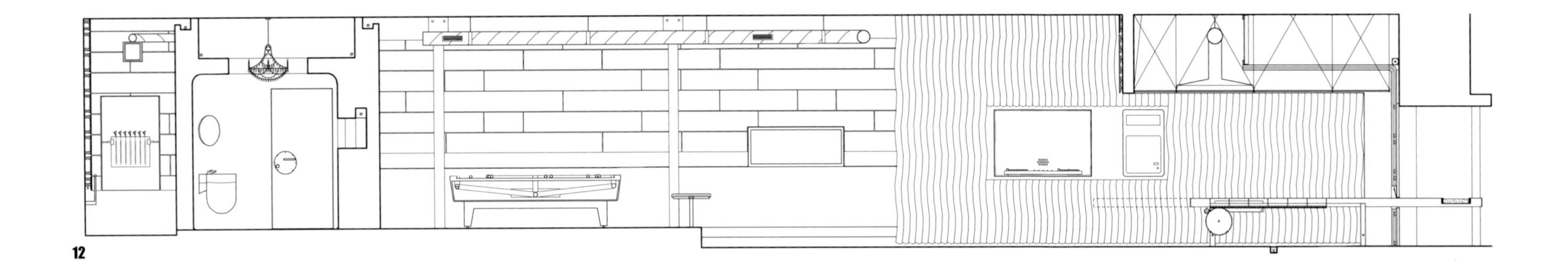

12

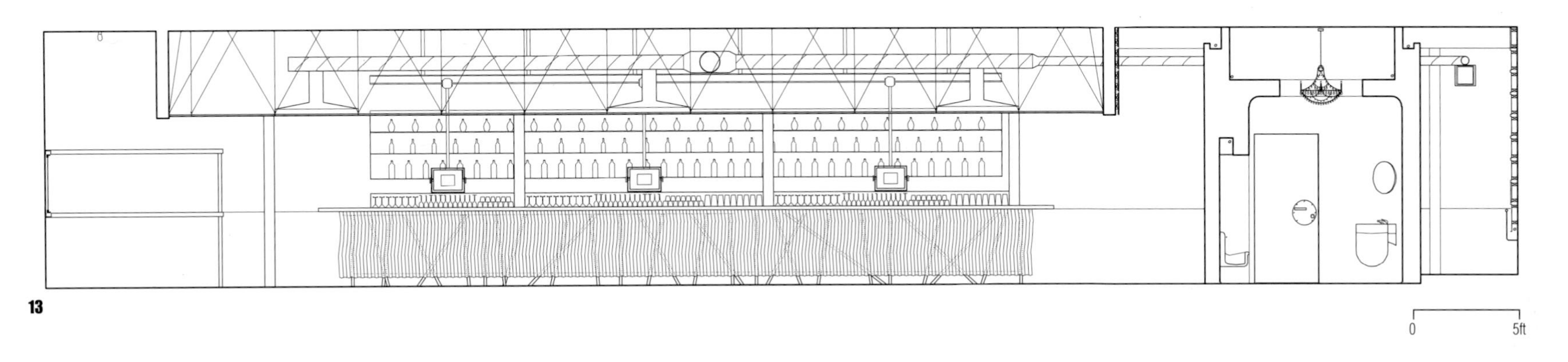

13

14

9 Women's restroom

10 Men's restroom hand sink

11 Acrylic vase

12 Longitudinal section looking east at DJ booth

13 Longitudinal section looking west at bar

14 Original photos and acrylic vase from ramp

Photography: Benny Chan / Fotoworks

1

2

3

4

5

6

7

ZAGREB, CROATIA

Buffet Vinica

3LHD

8

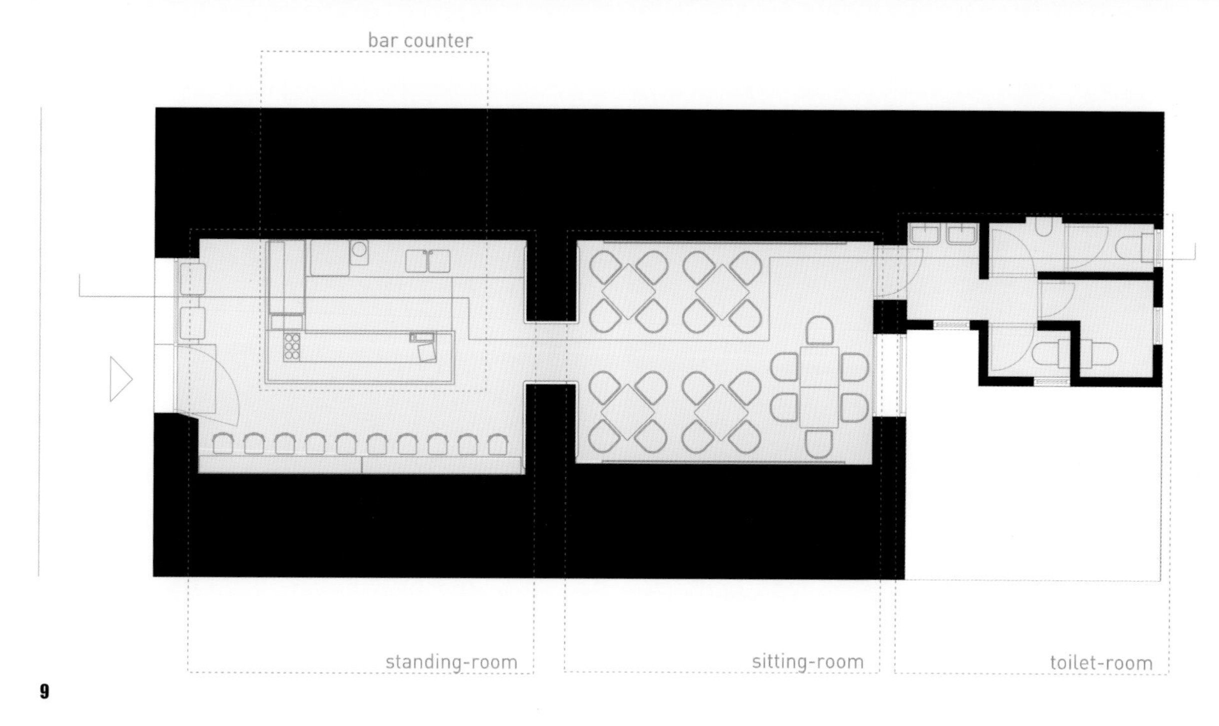

9

1 Horizontal mirrors capture details

2 Exterior night view

3 Exterior day view

4 Stainless steel bar with oak wood counter and chairs

5 Entrance with oak wood bench

6 Leather-clad walls, midnight-blue ceilings and 'zolja' lamp

7 Rear sitting room through two existing walls

8 Section

9 Floor plan

Photography: Gabi Fercic

Usage: Bar

Area: 506 square feet/ 47 square meters

This small bar that unexpectedly became a favorite hangout for Zagreb's local policeman was conceived from a very simple brief: the client wanted a central venue on a small budget.

Narrow, with high ceilings, and oriented in a downtown street, every patron can capture some flash of detail from outside. On both walls, three horizontal stripes of mirrors capture and reflect this movement from the busy street. The eye follows activity wherever the patron stands. The main bar is standing room only, with a room at the back that offers seating. Dark and intimate, the images from the front are repeated on three stripes of the same horizontal glass strips, but with photographs inside that capture movements of the street's activity. These are the mechanical reproductions of a lost ambience.

The ceilings are more than 4 meters high, which enabled the architects to hang an aluminum lamp installation. The pole-like lamps illuminate at two ends and are named 'zolja,' because their look and function is like that of the military shoulder rocket launcher of the same name. In contrast, two existing vertical column-like walls were clad in soft leather so that people may comfortably lean on them or touch them when passing by.

1 Catwalk

2 Bar

3 Caryatids

Photography: Alberto Ferrero

1

2

MILAN, ITALY

Café L'Atlantique

FABIO NOVEMBRE

3

Client: Ivano Fatibene

Usage: Bar/nightclub

Area: 12,920 square feet/ 1200 square meters

Materials: Fiberglass, tiles, plaster

Italian architect Fabio Novembre created Cafè L'Atlantique to satisfy the nocturnal desires of metropolitan nomads. The pale blue and pink color scheme celebrates lessons in sexual communication. On a refined blue mosaic floor, like an ocean that reminds us of how hard it is to communicate with one another, there floats an imperial round bar, with a chandelier made from optic fiber. It becomes a life-saving atoll, welcoming the 'shipwrecked' Milanese.

The VIP lounge has warm lights and blue velvet. The bar has soft vinyl stools, plastic lights, and a decorated floor. A gangway of crystal fragments spotted with 'caryatids and mutated omenoni' created by the Mutoid Waste Company becomes the symbol of this age of split identities.

This nightspot is a contemporary tale in which Novembre succeeds in expressing the problem of socializing in the city, with a futuristic collage of fashion, tastes, and souvenirs from trips elsewhere.

1

2

3

TRIESTE, ITALY

Caffé illy

CLAUDIO SILVESTRIN ARCHITECTS

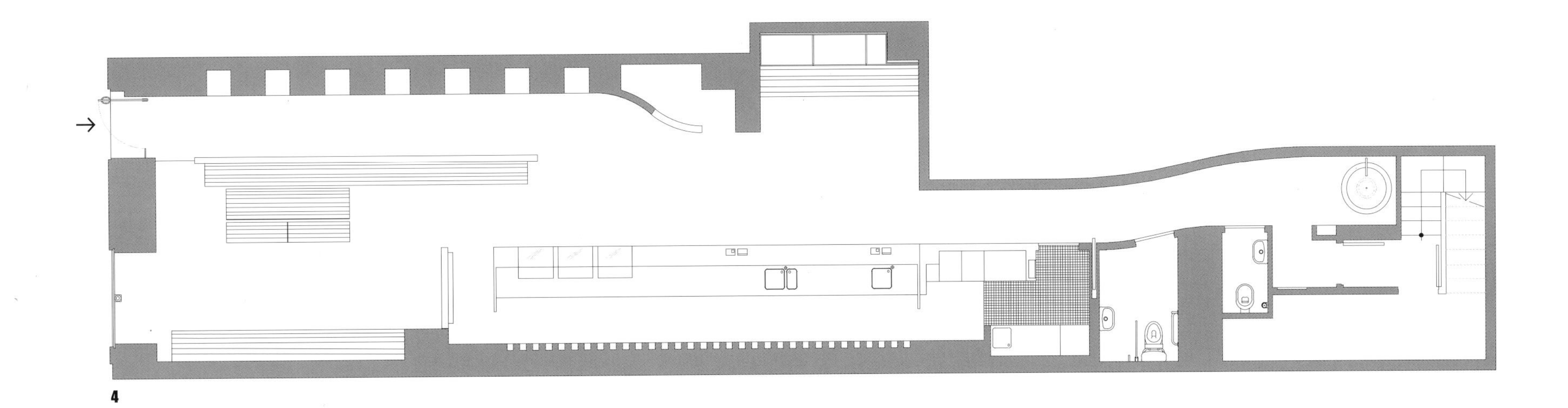

4

5

6

Client: caffé illy spa

Usage: Café

Area: 1614 square feet/ 150 square meters

The new image created for caffé illy generates comfort and serenity. The visual order of the elegant and simple design lines and natural materials induce the eyes and mind to relax, to salvage the 'lusso della pausa,' or the luxury of the break, far from the rush of everyday life. The use of timber and natural stone helps to create a warm, welcoming interior in a space that is both contemporary and timeless.

1&3 Interior

2 View from sitting area

4 Floor plan

5 Dwarf wall

6 View of corridor with water feature

Photography: Marco Covi

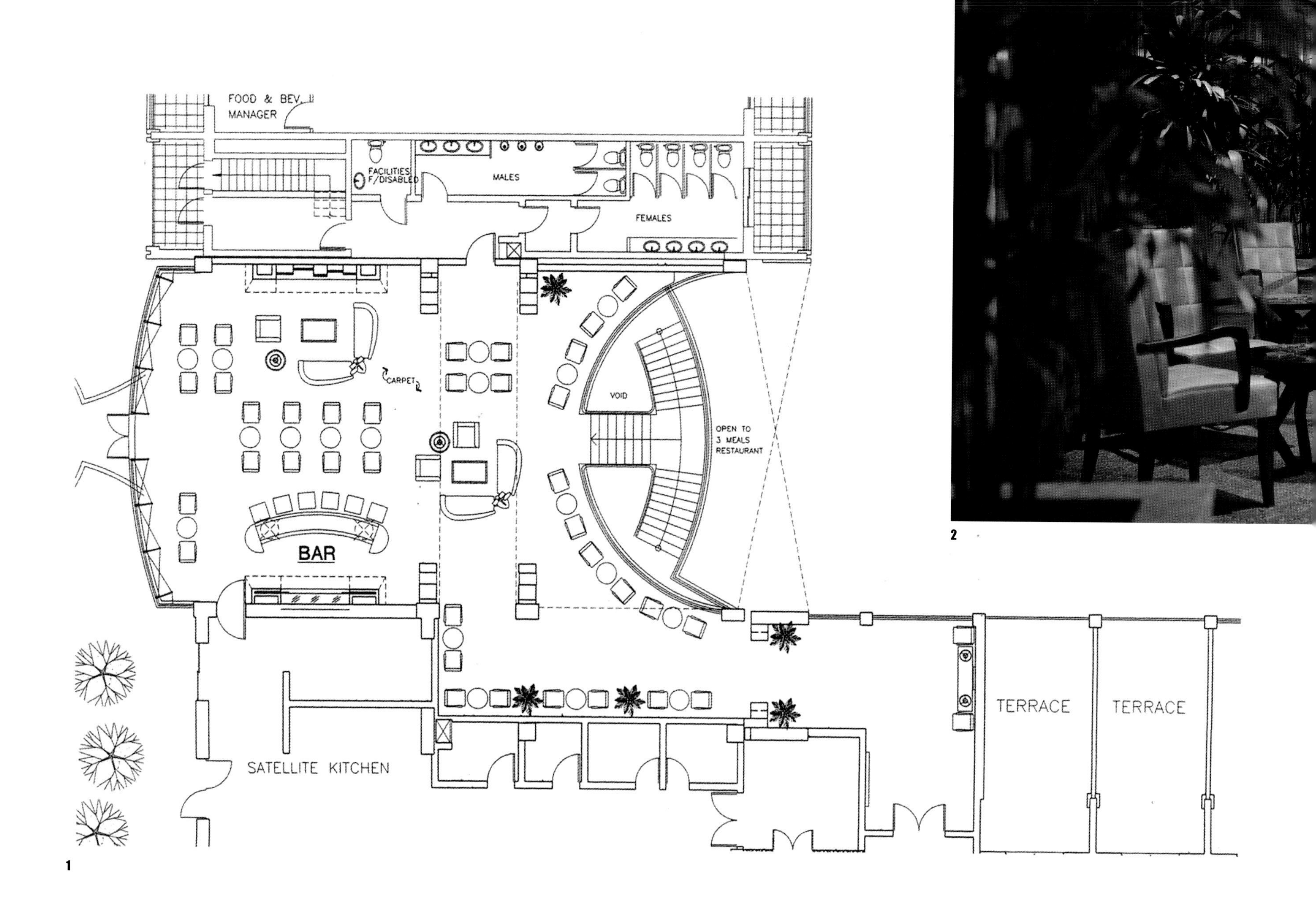

1 Floor plan

2 Lounge seating at window wall

3 Soft seating looking toward courtyard

4 Main bar at lounge

5 Lounge seating overlooking main lobby

6 Soft seating with framed mirror panels

Photography: Warren Jagger Photography

ST GEORGE'S BAY, MALTA

Carissa Bar and Lounge

DILEONARDO INTERNATIONAL, INC. WITH BEZZINA & COLE ARCHITECTS

4

6

3

5

Client: Eden Leisure Group
Usage: Bar/lounge
Area: 5381 square feet/ 500 square meters

The designer created a contemporary bar reminiscent of sleek ocean liners. The site was very complicated and resulted in interesting sectional relationships on the interior and exterior. An example of these sectional relationships is the stepped-level piano bar and exterior gardens, which are experienced at different elevations. This adds a dramatic and unexpected twist to an evening at the bar. Furnishings are sophisticated and contemporary and are a unique contrast to work by local artists.

The Carissa Bar and Lounge is a sophisticated yet casual experience with touches of modern elegance. Light woods and the creative use of mirrors open up the space and make it a suitable day or night environment. The color scheme is a fresh combination of violets, burgundy, teal, and gold with a combination of leathers, woven, and chenille fabrics. Unique materials were used throughout the building, and as much as possible, local materials were the preferred choice.

1

2

3

LONDON, UK

Cherry Jam

POWELL TUCK ASSOCIATES

4

Usage: Bar/restaurant

Area: 2712 square feet/ 252 square meters

Materials: Industrial resin, solid maple, galvanized steel, plaster

Powell Tuck Associates are particularly well known as the lead designers of the Metropolis Recording Studio complex in London and Metropolis/ Sterling Mastering studios in New York.

Their experience in music-related architecture in studios was considered invaluable in sorting out Cherry Jam's acoustic and sound isolation issues. Their architecture is also renowned for its space, light, and materiality, and they were confident that they could produce a robust space that felt good, and sounded good.

Cherry Jam works as an intimate, friendly, and robust venue with a simple design language that enables it to age well, and provides a flexible backdrop to the varying themes and events that it will host.

1 Dance floor

2 Street façade

3 Bar

4 View of dance floor from bar

5

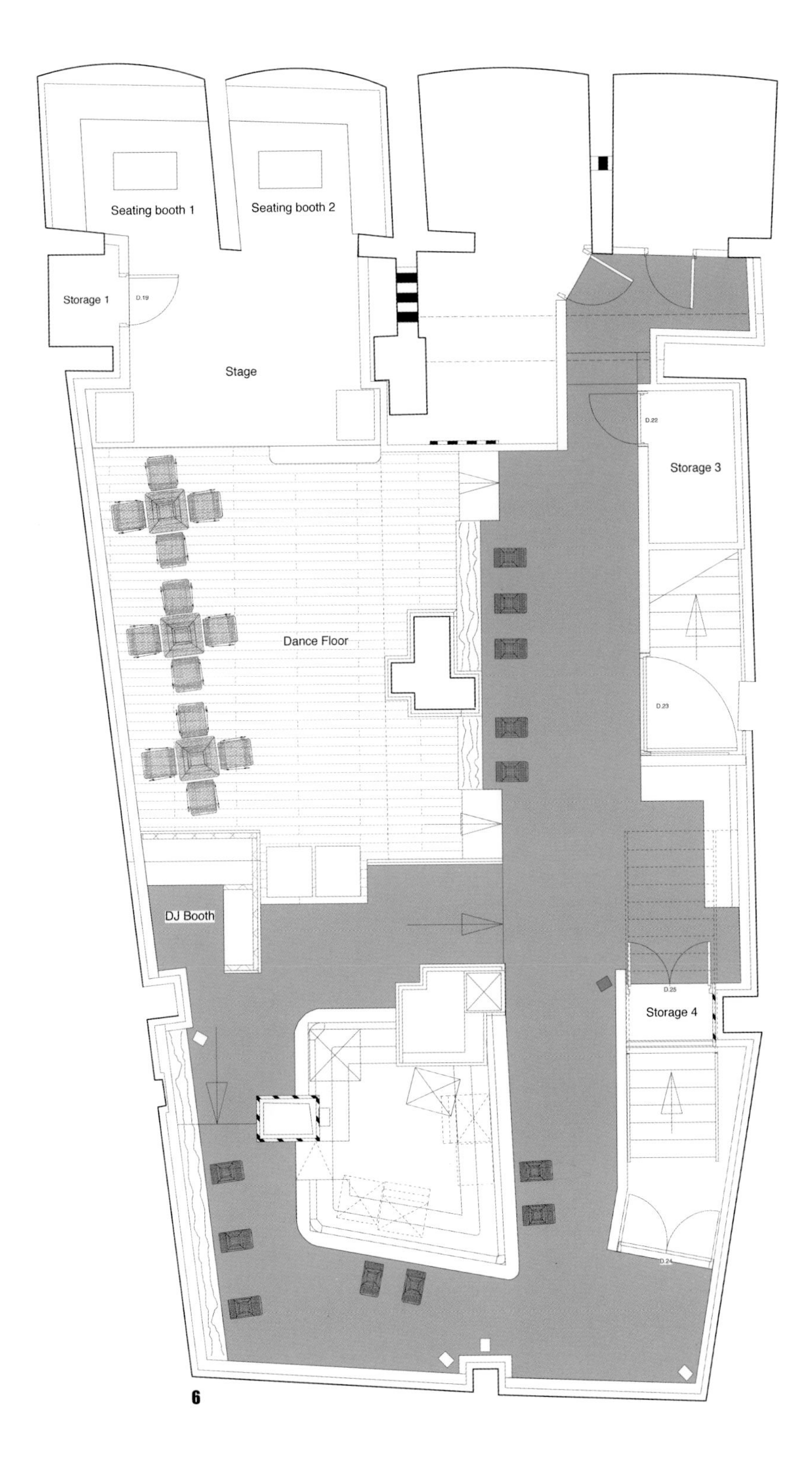

5 DJ booth and bar

6 Lower ground floor plan

7 Ground floor plan

Photography: Edmund Sumner

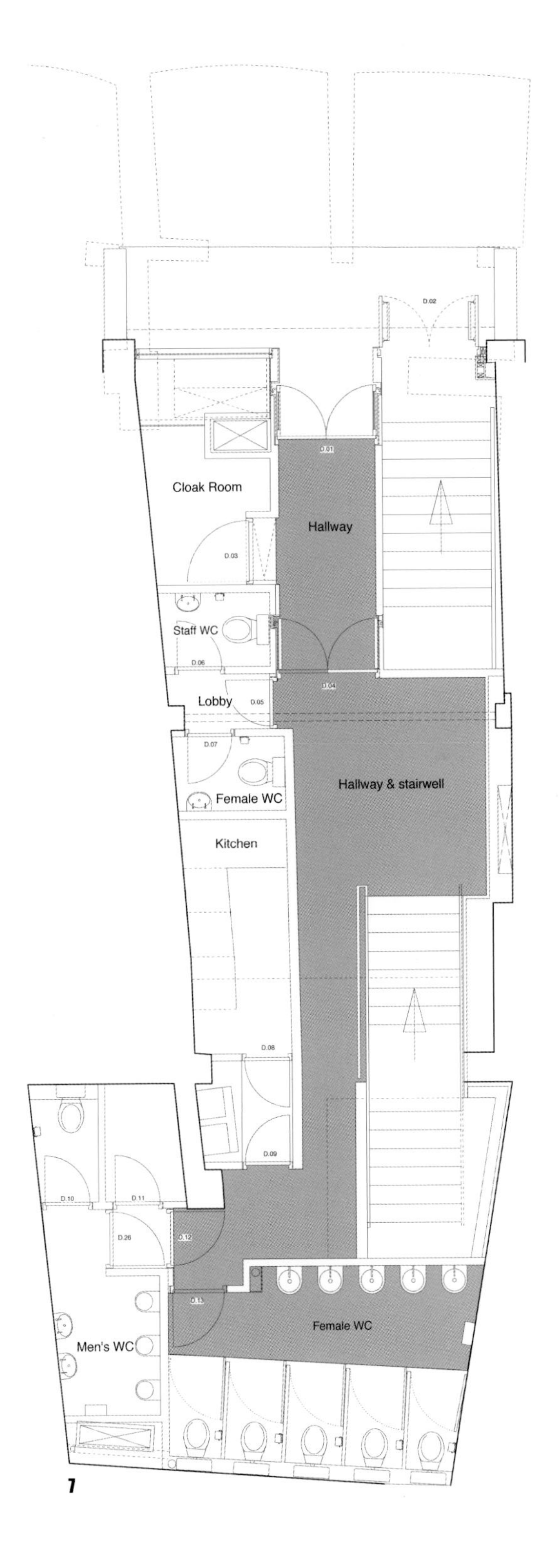

1

4

5

2

3

TOKYO, **JAPAN**

Chika

CLAUDIO COLUCCI DESIGN

6

7

1&3 Entrance
2 Exterior
4 Back room
5 Bar
6–8 Seating
Photography: Mitsutaka Kitamura

8

Usage: Wine bar

Area: 62 square feet/ 6 square meters

Formerly a well-known geisha's house, the new interior is thoroughly modern, while the façade retains traces of the venue's residential features. These existing elements created many problems for the architect, who was faced with an old and fragile structure, and countless small rooms. The pre-existing walls were removed after the structure was reinforced from the basement to the roof. The architect used many of the current materials, while implementing new and modern features. The result is a visible 'morphing' between a traditional Japanese house and a contemporary interior.

1

LONDON, UK

The Cinnamon Club Bar

MUELLER KNEER ASSOCIATES

1 View from cocktail bar to arches and 'cocoon seating'

2 View from entrance toward projection wall

3 Main seating area

2

3

Client: Iqbal Wahhab for The Cinnamon Club

Usage: Bar/restaurant

Area: 12,000 square feet/ 1115 square meters

The Cinnamon Club Bar is situated in the Old Westminster Library close to Westminster Abbey and the Houses of Parliament. The brief was to create a new members' bar that would complement the style of the existing spaces while offering a natural transition into a totally new environment. Inspired by Indian and Art Nouveau references, yet thoroughly contemporary, the new bar space is embraced by gentle parabolic curves.

Specially commissioned handcrafted tables were imported from Rajasthan. Made from rare sheesham wood, they change color during the different seasons of the year. The material selection generally focuses on opulence with intimacy: dark leathers, rubber, glass, and free-flowing fabrics are combined with carefully choreographed lighting, and a dramatic large-scale video projection.

The main feature of the bar is its use of projection technology: a floor-to-ceiling glass screen is the first element the visitor perceives when entering. The screen is animated by a bank of coordinated video projectors: one single moving image stretches over the entire length of the wall, an ever-changing backdrop or 'live wallpaper' for the bar. Specially commissioned video work such as feature films or still graphics can be shown here. India's most celebrated contemporary musician and Mercury prize winner Talvin Singh made a special on-screen appearance performing live from Dehli on the opening night.

Since opening, the Cinnamon Club Bar has received the THEME award for 'Best Use of Technology.'

4&6 Main seating area

5 View from cocktail bar to arches

7 Section through curved leather wall, cocoon seating, arches, and projection wall

8 Floor plan

Photography: Marq Bailey

4

5

6

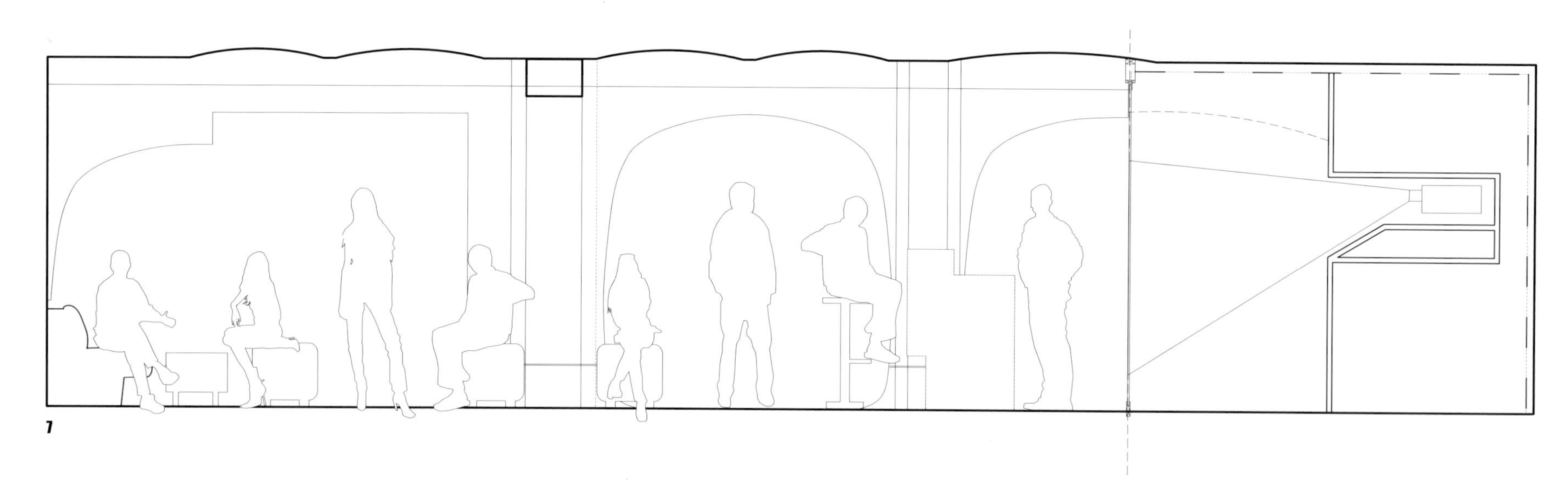

7

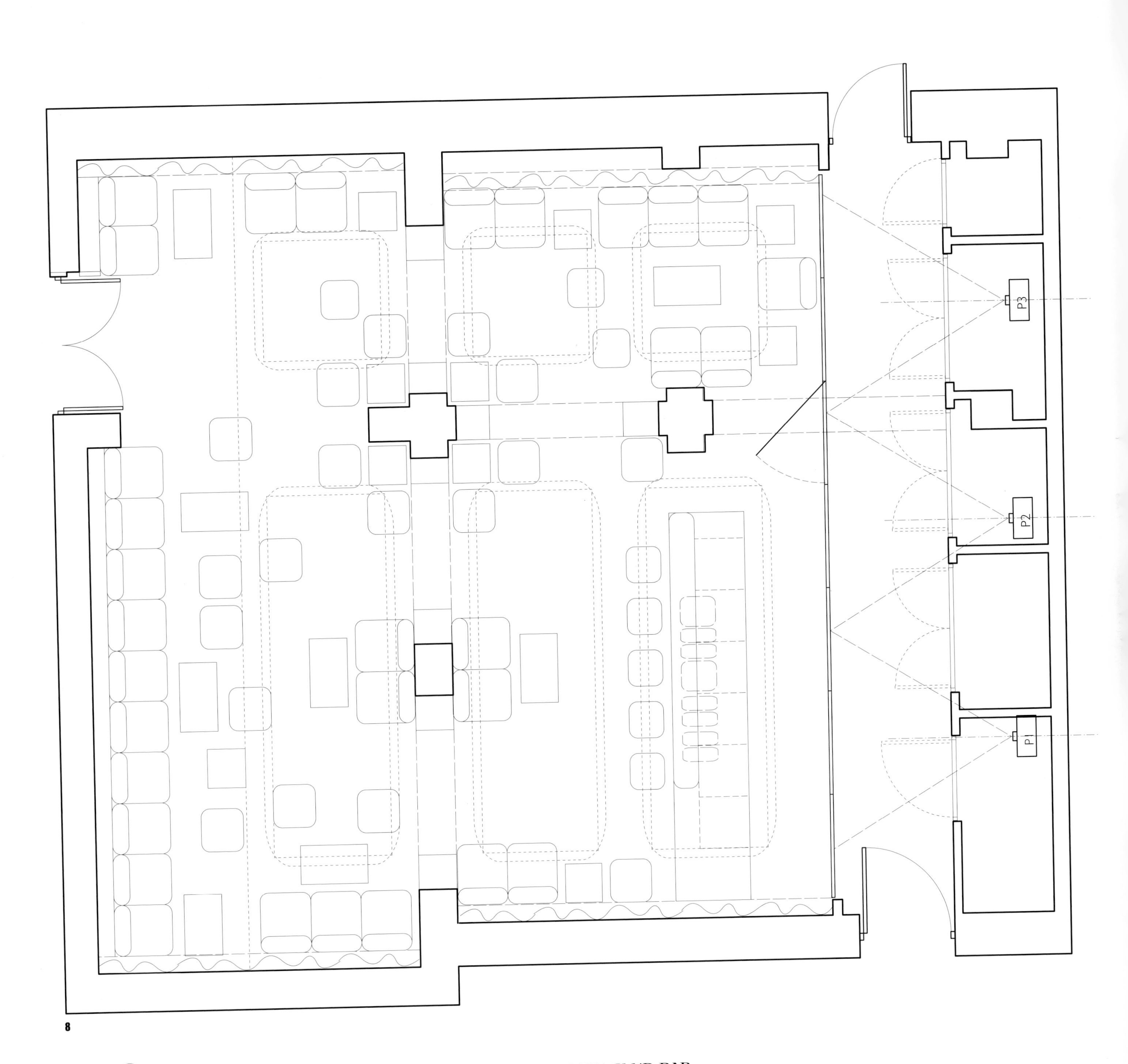

8

1

2

3

4

SÃO PAULO, **BRAZIL**

City Hall Bar

BRUNETE FRACCAROLI

1 Skyline view

2 Stage

3 Bar and seating

4–6 Bar views

5

6

Usage: Bar/restaurant

Materials: Wood, glass, steel, acrylic

A large glass door opens into a tunnel lined with mirrors and a view of the metropolitan skyline. The transparency and fluidity of the spaces were a bonus, creating an ambience in the bar, lounge, dance, cabaret, and banquette areas.

The architect has taken advantage of the venue's double-height ceiling to create a bar, which marks and delineates the space as a big lighting panel. It is a symmetrical project: the cabaret area has been placed in front of the bar, generating better visibility and extra space for the dance area. Specially designed wool–glass panels on the walls, with curved forms and different levels of depth, aid acoustics in the space.

9

7

8

10

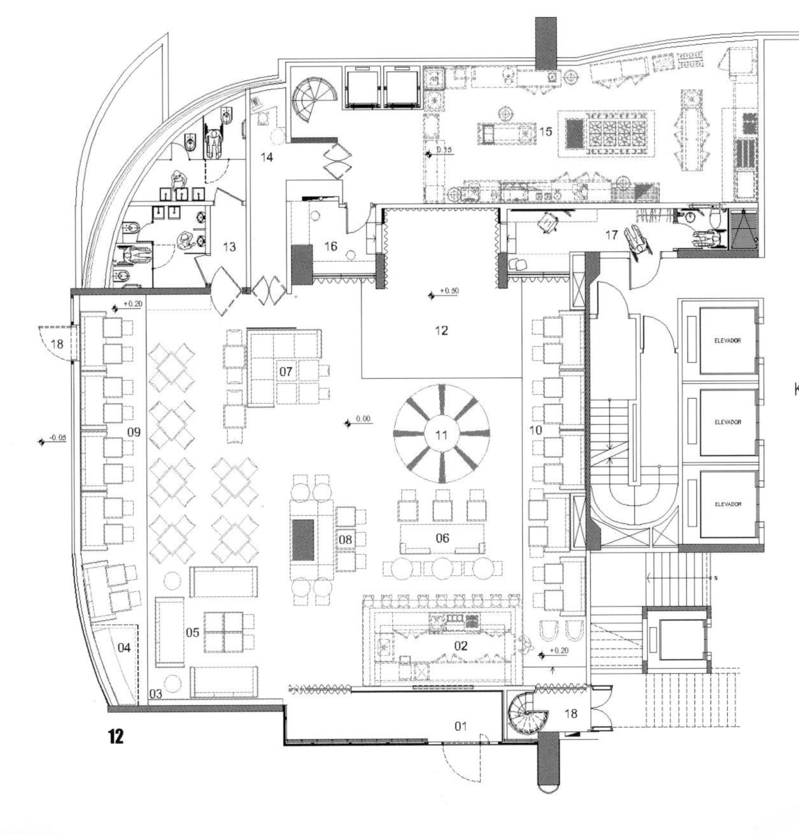

12

11

7 Lounge

8&10 Main seating and lounge

9 Seating detail

11 Restroom

12 Floor plan

Photography: Tuca Reinés

1

2

3

4

1 DJ booth from entry

2 Members' lounge

3 F4 chair, logo application on back wall in members' lounge

4 View from behind bar

5 Main room from dance floor

6 Semi-outdoor patio

7 Wash basin in women's restroom

Photography: Drek Swallwell

MELBOURNE, **VICTORIA, AUSTRALIA**

Club F4

PLAYGROUND MELBOURNE PTY LTD

5

6

7

Usage: Bar

Area: 5113 square feet/ 475 square meters

Materials: Wood, glass, stone

A cross-section of F4 reveals a rectangle with an angle void subtracted from it, a symmetrical diamond shape with a convex folded ceiling. Angled walls, ceiling and tiered floor converge to a focal point, creating a false perspective. Elements reflect not only form but also function. For example, a chair need not only be a type of seating arrangement, but also a sculpture that stands alone as an art piece, linking it to the Bauhaus and Russian Constructivist ideals, the primary design influence. F4 creates the form, structure, and movement to allow patrons to become part of and interact with the venue. Organic materials, for example stimulate a sense of well being, through sight, smell, and touch.

The main space within this venue revolves around the principle of functionality. The daily or weekly usage of F4 can be adapted to suit the needs of the clientele. Tiered flooring and ceiling give a theatrical feel to the whole place, creating depth and perspective as well as being useful when a seated function requires patrons to face one direction of the room. The bar is huge and central in its position, allowing for greater fluidity in access and service.

Overlooking the historic buildings of Little Collins Street, the members' room has its own semi-outdoor patio. Totally encased in glass, the members' area represents refinement and flair. Diacritic down-lights located at each end of the space wash boldly decorated walls, where axonometric illusions hand painted onto canvas evoke 1920's communist Russian poster art. This area can be dedicated for any private function or as a backstage area for a catwalk or live music situation.

1

SANTA MONICA, CALIFORNIA, USA

Club Sugar

JOHN FRIEDMAN ALICE KIMM ARCHITECTS

1 Dance floor

2 Tunnel with restroom doors and dressing room beyond

3 Bar with raised seating area, aquarium beyond

2

3

Usage: Nightclub

Area: 3000 square feet/ 278 square meters

Club Sugar was designed to both facilitate and confuse the voyeuristic and narcissistic activities of seeing, looking, and gazing, in an attempt to create a series of spaces that would not only enhance the conditions for desire in a sexually charged atmosphere, but whose very design would arouse the sensibilities of the club's patrons.

The design was initiated with the selection of numerous new plastic materials with the intention of exploiting their contradictory qualities of transparency and reflectivity, as well as varying degrees of translucency, distortion, and color. These hard materials were juxtaposed against softer and warmer materials such as drapery, exposed brick, and the exposed wood ceiling structure.

The dance floor is separated from the bar by a stainless steel coil screen that is closed at the beginning of each evening, so one sees an empty, but steam and light-filled dance, floor through it. As density increases in the bar, it is parted gradually until the club is full and it settles into its completely open position.

Rest rooms are accessed by a polycarbonate-clad 'tunnel' that creates a distorted view of the dancers. Each of the restrooms has a clear acrylic door allowing direct views into the lavatory areas. The walls and ceilings of these spaces are of identically colored acrylic panels so that the patrons are enveloped in a warm, colored glow that the architects refer to as 'saturated psychological territories.' ►►

This is also true in the restrooms, where walls and ceilings are completely clad with identically colored mirrors. A slot in the wall between the men's and women's sides allows the lavatory counter to slip from one side to the next, as well as creating space for a peeping Tom or Jane to get a glimpse into the other side.

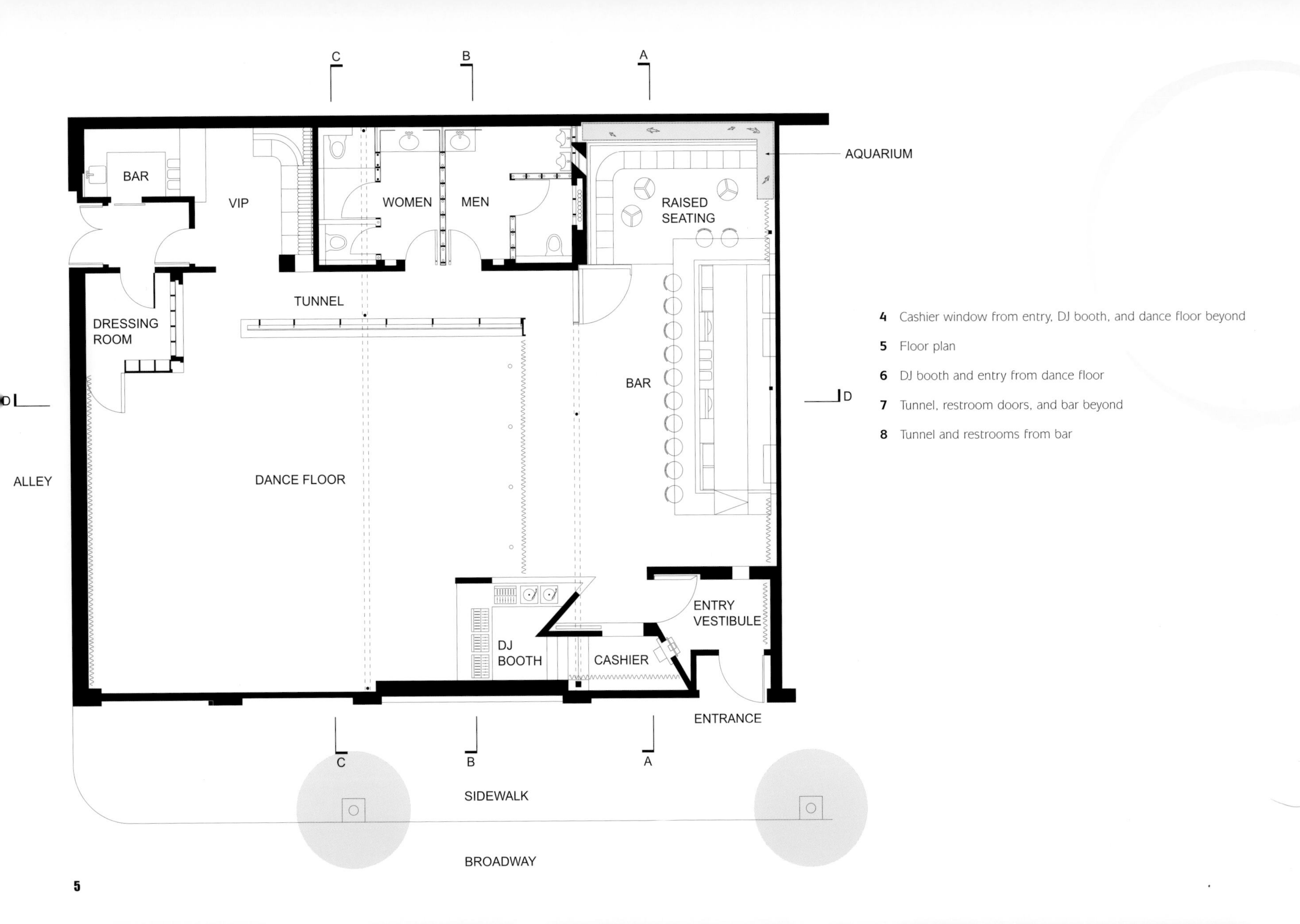

5

4 Cashier window from entry, DJ booth, and dance floor beyond

5 Floor plan

6 DJ booth and entry from dance floor

7 Tunnel, restroom doors, and bar beyond

8 Tunnel and restrooms from bar

6 7 8

9

10

11

12

13

9 Men's and women's restrooms through clear acrylic doors

10 Women's restroom

11&12 Bar and tunnel wall (with glowing restroom doors) from dance floor

13 Bar and dance floor from DJ booth

Photography: Benny Chan / Fotoworks

1 Lounge bar

2 VIP Room with peacock feather walls

3 Men's restroom

Photography: Satoshi Asakawa

1

BEIJING, PRC

Commune at the Great Wall

LEIGH & ORANGE LTD

2

3

Usage: Bar/lounge

The club for the Commune at the Great Wall forms the center of a residential development devised by SOHO China on a hilly site outside Beijing. This development has received worldwide media coverage, having been awarded a special prize at the 2002 Venice Biennale, and was designed by cutting-edge architects working in the Southeast Asia region.

The interiors are set out in a series of different rooms with different moods. A lounge bar, with stunning views of the Great Wall from a connecting terrace, has these views reflected back into the room off an apricot-colored mirror. Adjoining this is a VIP room finished in peacock feathers that shimmer with iridescent color as they catch the light from surrounding floor and table lamps.

The adjoining restrooms have views of the surrounding countryside and as requested by the client, have reversed sexual stereotypes. The men's room has pink mirrors with crystal chandeliers and sheer curtains, while the women's has black leather, gray flannel, dark veneer, and stainless steel.

1

SYDNEY, **NEW SOUTH WALES, AUSTRALIA**

The Cruise Bar and Restaurant

LANDINI ASSOCIATES

2

3

Client: Chris Cheung
Usage: Bar/restaurant
Area: 3229 square feet/ 300 square meters
Materials: Polyurethane panels, mirrors, white terrazzo

Cruise, designed by Landini Associates, sits on the water's edge opposite the Sydney Opera House on Circular Quay. The building that houses it also hosts a passenger terminal for visiting ocean liners too large to pass under the cities bridge, hence the name.

Landini Associates commissioned UK artist, Jeremy Lord to build a 13-metre-long kinetic light wall, which gently moves between seemingly random color combinations, winking at passing ferries and painting the white space with a hypnotic light.

A white terrazzo island bar with custom-made stainless steel beer fonts is in front of the light wall. White plastic dry bars at the bar entrance introduce visitors to the linearity of the scheme and the remainder of the space is left clear. Sets of colored images are reproduced on matchboxes, business cards, staff T-shirts and coasters to remind customers of their visit.

1&2 Exterior

3 Cruise Bar identity is communicated consistently throughout

EXIT

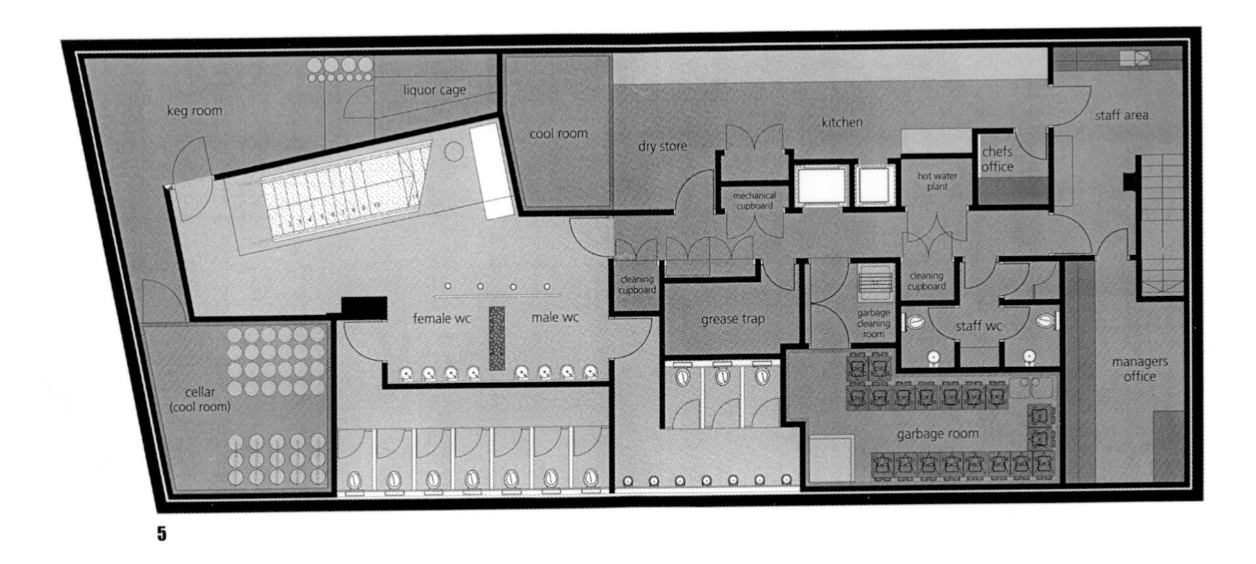

5

6

7

4 Main area cast in colored mood lighting

5 South end, basement floor plan

6 Custom-made benches

7 Kinetic light wall

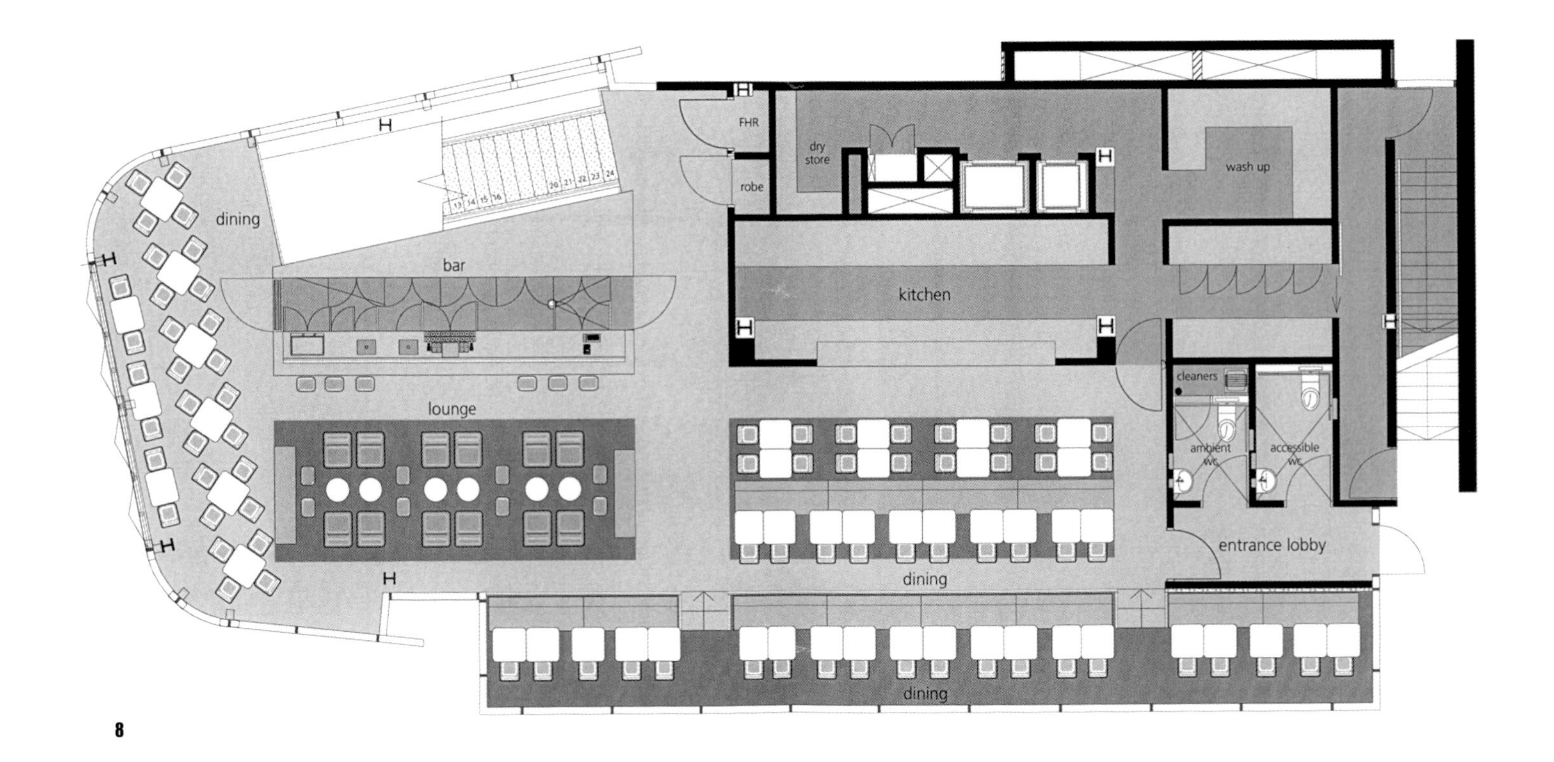
FHR
dry store
robe
wash up
dining
bar
kitchen
lounge
cleaners
ambient wc
accessible wc
entrance lobby
dining
dining

8

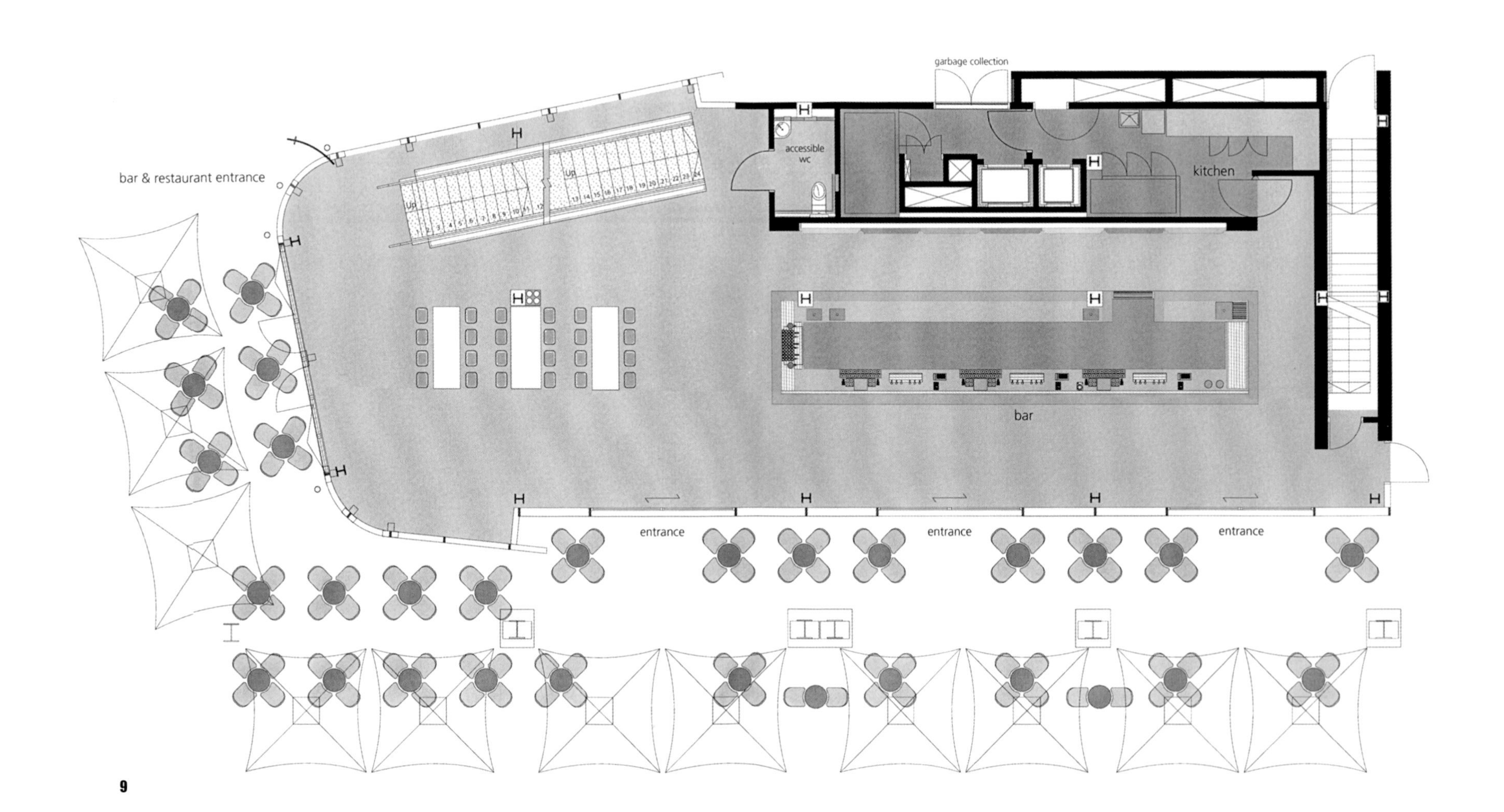
garbage collection
accessible wc
kitchen
bar & restaurant entrance
Up
Up
bar
entrance
entrance
entrance

9

8 South end, level two floor plan

9 South end, level one floor plan

10 Seating area

Photography: Ross Honeyset

1

2

VANCOUVER, **BRITISH COLUMBIA, CANADA**

Crush Champagne Lounge

EVOKE INTERNATIONAL DESIGN

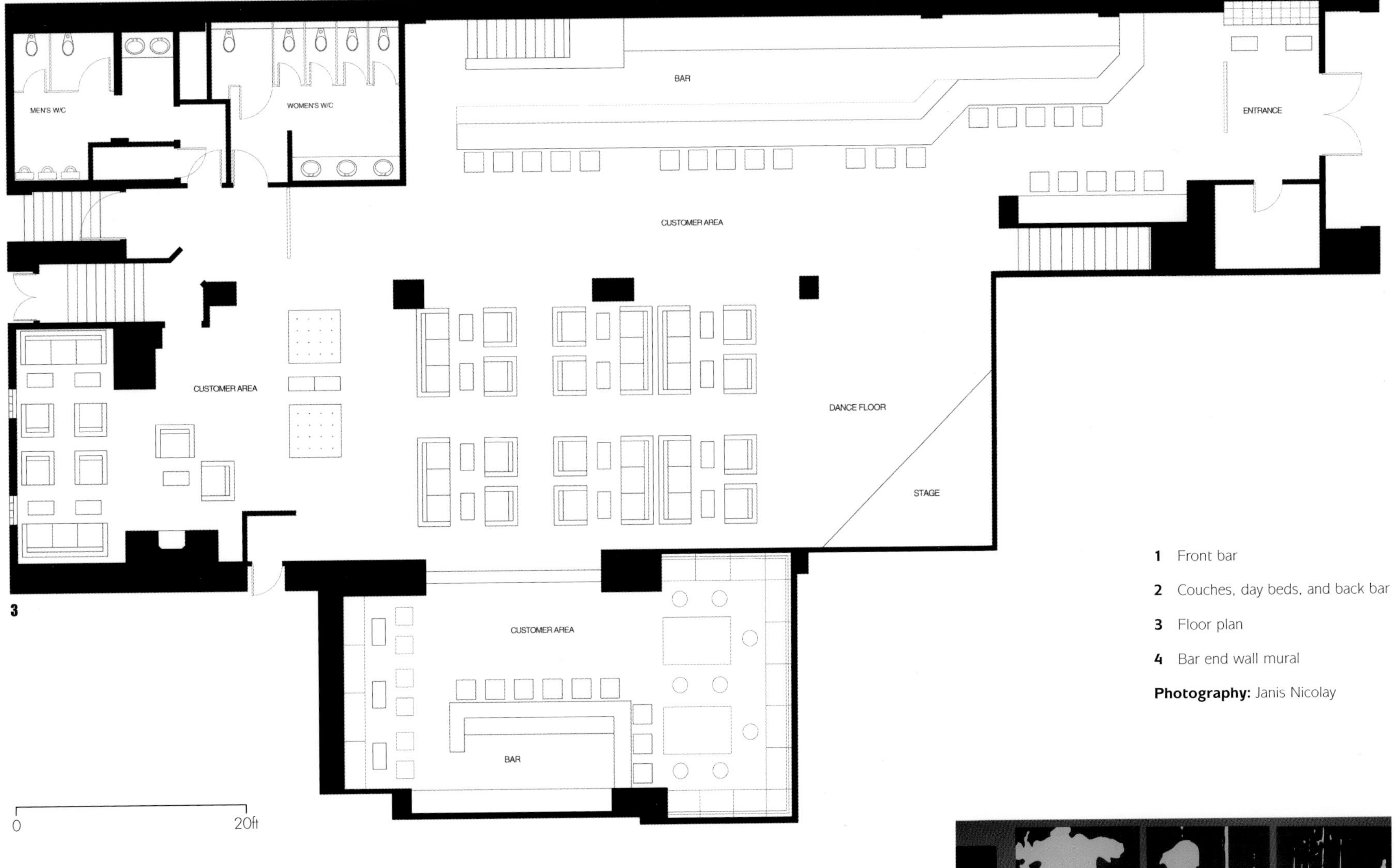

3

1 Front bar

2 Couches, day beds, and back bar

3 Floor plan

4 Bar end wall mural

Photography: Janis Nicolay

Usage: Bar/lounge

Area: 4500 square feet/ 418 square meters

Materials: Birch veneer, white Corian, steel, glass

Crush Champagne Lounge was designed as a sophisticated lounge/bar aimed at attracting a discerning clientele. The objective was to create loungeroom 'pods' throughout the area where up to eight people could sit comfortably and converse in their own space. Large lights were installed over each grouping to further enhance the individual loungeroom concept. The soft gray and brown hues of the Milliken 'Oxygen' carpet, and sofas and settees designed by Bombast, Vancouver, are accented with splashes of color from the oversized orange day beds. Bubble lamps by Foscarini hang over the white Corian bar that runs the length of the room.

4

1

2

3

ISTANBUL, **TURKEY**

Dada

AUTOBAN

1&5 Main dining room

2 DJ table

3 The 'cozy' room

4 Cigar room/lounge

4

5

Usage: Bar/restaurant

Dada is located on the ground level of a high-rise residential tower and has the most sought-after tables in Istanbul. On the ground floor, the bar and lounge section is furnished with a mirrored screen, a 5-meter-long bench, and *darbukas* (a Turkish percussion instrument) as coffee tables. The area is illuminated by large chandeliers and tiny spots placed in between mirrored panels on the ceiling, made complete with the addition of large, comfortable leather armchairs to create a laid-back feeling.

The restaurant, located on the first floor, consists of three interconnecting sections; the main dining room, the VIP room, and the cozy room. White gauze curtains hang from a 6-meter-high ceiling, a large bookcase covers a wall, tables are illuminated by large pendant lights, and there are large sofas with cushions. The entire floor is decorated to reflect the glamour of yesterday's mansions.

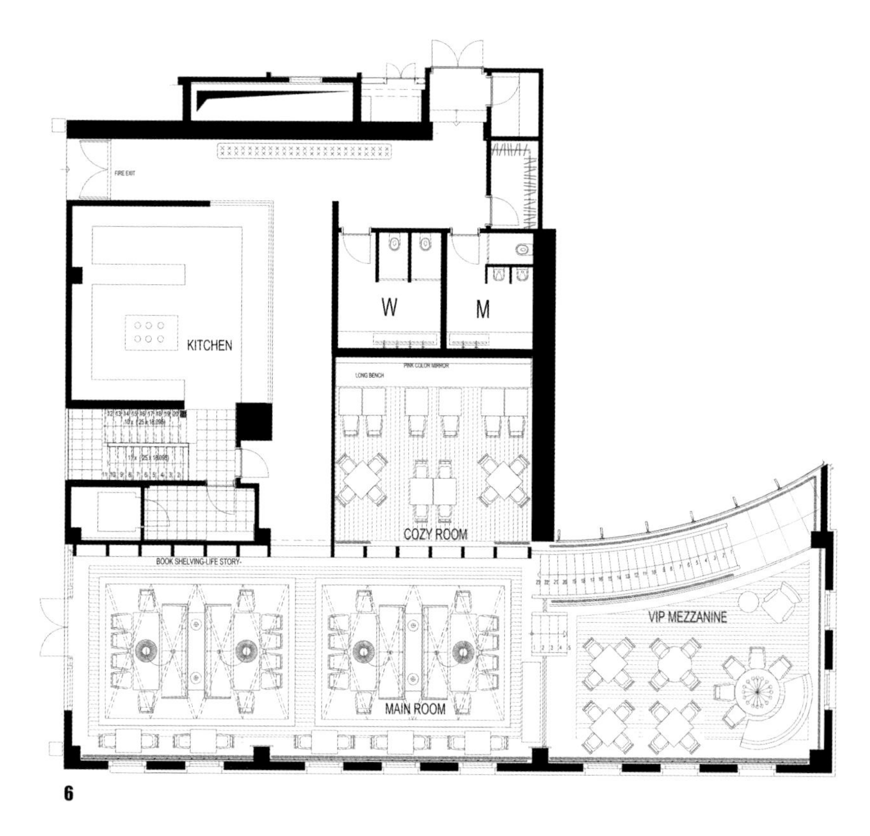

6

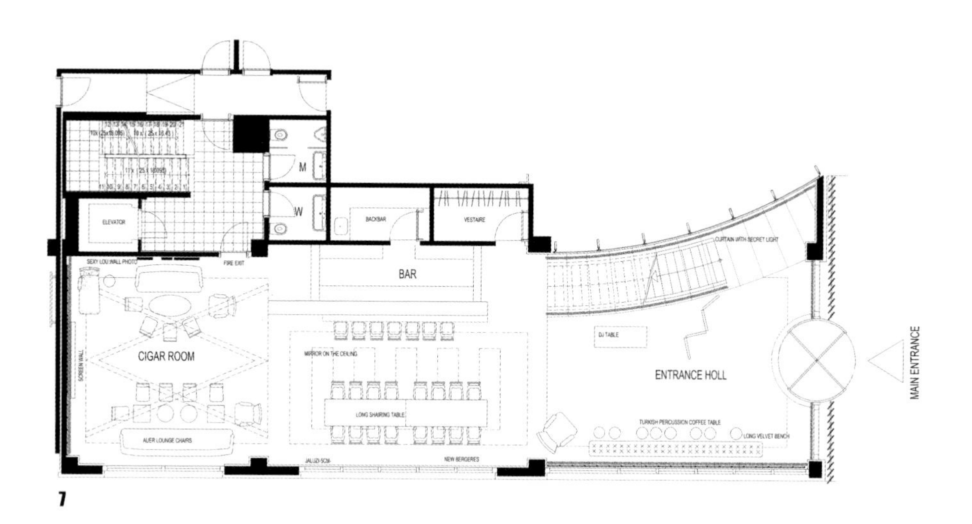

7

8

6 First floor plan

7 Ground floor plan

8 Bar stools and tables

9 Bar

10 VIP mezzanine

11 Entrance area

12 *Darbuka* coffee tables

Photography: Ali Bekman

9

10

11

12

1

2

TORONTO, **ONTARIO, CANADA**

Distrikt Nightclub

SUPERKÜL INC ARCHITECT WITH UW DESIGN GROUP INC

Area: 14,000 square feet/ 1300 square meters

Materials: Tempered clear glass, American walnut veneer, plastic laminate, fir wood slats

The venue is located in Toronto's entertainment district among the theaters, restaurants, and multitude of nightclubs. It has a design that speaks of warmth, grandness, and cool. The entry sequence begins via an exterior stair that leads down to a long tunnel. The mood in the tunnel is subdued, lit by slivers of colored light emanating from slanted walls, at the end of which is a stair that leads up to the nightclub.

There are two VIP areas upstairs: the first has private, intimate banquettes, glass guards, and suspended glowing drink rails. The second, at the other end of the space, is raised and helps to contain the large dance floor. A 28-meter-long walnut bar connects the VIP areas. A sculpted ceiling hovering above reinforces the bar's presence in the space. Multi-colored beams of light shoot down from the ceiling onto the bar surface.

1 Walnut bar

2 Island bar

3

4

3&4 Bars and dance floor

5 Dance floor

Photography: Tom Arban

5

1

2

3

SHANGHAI, PRC

DR Bar

WOOD-ZAPATA, INC.

1 Bar entry

2 Black lacquered front door

3 Small intimate space for drinks and conversation

4 Silver woven-mesh bar top

5 Brick wall detail

4

5

Usage: Bar

Area: 753 square feet/ 70 square meters

A quiet place for casual conversation and relaxation, the DR Bar offers fine wines, champagne, the best martini in Shanghai, and a collection of premium spirits. The interior design features works by many of the architects and designers who came together to create the distinctive contemporary Chinese style that has become synonymous with Xintiandi.

The DR in the name stands for 'design resources'. This small bar endeavors to promote awareness of some of the extraordinary design resources available in China. The designers (and owners) include the chief architect of Xintiandi, Ben Wood, and Francis Yum, the builder/producer of many of Xintiandi's best restaurants. All the materials, furniture, and finishes in the bar are from sources within mainland China. The millwork is matte-finish black lacquer, and the bar top and vodka trough is made from Tibetan silver mesh. The back bar is made using five slabs of Anhui ink stone, the ceiling is of Yunnan saddle leather, and the long wall is made from sliced Hang Zhou black roof tiles.

6

6 Wall made of sliced Hangzhou black roof tiles

7 Bar and seating

8 Black lacquered walls

9 Custom-made furniture

10 Skylight fills space with filtered light

11 Silver woven-mesh bar top

Photography: Liu Shen Hui

7

8

9

10

11

1

1 Bar, toward store

2 Bar

3 Bar section

4 Bar and store plan

Photography: Yael Pincus

BOLOGNA, **ITALY**

Energie **Bar**

STUDIO 63

2

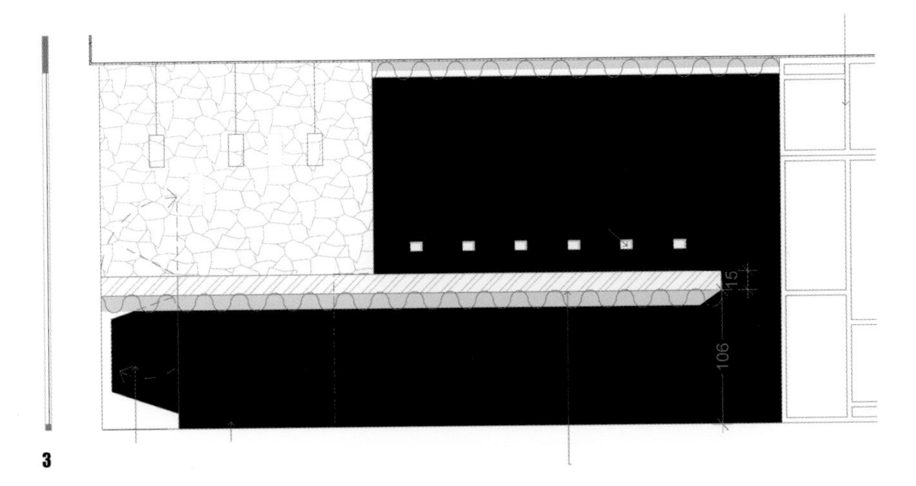

3

Usage: Bar

Area: 269 square feet/ 25 square meters

The Energie Bar is part of the Energie retail design store but has its own separate entrance. The bar serves as a brief pause during the day and a fashionable hangout at night. Small plasma screens offer a personal peek into the latest fashion and music trends.

4

1

2

3

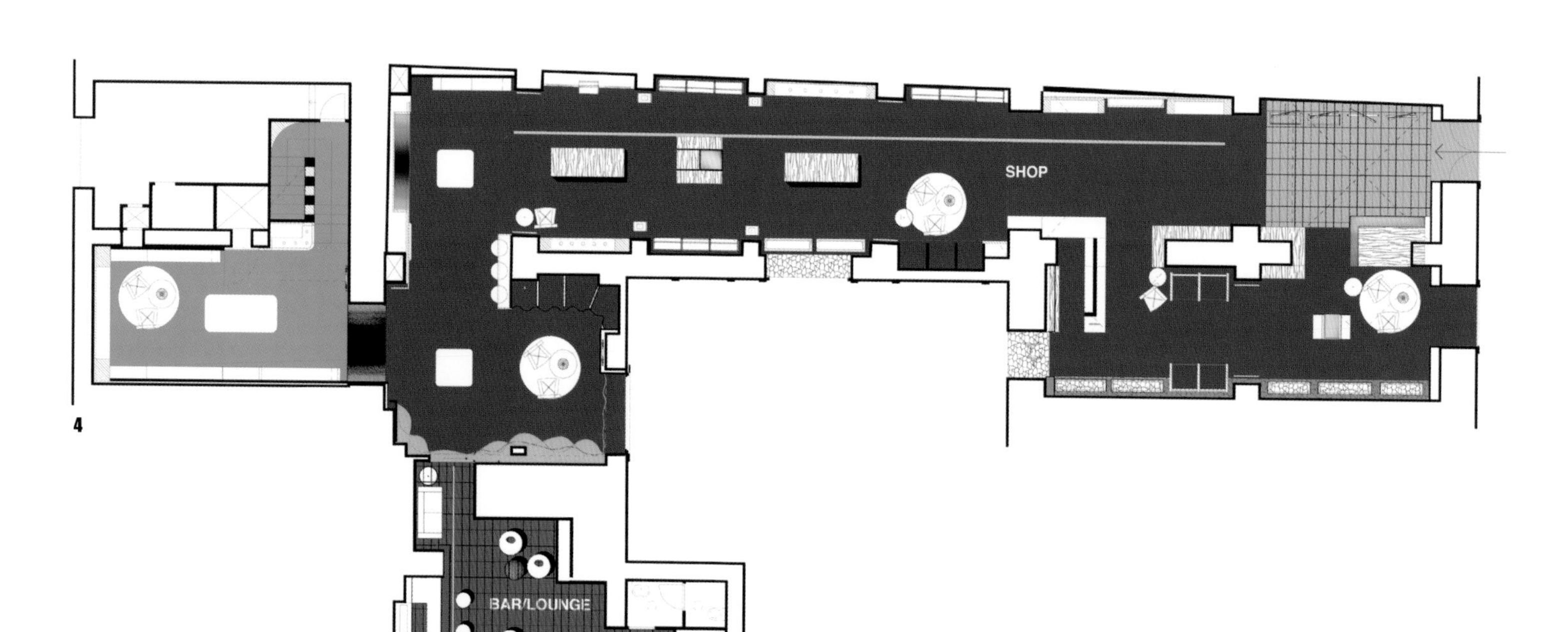

4

CATANIA, **ITALY**

Energie Café

STUDIO 63

5

1–3 Lounge

4 Store, bar, and lounge floor plan

5&6 Bar

Photography: Yael Pincus

6

Usage: Bar/lounge

Area: 538 square feet/ 50 square meters

Completed in May 2003, the Energie Café in Catania is a lounge/bar part of the Energie/Miss Sixty retail design store. It is located inside the store but has its own entrance as well. Traditional materials together with vintage pieces from the 1950s create this intimate and friendly atmosphere.

Located in one of the most vivid cities of Sicily, this is an interpretation of the old-fashioned bars and cafés that still exist in this area. They are called 'il circolo' in Italian, meaning the conversation circle: a place where people gather to talk about politics or soccer.

1

2

3

1 Entranceway, dining room, and lower level bar

2 Lower-level bar

3 Decorative sculpture and upper-level bar

4 Hallway, ceiling swoop, and lighting detail

5 Lower-level dining area

6&7 Dining table and seating detail

8 Tables, seating, and wall partition

9 Women's room vanity

10 DJ booth

Photography: courtesy Flux Design

4

5

MILWAUKEE, WISCONSIN, USA

Eve

FLUX DESIGN

7

8

6

9

10

Usage: Bar/ nightclub/restaurant

Area: 5600 square feet/ 520 square meters

Materials: Steel, concrete, glass, plastics

The innovative team of artists and designers at Flux Design developed the interior theme of Eve. An elegant balance of taste and temptation accents this contemporary interpretation of the Garden of Eden. The graceful lines and contrasting textures of the design grew from a series of tables developed and built by Flux Design owners Jeremy Sham and Jesse Meyer. Their comparatively humble Hobbit Series tables sprung forth into sweeping entranceway and wall structures and trickled all the way down to the candleholders and door handles.

Completed in December of 2001, nearly every interior feature of this upscale restaurant and nightclub was designed and handcrafted by Flux Design and took nearly one year to complete. The first-level restaurant and lounge is rich with organic lines and forms of hand-bent steel, featuring a backlit drinks bar with a layered concrete and glass top, supported by more than 50 miniature steel trees. More than 170 concrete forms were poured and beautifully finished for the bar tops, drink rails, dining tables, and bathroom sinks.

The upper-level nightclub is notably contemporary, with geometric yet whimsical structures. The two bars, along with the DJ booth and dance platform, are noted by crisp contrasts of shape, texture, and color. A twisting steel sculpture snakes out of the floor, from the garden below, and leads from room to room as it swallows aluminum orbs along its path.

1

NEW YORK, **NEW YORK, USA**

Fusion Bar and Lounge

RIVER ARCHITECTS

2

3

4

1 Exterior

2&3 Front area of bar

4 Entry to rear lounge

Client: Oscar Riba

Usage: Bar/lounge

Area: 834 square feet/ 77 square meters

Materials: Stained maple, glass, exposed brick, oak

The client requested a design that was unpretentious, comfortable, warm, and sensual with a retro-Cuban feel. Working with the limited construction budget of US$32,000, the architects used simple materials, bold colors, and dynamic lighting to create a rich atmosphere.

To emphasize the long and narrow space, River Architects designed a bar that angled out of the southern wall and gradually led patrons into the cozy lounge in the back. To accommodate the narrow bar area and to relate to the mid-century modern furniture, the padded-vinyl bar front was designed to cushion the knees against the hard surface of the wood. One aged cast-iron column caked with paint, located by the front windows, was left untouched. Since the new ceiling level had to drop below its capital, the ceiling was framed around the capital, accenting it with a hidden light. A cozy Cuban cigar lounge was emulated for that retro-Cuban feel.

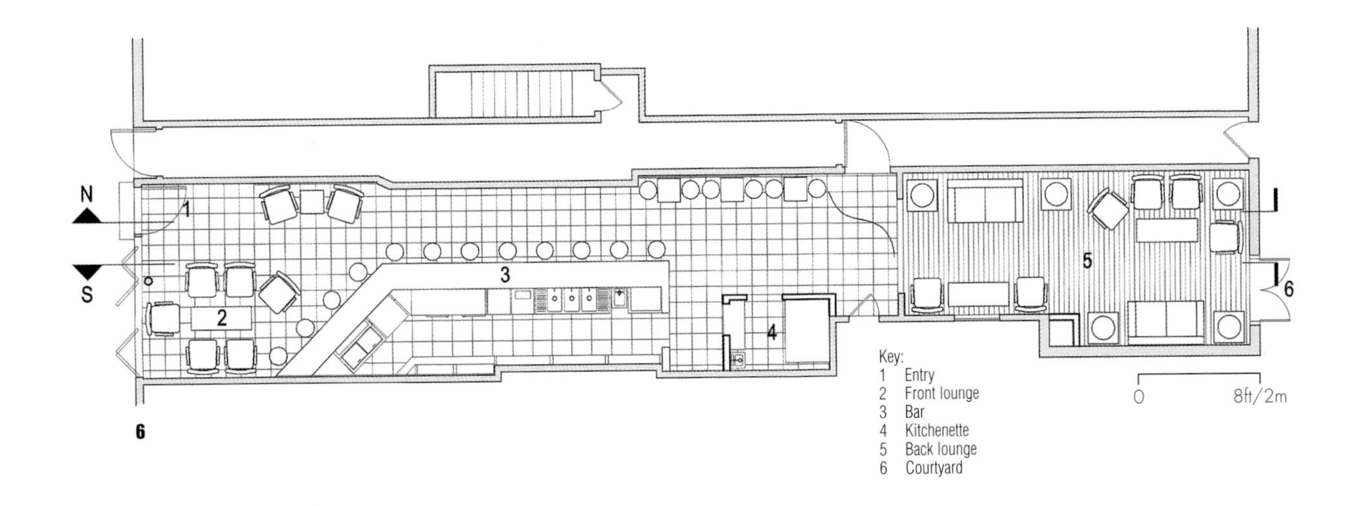

6

7

Opposite View from entry

6 Floor plan

7 Rear lounge

Photography: Juhee Lee-Hartford and James Hartford

1 Reception and cloakroom

2 Lounge overlooking dance floor and stage

3 Main bar

4 Bar detail, walnut surface

5 Glass bar rack

1

2

MUNICH, GERMANY

The Garden

STUDIOACHT.

3

4

5

Client: Milch und Bar GmbH

Usage: Nightclub, live music venue

The Garden is situated near Theresienwiese, home of the famous Oktoberfest. A brilliant green light on the exterior and a soft light shining through the entry doors are the only indication that there is a nightclub inside the otherwise plain building.

The main bar is constructed from natural stone and walnut, with a soft-form ceiling above. An indoor garden featuring Japanese bamboo trees, grass, and volcanic stones is located opposite the bar. A movable stage features red curtains that can be closed during live acts.

The lounge area is raised and furnished with comfortable seats and small handmade high-grade steel tables. The backstage area features a small bathroom, a wardrobe with tall mirrors, and a small private lounge for the musicians, which is furnished with divans.

6

7

6 Main bar

7 Second bar

8 Indoor garden with volcanic stones

Photography: Tobias Kreissl

8

1

2

3

1 Fabric panels
2 Illuminated screen provides backdrop
3&4 Bar
5 Ramps lead patrons to bar and elevated lounge platform

SYDNEY, NEW SOUTH WALES, AUSTRALIA

Glo Bar, Star City Casino

BATES SMART PTY LTD

4

5

Usage: Cocktail bar

Area: 5382 square feet/ 500 square meters

Materials: Marble, anodized aluminum wall paneling, wood

Glo Bar has been designed to be the signature cocktail lounge and visual centerpiece of the main gaming floor at Sydney's Star City Casino. Set in a sea of hyperactivity and high energy, its unique design allows it to transcend its surrounds to achieve a sense of relaxed sophistication.

Glo is set on a viewing platform surrounded by a patterned metal screen, enhancing the sense of elegance and luxury delivered by high-end finishes and opulent fabrics. Glo invokes a sense of theater through the spectacular diaphanous 100-meter-long chandelier that spirals down over the lounge area, creating a dramatic and seductive atmosphere. The chandelier is composed of 2-meter-long acrylic rods suspended from a 6.8-meter-high ceiling lit by fiber optics.

This exquisite bar realizes a level of sophistication unsurpassed in both context and form. Patrons can circulate and communicate in a seductive environment unparalleled in any other urban setting.

The Glo Bar achieves what so many strive for: delivering a real experience to patrons, with its ambience lit by the truly breathtaking chandelier. Its design and location make it a haven for casino guests looking for respite and sophistication, and what better respite from the hustle and bustle of the gaming floor than a five-star 1950's style cocktail lounge.

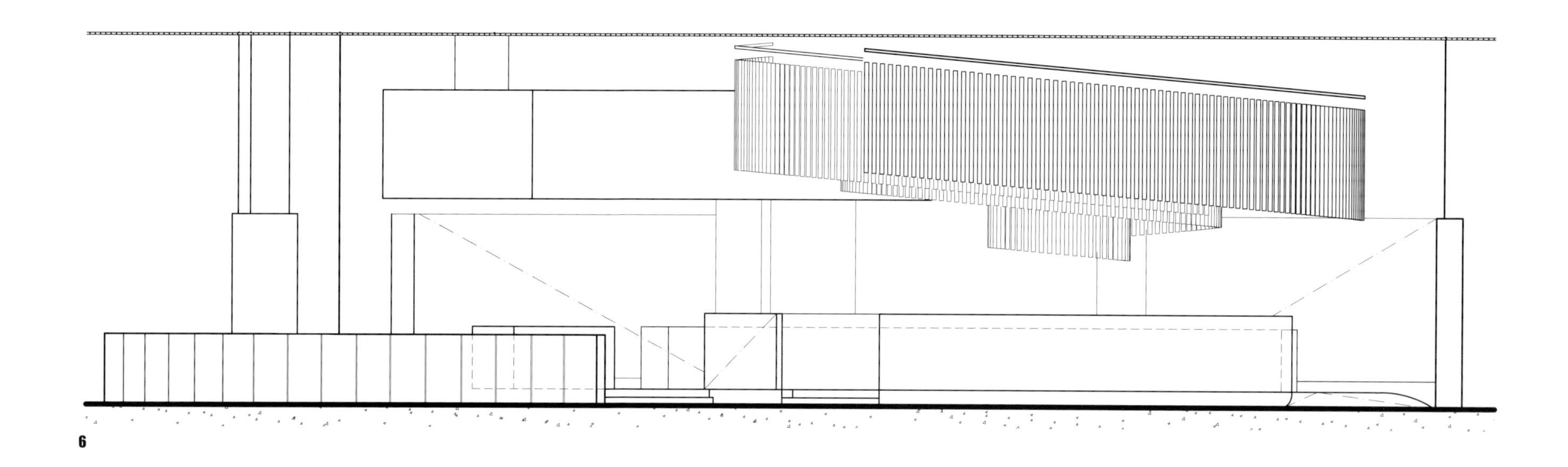

6

7

8

6 Elevation

7&8 Chandelier hovers over lounge seating area

9 Floor plan

Photography: Sharrin Rees

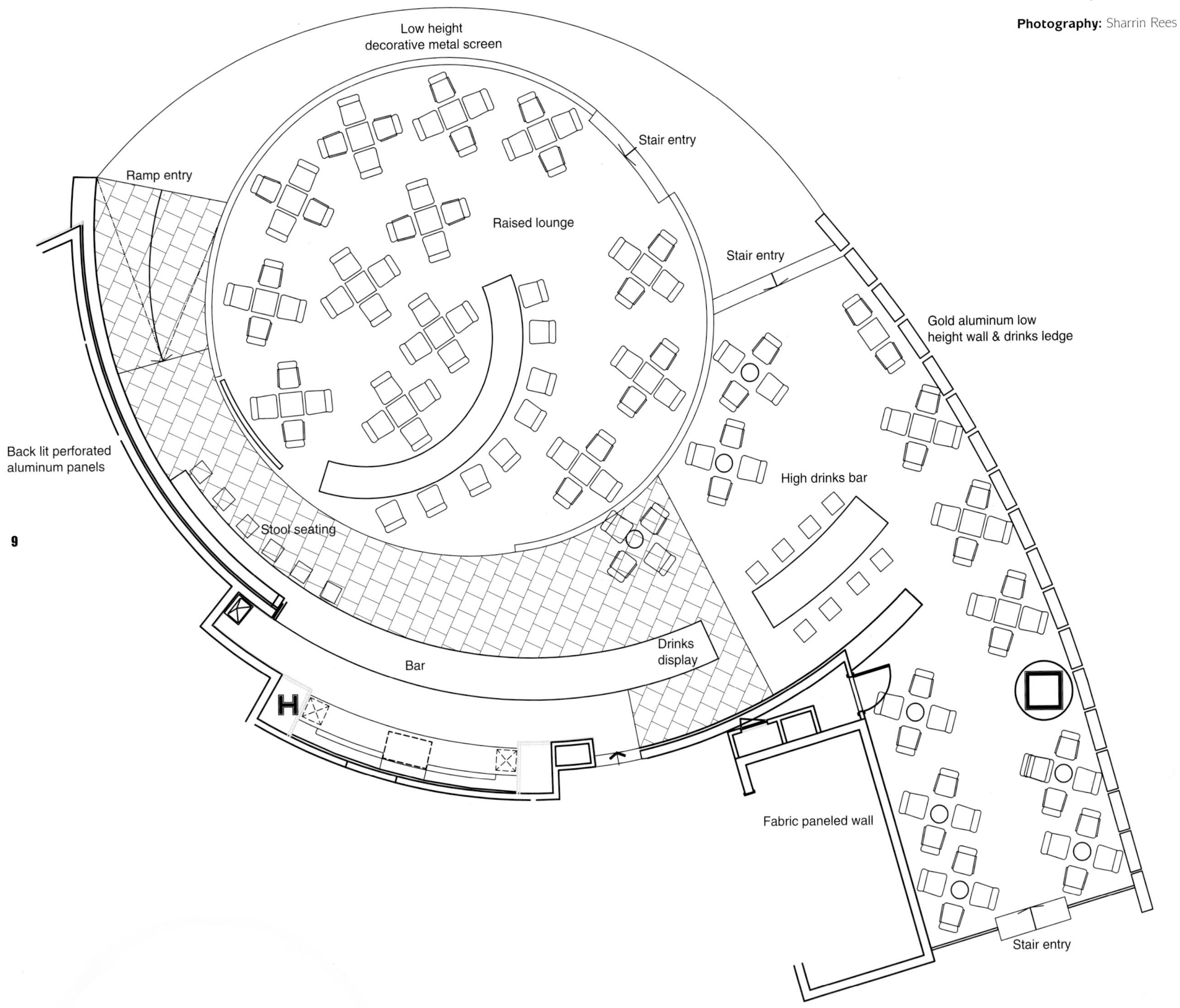

9

1 Exterior

2 View toward seating area

3 View toward bar

4 Bar detail

5 View toward entrance

6 Bar

1

2

LONDON, UK

Grand Central Bar

BLOCK ARCHITECTURE

3

4

5

6

Usage: Bar

Area: 1937 square feet/ 180 square meters

Materials: Bespoke laminated Perspex, galvanized steel lighting, perforated leather

The architects wanted to create a space that used light, movement, and electricity as physical building elements rather than applying a new architectural surface to an existing one. The primary aim was to draw in the dynamic exterior condition to the interior of the space.

The bar is situated on a busy road junction in Shoreditch, so the architects' proposals drew directly from this context of road junctions, traffic lights, and city movement. They wanted to tap into the ebb and flow of this, while at the same time providing a means of retreat from the perpetual 'stop, wait, and go' punctuation of urban life.

To visualize these ideas, Block Architecture drew its influence from long-exposure photographs of night time traffic movement and froze this into interior wall surfaces within the bar, constructing 'lightstream' walls suggestive of this movement and flow. These were manufactured from strips of live edge and colored Perspex, laminated together and lit from behind to create the extruded light path of car headlights and tail lights.

Translucent-resin tabletops, restroom sinks and the urinal (lit from underneath), and the wall-mounted light were designed by the architects. The chairs in the central space were modified to be made with perforated leather padded seats and seat backs, and gray powder-coated legs. The chairs and stools on the upper levels were also designed using the same perforated leather that is again repeated on the upholstered booth seating on the raised levels.

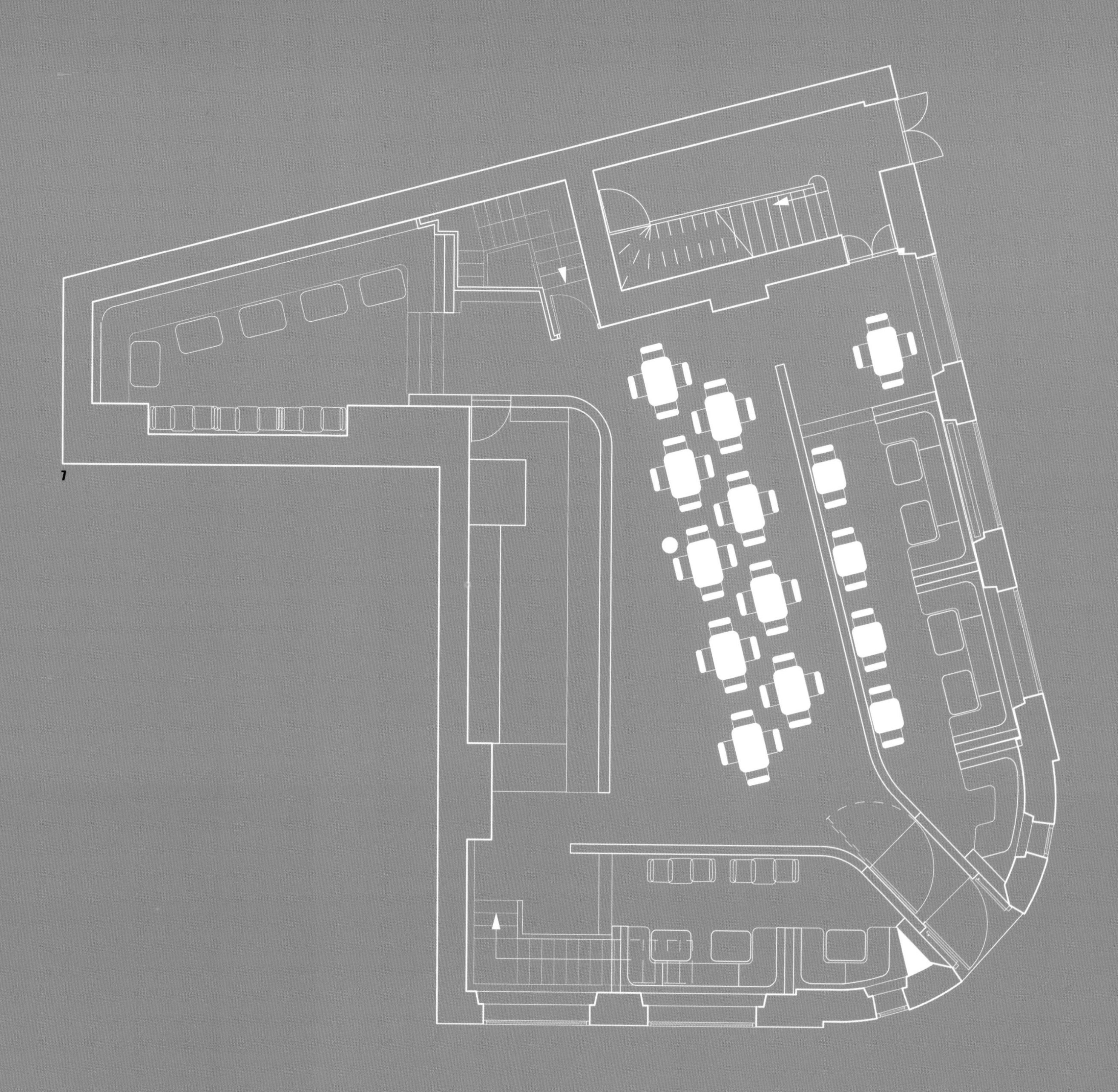

7 Floor plan

8&9 Seating

10 Corridor to restrooms

Photography: Leon Chew

8

9

10

1

2

SYDNEY, **NEW SOUTH WALES, AUSTRALIA**

Guillaume at Bennelong

DALE JONES-EVANS PTY LTD ARCHITECTURE

1 Exterior

2 Exterior, Sydney Harbour Bridge backdrop

3 View into restaurant

3

Usage: Cocktail bar/ restaurant

Area: 11,840 square feet/ 1100 square meters

The re-designing of Guillaume at Bennelong involved the use of light to reinforce the drama and scale of the ribbed shell structure of the Opera House that encases the restaurant. While reinforcing this overwhelming architectural gesture, it was necessary to design a low layer of intimacy, which was achieved using light. A series of small- and large-scale lamps were designed and placed throughout to ensure that an intimate and sensually illuminated ambience occurred.

The architect collaborated with Australian indigenous artists to introduce a direct and abstract sense of aboriginality throughout the space. The aboriginal elements: large- and small-scale painted lamps (painted by Central Desert, Utopia, artist Barbara Weir) and the hollow log-painted memorial poles (*larrakitj*) from the Yolnu people of Gove Peninsula, appear to come from the land below the Opera House and penetrate the ground plane of Utzon's architecture. The eight *larrakitj* (also approached as objet d'art) command center space under the shell, like Captain Cook's flag which was stuck into the shores of Botany Bay more than 200 years ago. The lamps and *larrakitj* seek to remind us of the aboriginal place on which the Opera House and restaurant now stand.

Three terraces flow in open plan from the upper-level cocktail bar. The mid-level central bar is flanked by two large sculpted bronzed vases designed to carry Australian flower arrangements (by Sydney's floral artiste, Grandiflora). The *larrakitj* are also located at the center and ►►

4

heart of the ribbed-shell structure. The color palette of fabrics, furniture, and joinery ranges from muddy browns to saffron orange and anchors the space in contrast to Utzon's white shells. The color scheme also reduces glare and over-lighting and generates a layer of warmth for the restaurant.

4 Overview from lower level

5 Hand-painted lamp and bronzed vase

Opposite Lower-level banquette seating

5

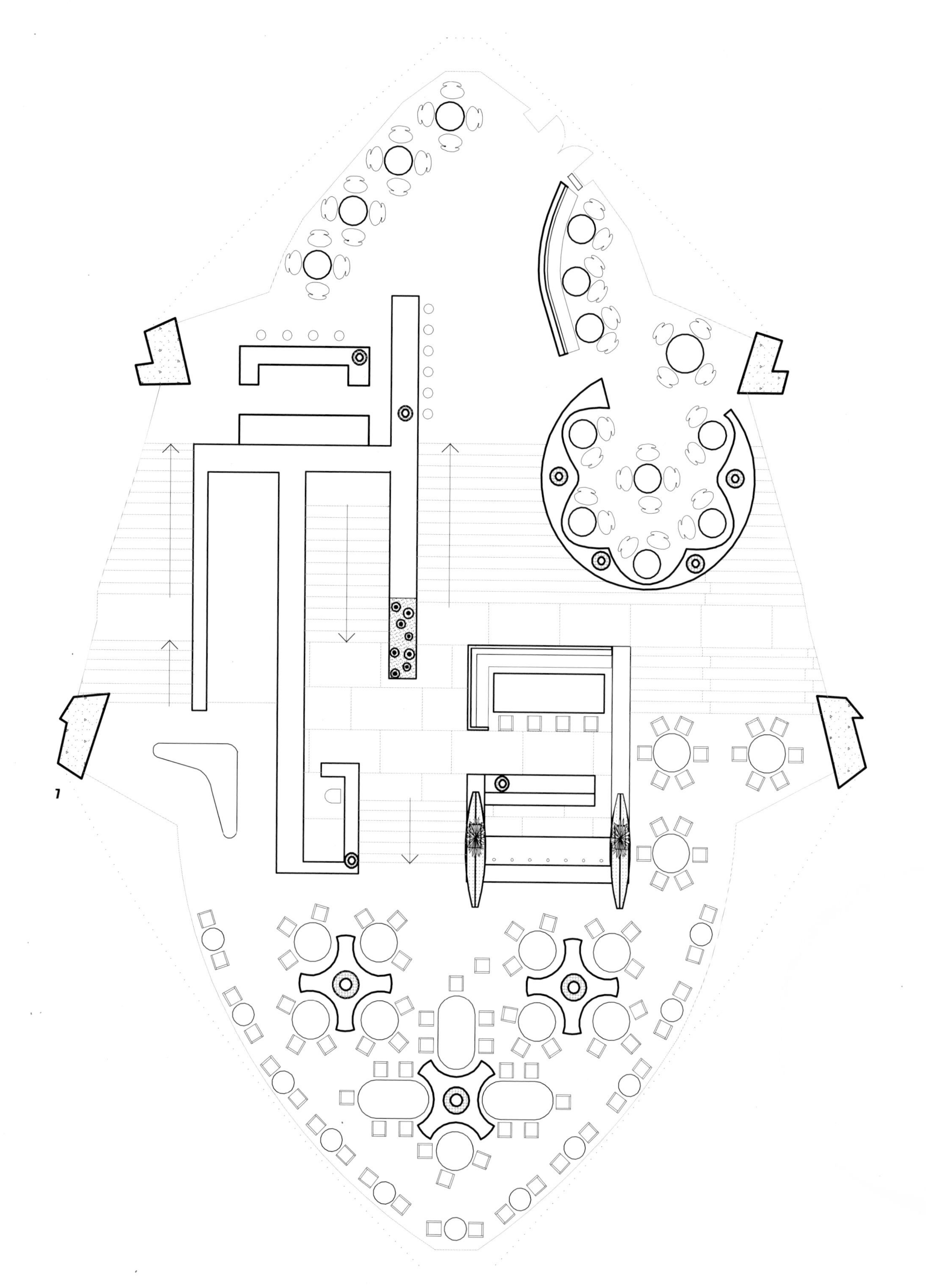

7

8

7 Floor plan

8&9 Memorial poles (*larrakitj*)

10 Bronze vases with sculptural Australian flower arrangements

Photography: Paul Gosney

9

10

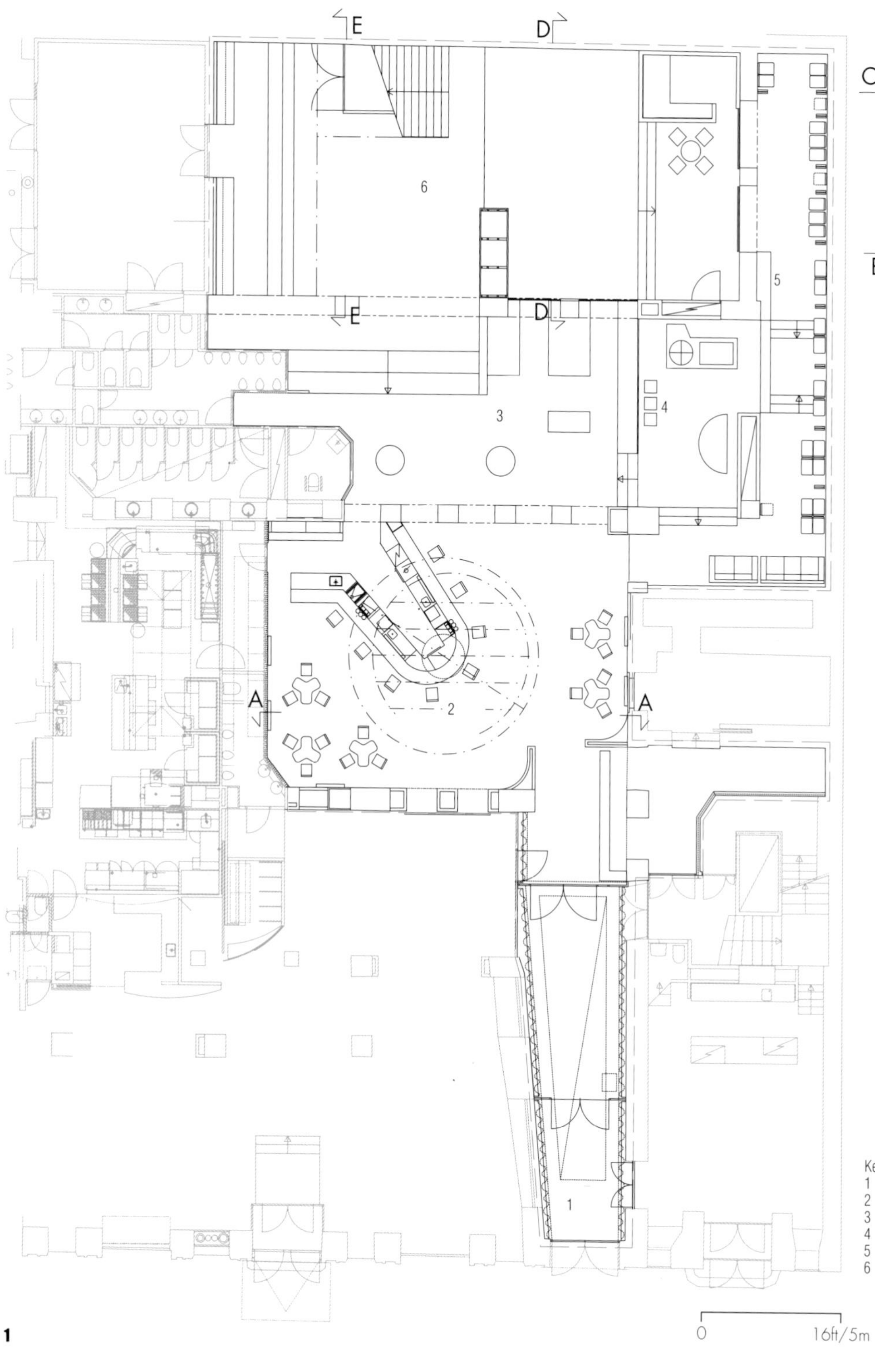

1

2

1 Floor plan

2 Central lounge, featuring extensive use of carpet

3&4 Main dance area with different lighting effects

5 Corridor

Photography: Matti Pyykkö

HELSINKI, FINLAND

Helsinki Club

M41LH2

3

4

5

Client: Sokotel Oy

Usage: Nightclub

Area: 6996 square feet/ 650 square meters

M41LH2 created a luscious and rich atmosphere in one of Helsinki's oldest nightspots, with the assistance of designers from the agency Anteeksi. Together, they refurbished the interior (with the exception of the restrooms and the entrance) of what was originally a 1970's nightclub and casino.

With the use of opulent carpet, mirrors, and gold wallpaper, the new interior appears inviting and luxurious, giving life and warmth to the space. The main dance floor is located beneath a glazed ceiling and features a white bar—a stark contrast to the red and orange tones of the other areas. A lounge room and VIP room continue this color scheme, while 'the back room' features vintage furniture, decorated entirely by the staff for their own use.

1

2

3

HAMBURG, GERMANY

Herzblut

JORDAN MOZER AND ASSOCIATES, LIMITED WITH UDO ULRICH

1 Reinforced concrete façade

2 Dining room doubles as dance floor when seating is removed

3 Balcony seating area

4&5 View toward bar from raised seating areas

6 View toward raised seating area from bar

4

5

6

Usage: Bar/restaurant

Area: 3767 square feet/ 350 square meters

Herzblut was developed to promote Astra Beer for Strenger's clients at the Holsten Brewery in Hamburg. The Astra Beer logo is a heart with an anchor inscribed in it, a celebration of the harbor neighborhood where the beer is brewed. This area is noted for the Reeperban: the famous street filled with theaters and cabarets, and the place where the Beatles played their earliest shows.

The façade and interior are warm, a modern take on an old tavern with surprising details. Inspired by the curve of the hulls of big ships in the Hamburg harbor, the façade is composed of steel reinforcing and painted concrete with front doors made out of rusty steel.

Two arches near the entry are made of glass Bisazza tiles. The stripes suggest the jerseys worn by the St. Pauli football club, one of the sponsors of Herzblut. The illuminated mural, composed and manufactured by Jordan Mozer and Associates, Limited (JMA) along the wall is a series of hearts, another riff on the Astra logo.

The façade and many of the interior walls, are composed of traditional plaster. The plaster forms were designed on computer, then sent via email to Martin Ranft, a master-plasterer, who developed the framing elements at his studio near Frankfurt and shipped them to Hamburg where they were set in place, tied together with lathe, and plastered by hand.

►►

The floor, the bar, and the seating are composed of smoked oak. The light fixtures, composed of spun metal, cast resin, etched acrylic, and blown glass, were designed and fabricated in Chicago and shipped to Hamburg. The back bar shelving is also composed of cast aluminum-magnesium alloy brackets with wood shelves created especially for Herzblut by JMA. The railings are made of raw steel, suggestive of the materials in the Hamburg shipyards. Custom barstools were made by JMA in raw steel tube for the project.

7

7 Bar

8 Barstools custom-designed for Herzblut

9 Heart sculpture

8

9

10

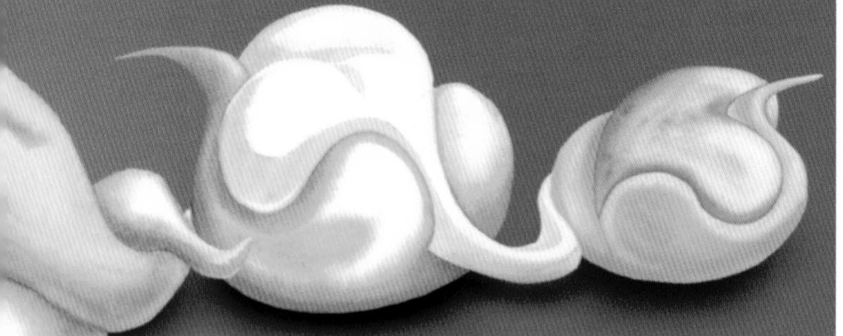

11

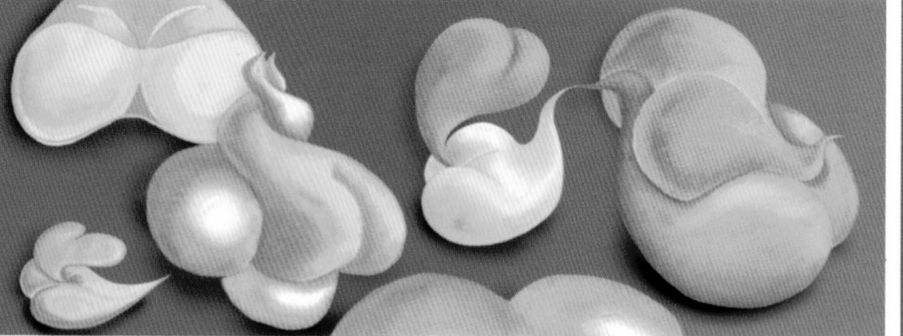

12

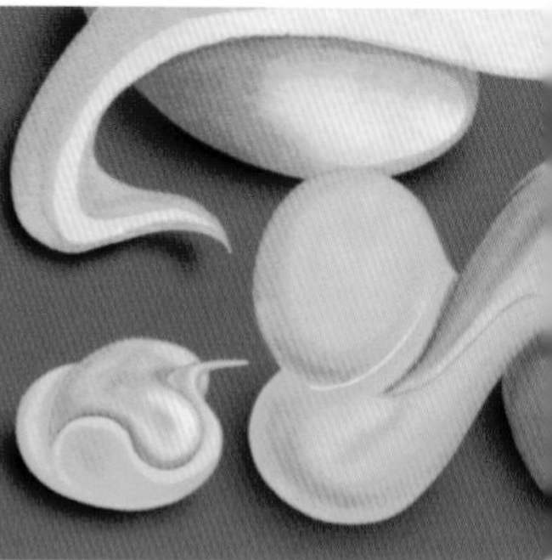

13

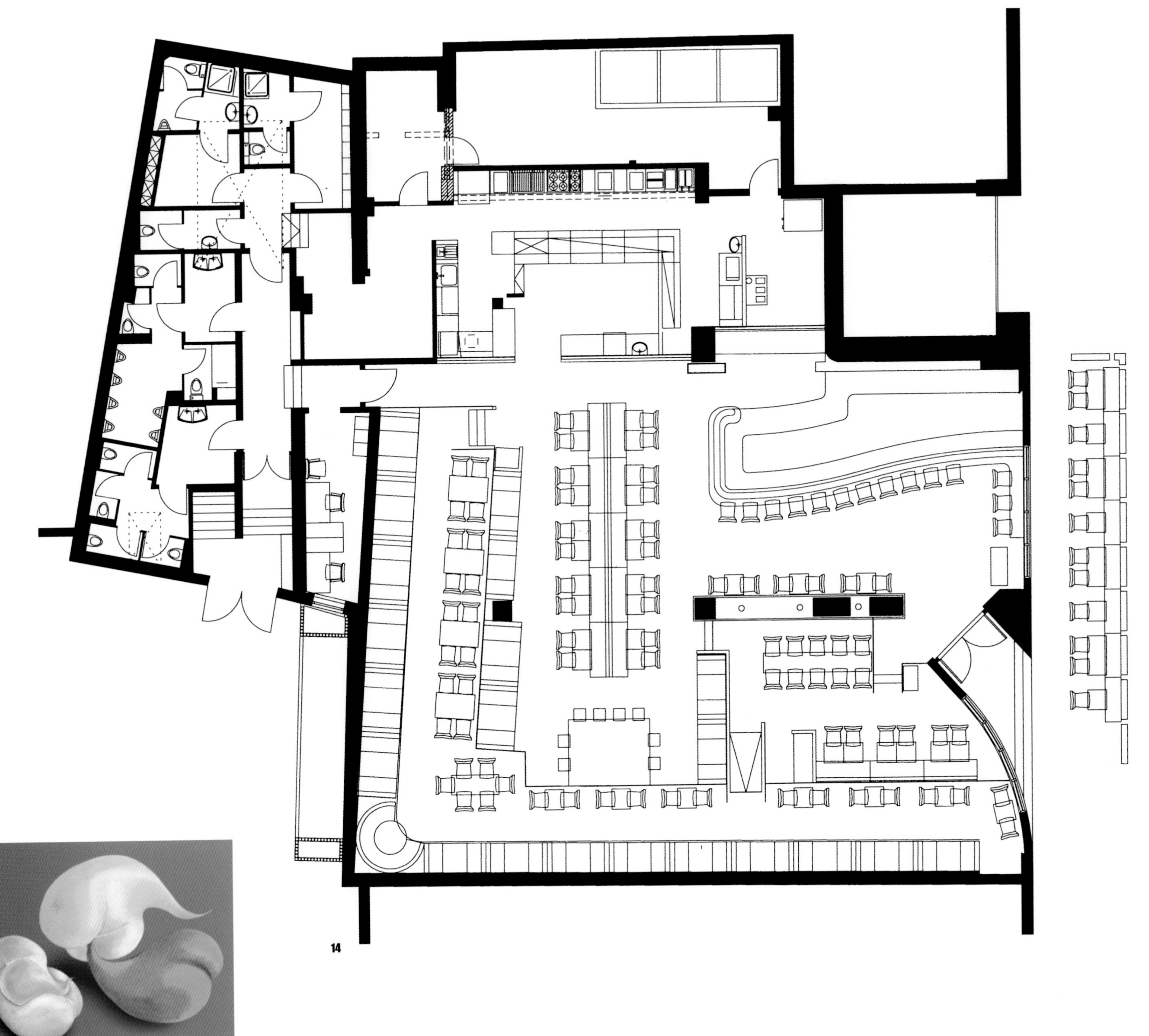

10 Raised seating area with illuminated mural above

11–13 Mural

14 Floor plan

Photography: Klaus Frahm

1

2

MUELHEIM, GERMANY

Himmelreich

JORDAN MOZER AND ASSOCIATES, LIMITED

Client: Karstadt

Usage: Bar/café

Area: 6458 square feet/ 600 square meters

JMA was responsible for the development of the design for the new Karstadt Lifestyle Prototype Department store. Himmelreich is located within the women's fashion zone. The venue features a very long bar, which has a parallel bar-height banquette, encouraging density. The café area is filled with tables and overlooks the street, while the lounge area is toward the rear. The café is accessible from the parking lot, so it can remain open later than the store, operating as a separate business.

The ceiling of Himmelreich was built in plaster, and is composed of four different melted and perforated planes. Like most of Jordan Mozer's projects, there are a number of elements that were designed exclusively for the project. The light fixtures and enormous lanterns that are curved and perforated, were designed in CAD in Chicago and cut using CAM in Germany, and then sanded and lacquered. The flooring, composed of Amtico vinyl tile, was also designed this way.

1 Raised lounge overlooking café

2 Bar-height seating area

Lager
WC
Vorraum
WC
Spülküche
R11/A/4
Kellner-
gang
Müllraum
Topfspüle
Dispo
R10
Warme Küche
AFG
Kühlraum
Kühlraum
Tiefkühlraum
Kalte Küche
AUSGABE
NA
NA

3

4

3 Bar floor plan

4 Café toward bar

Photography: Doug Snower

1

2

3

CHICAGO, **ILLINOIS, USA**

Hudson Club

JORDAN MOZER AND ASSOCIATES, LIMITED

1&5 Entry door

2 Façade at night

3&4 Façade detail

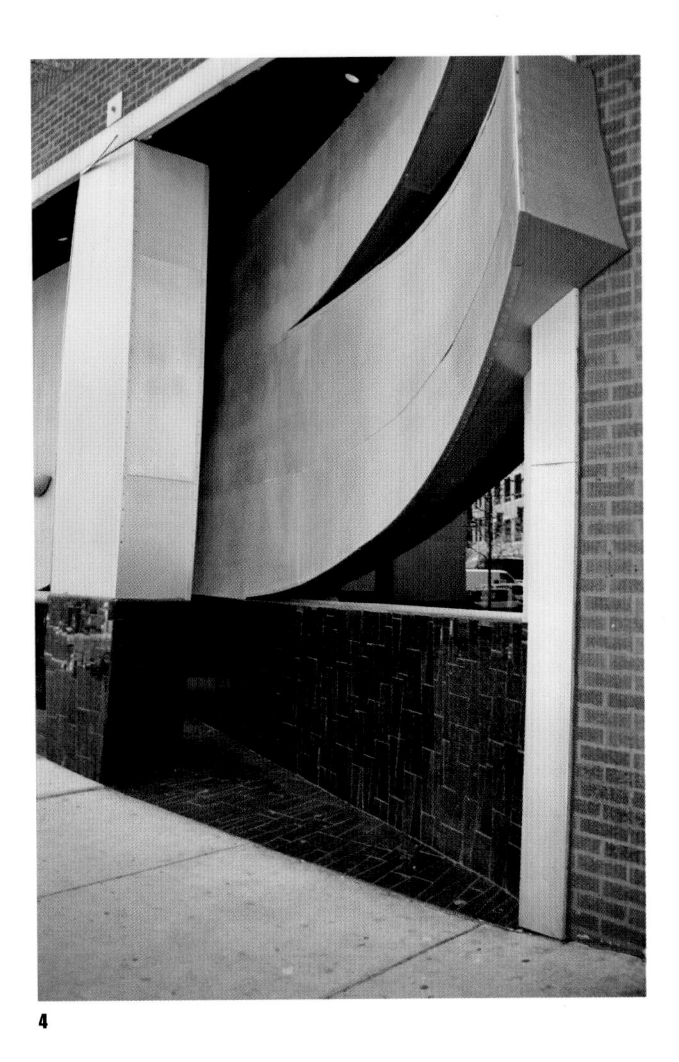

4

5

Usage: Wine bar

Area: 10,765 square feet/ 1000 square meters

Materials: Drywall, aluminum, velvet, vinyl

The owners asked JMA to assist them in the development of a modern American brasserie and bar that would offer 'flights' of wine. The new environment was to be a mixture of 'tomorrow' and 'once upon a time', with an emphasis on the 1930s. During its research the design team became transfixed not by the architecture of the period, but by the design of airplanes, dirigibles, and fantasies about spacecraft.

The existing building was built like an airplane hangar, with 75-foot-long wooden trusses in the ceiling. One long speedy room was developed that had terraces and rooms opening onto it. Wings sprouted from walls and window openings became 'pushed' ovals, egg-like—inspired by blurred photographs of airplane windows in flight, and by the dynamic forms of teardrops, airplane wing sections, and whales. A sense of movement and flight was invoked for the design of chairs and barstools, again employing sections used in airplane fuselage and tail design.

6 Bar, custom-framed mirror above

7 Bar with maple counter

8 Entry to lounge

9 Raised booths

10 Aluminum railing at raised platform

11 View of restaurant from rear

12 Table detail

13 View from behind bar

Photography: Doug Snower (1,3–5,12); David Clifton (2,6–11,13)

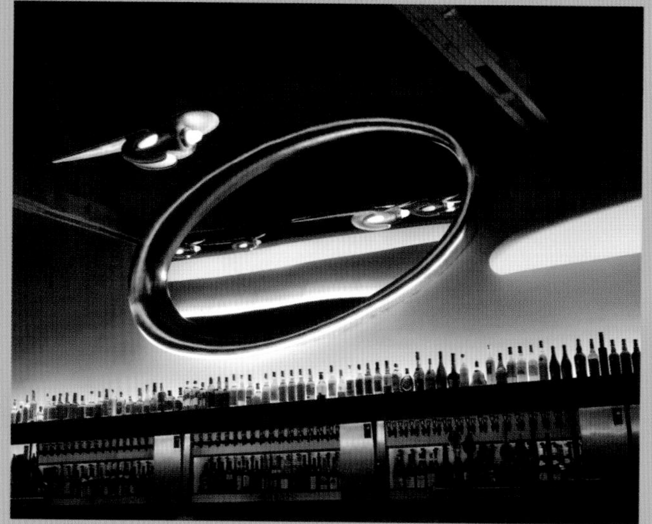

6

8

7

9

10

11

12

13

1

2

HONG KONG SAR, PRC

Isola

LEIGH & ORANGE LTD.

1 Bar pod, view from street

2 Fourth-level terrace

3 Interior showing Hong Kong harbor at night

3

Usage: Bar/restaurant

Area: 7500 square feet/ 696 square meters

Materials: Corian, pine

Situated on levels three and four of IFC Two, this restaurant and bar has spectacular views of the Hong Kong Harbour. The bar, placed within a 7-meter-high glass box, is associated with a large landscaped terrace, designed for casual outdoor drinking.

The bar, completely finished in white, has been left very simple to allow the view outside to take prominence. The ceiling is an exposed, painted steel structure with aluminum profile sheeting. The bar wall is finished in painted timber perforated acoustic paneling that counteracts the acoustically hard finishes of the glass walls. The flooring is in antique reclaimed pine planks from London. Giant mirror balls hang from the ceiling, providing a soft dappled light, as the bar goes from being a lounge to a venue for late-night dancing.

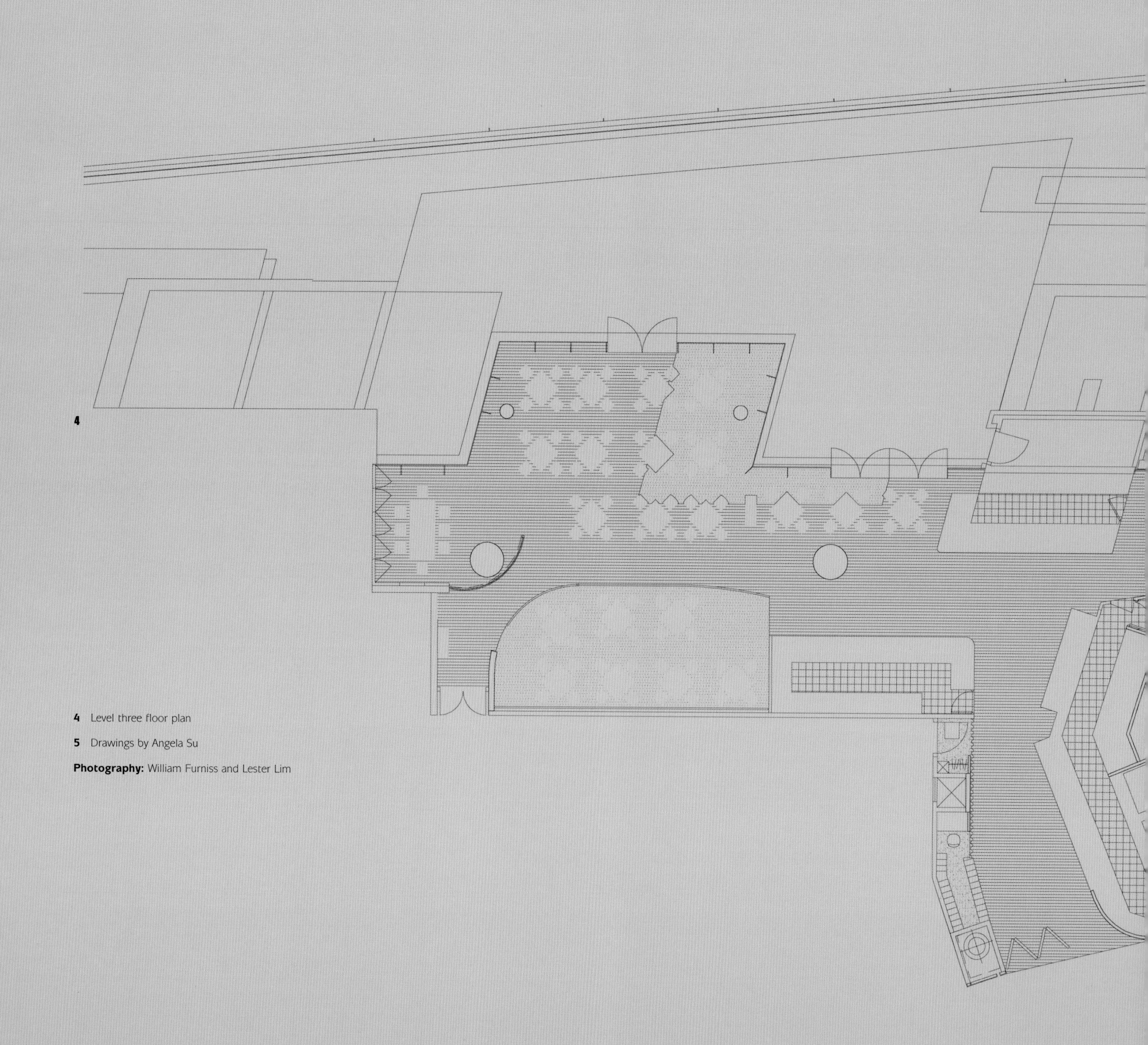

4 Level three floor plan

5 Drawings by Angela Su

Photography: William Furniss and Lester Lim

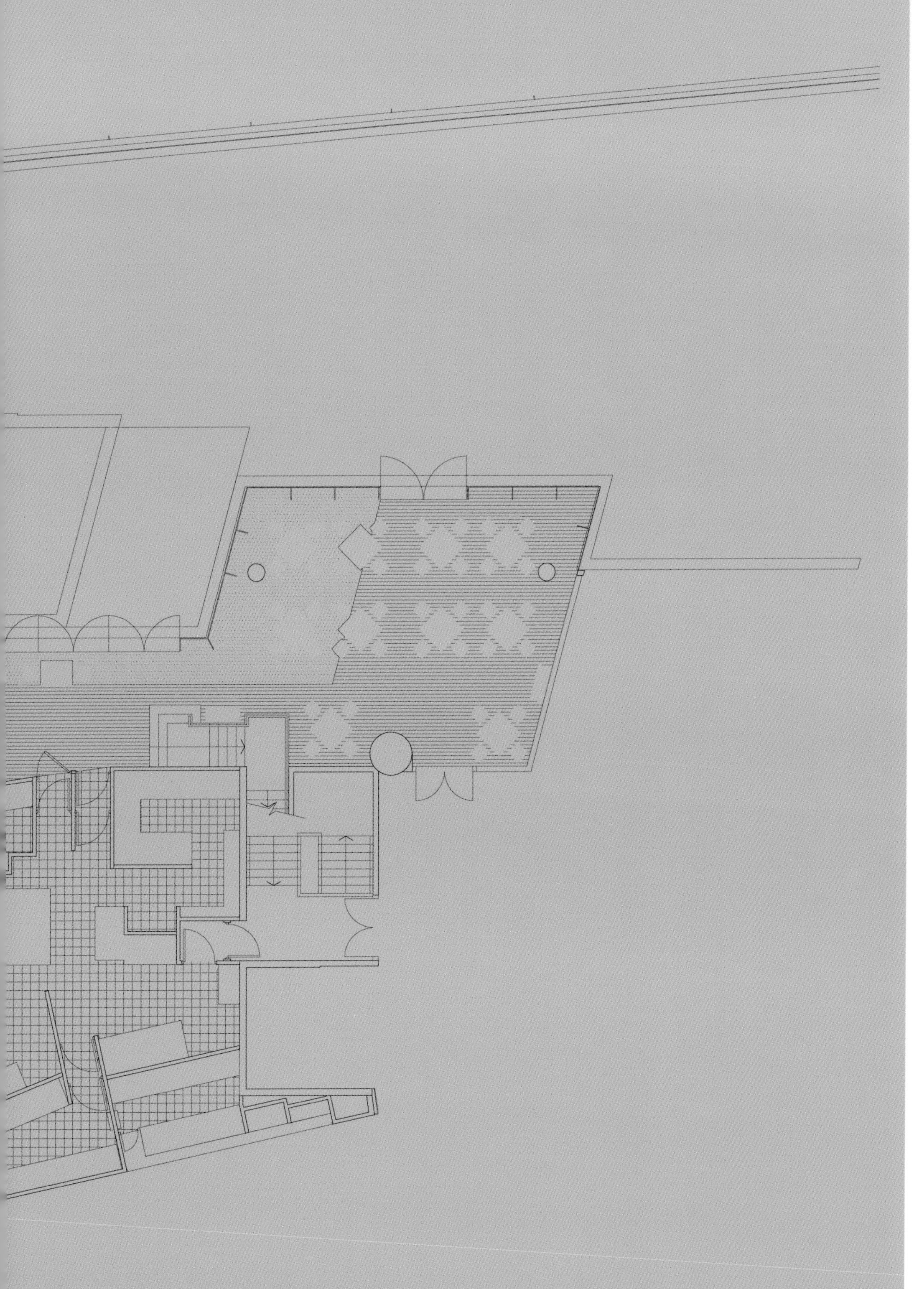

5

1

2

3

CONSTANTA, ROMANIA

Kat Café

TWINS DESIGN

4

5

1&3 Café seating

2 Bar and counter link café and music shop

4 Concrete and wood contrasted

5 Tunnel of sound: backlit aluminum panels, DJ booth at rear

Client: Dan Popi
Usage: Café/music store
Area: 3229 square feet/ 300 square meters

Designed by Mihai Popescu inside a mall in Constanta, Kat is a fusion between a music store and a café, promoting quality music and the pleasure of coffee. The entrance is made through a tunnel of sound, bordered by specially designed wooden panels, covered with stiplex finishing. The central panels on which the CDs are displayed are made using a sliding system and serve as the border between the café and the music store. These sliding panels increase or decrease the café space for special events.

The café area is a warm zone, created by use of wood on the floor and walls. Its tables are made of veneered wood with a glass plate and are complemented with leather sofas and chairs. The large bar binds together the highlighted areas and the lighting objects: matt glass spheres that create Kat's cozy atmosphere.

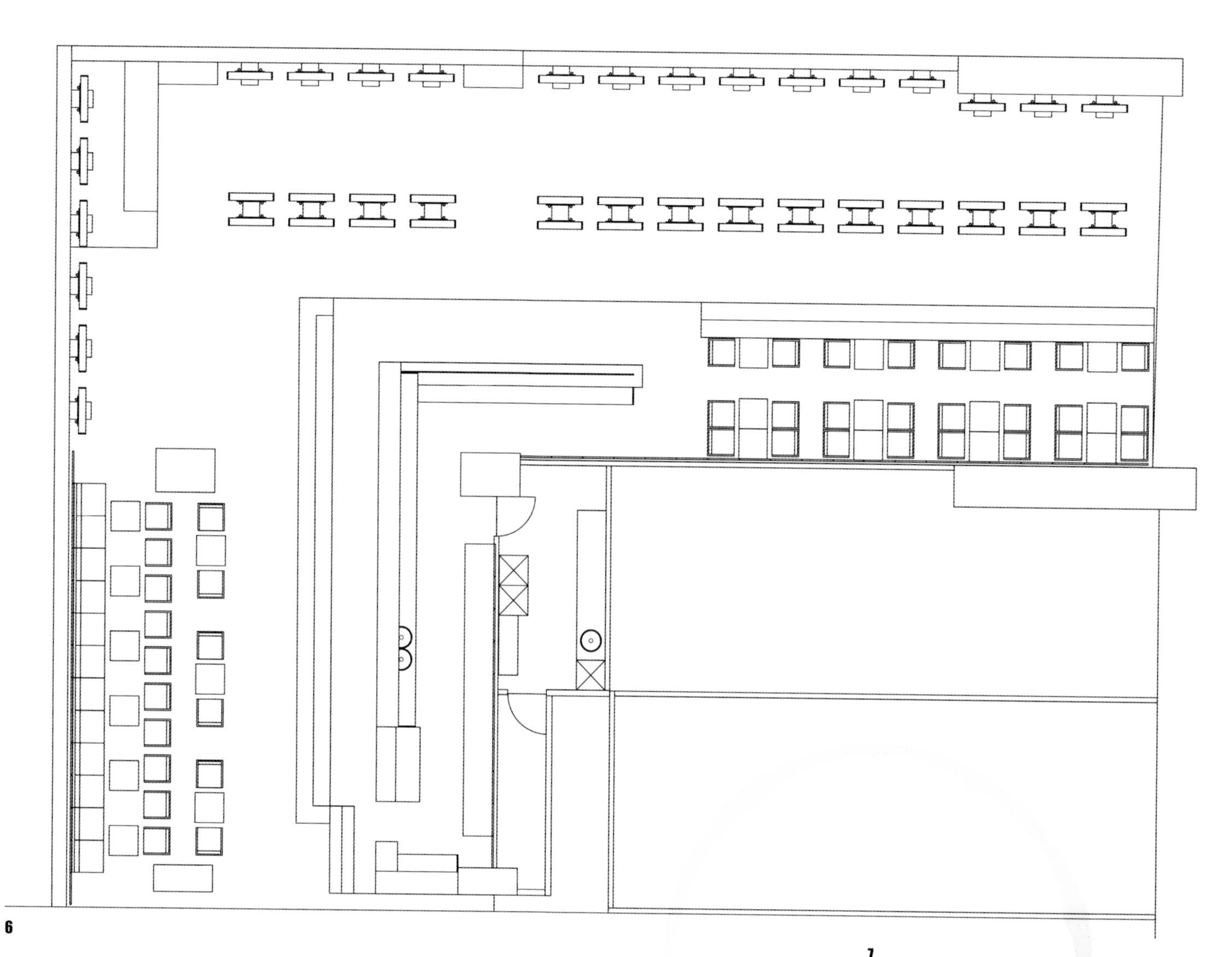

6

7

6 Floor plan

7 Graphic design

8 CD shelves

9 Bar

10 General view

Photography: Cristian Tanase

8

10

9

1

2

3

1 Night view of chandelier

2 Central bar

3 VIP area

4 View from dance floor toward seating

5 Numerous video screens, wooden dance floor, and chandelier

6 VIP area detail

Photography: Christian Tanase; Marius Bercu

BUCHAREST, **ROMANIA**

Kristal Glam Club

TWINS DESIGN

4

6

5

Usage: Nightclub/ events venue

Area: 6996 square feet/ 650 square meters

Bucharest was in need of a venue that would house more than 1200 people and feature international performers and DJs. After an extensive search, the owner discovered a former cinema hall located in a residential area that was well suited to house Romania's biggest, newest, and most popular nightclub. The structure, foyer, lobby, and cinema were retained while a luxurious new interior was created.

The bar is built of wood and quilted with a golden fabric. The surrounding walls are wood-veneered and offer a sense of grandeur and very good acoustics. Archways and ornamental work surround classic sofas in the VIP area, and an enormous picture frame highlights the DJ booth.

The design is classic, yet quite simple: there is a central dance floor, a bar, and surrounding sofas with tables, as well as a VIP area. The most extraordinary feature is the club's light source—an enormous 6 x 3-meter chandelier, with more than 7000 brilliant parts. Lasers project onto the chandelier, which by reflection distributes the light throughout the entire club, taking it to the screens and beyond. Sixteen video projectors that surround the space assist the drama chromatically and visually.

1

TORONTO, ONTARIO, CANADA

Lexus Lounge in Roy Thomson Hall

KUWABARA PAYNE MCKENNA BLUMBERG ARCHITECTS

1 Curved ebony wall at entry

Client: The Corporation of Massey Hall and Roy Thomson Hall

Usage: Bar/lounge

With the successful completion of the auditorium enhancements to Roy Thomson Hall, attention was directed to other areas of potential improvement. In a gesture of appreciation for the contributors of the ongoing facility investments, the decision was made to transform the former rehearsal hall into a sponsor's lounge.

The proposed location of the lounge posed several challenges, not in the least another incursion into the strong architectural framework of Arthur Erickson's original design. Although this phase was of a dramatically smaller scale than the concert hall enhancements, the same measure of sensitivity and respect toward the design legacy of the building was taken. Two particular impositions of the existing environment were apparent from the onset: the geometry of the curved wall and the materiality of the concrete.

As a transposition of the sweeping curve of the existing north wall, a second curved element was introduced. The convex surface of the ebony wall leads one in from the vestibule and deflects the circulation into the lounge. In response to the predominant presence of the concrete, the same strategy in the main auditorium was redeployed here. A sleeve of maple was inserted into the volume to add warmth and to lend a material resonance with the concert hall.

In keeping with the mirrored pageantry of the main lobby, the lounge was conscientiously designed as a place to see and be seen in. ►►

2

3

The clear strip of glazing at the vestibule wall invites the cinematic panning of the room, and the lighting at the bar receives its inspiration both from the diffused side illumination of photographic studios and the dramatic overhead point lighting of theatrical stages.

Ultimately the success of the lounge depends on its ability to impart to the patron a sense of the importance of their contribution. As such, the space does not seek to draw overt attention to itself, but to serve as a sumptuous backdrop that compliments the patron and elevates their concert-going experience.

2 View to exterior

3 Ebony bar and sandblasted glass partition with clear glass window

Opposite Entry vestibule with new glass partition juxtaposed to existing curved concrete wall

5 Bar end detail

6 Bar with view to lobby

7 Bar with view to sandblasted-maple art wall

Photography: Peter Sellar/KLIK, 2004

5

6

7

1

2

EDINBURGH, UK

The Links Bar

LEE BOYD

3

4

1 Exterior

2 Curved ceiling above bar

3 Curved ceiling above seating

4 Seating

Client: Festival Inns Ltd

Usage: Bar

Lee Boyd was commissioned to design a new bar for Festival Inns Ltd, the owner of the venues, formerly named Park Bar and Alvanley Hotel. Sandwiched in between was the rather run down Bruntsfield Links Hotel and Bar. When Festival Inns purchased the Bruntsfield Links, the opportunity arose to join all three properties together to create one large bar with a 30-bedroom hotel above.

The creation of a double-height pool hall between two existing extensions to the rear created additional floor space, and removed the intermediate floor from one of the extensions. The rear extension features transparent Kalwall to bring light into an otherwise dark recess, while minimizing sound and heat loss.

The new bar, clad using oak strips with wenge stain, links the existing bar through to the new area. The stained-glass window feature in the central space, designed by local artist Inge Paneels, hints at the sports theme and provides a link to the older bar.

Externally, a terraced area is expanded over the full elevation of the building. Traditional railings have been reinstated at each end but then step down to reveal the landscaping behind the low stone wall. The boundary walls between each plot have been finished in hardwood timber slats to provide supplementary seating. The Links Bar now offers a continuous series of spaces with different characters to suit all forms of bar life.

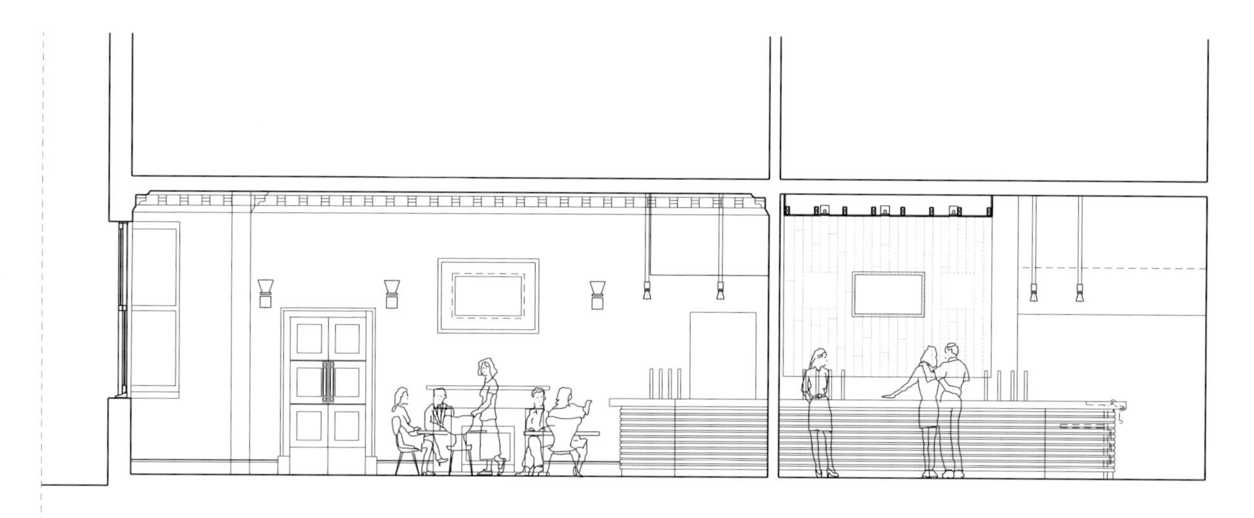

5

6

9

7

8

5 Section

6 Lounge/dining area

7 View toward rear

8 View toward entrance

9 Stained glass panel by Inge Paneels

10 Ground floor plan

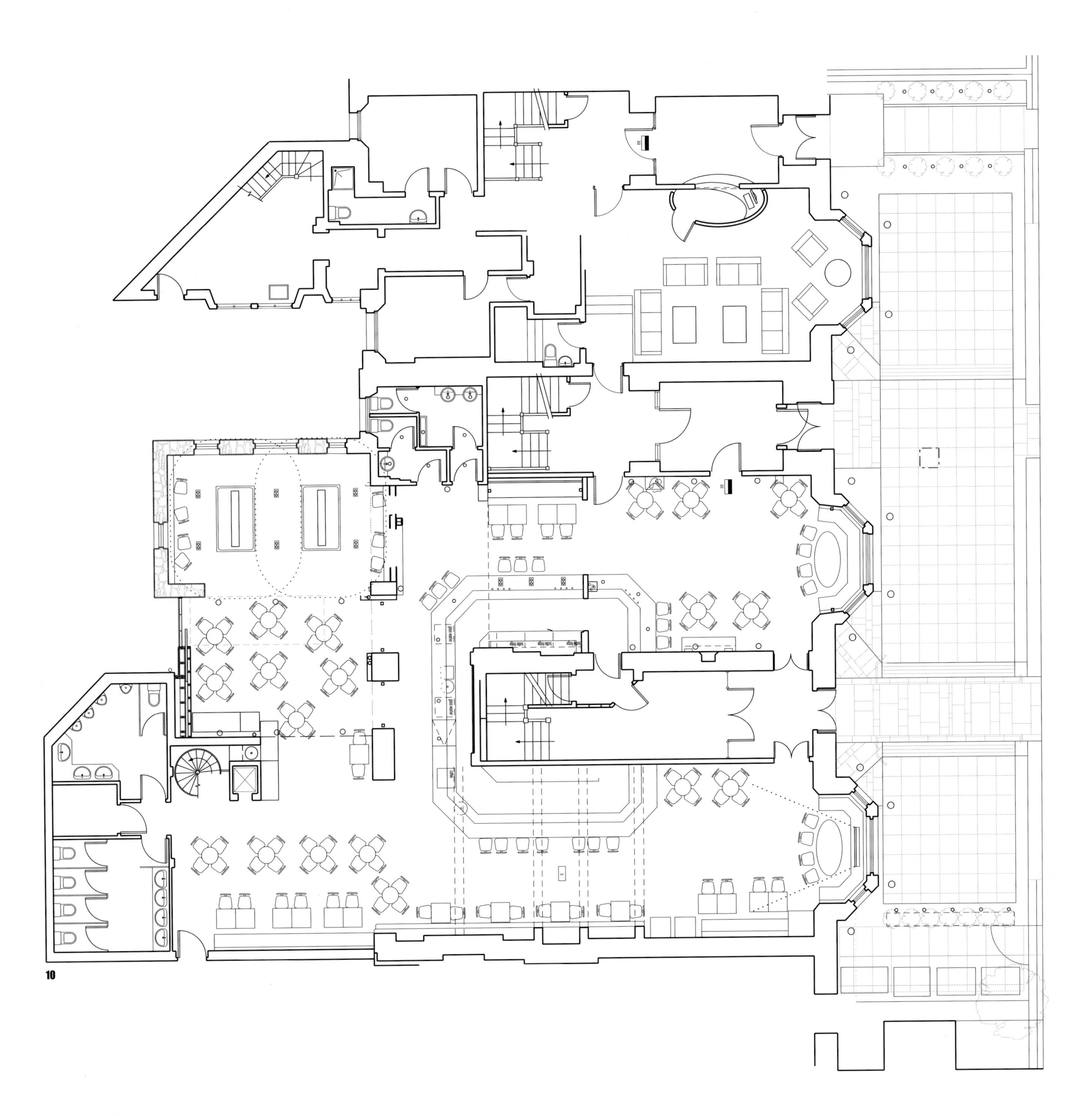

10

12

11&12 The Pool Hall

13 Stained glass panel and restrooms

14 Elevation

Photography: Paul Zanre

13

14

1

2

1–3 Bar, with bamboo ceiling and paper lanterns, bungalow8

KING STREET WHARF, **NEW SOUTH WALES, AUSTRALIA**

the loft and bungalow8

DALE JONES-EVANS PTY LTD ARCHITECTURE

3

Usage: Bar/restaurant

Materials: Glazed split bamboo, zinc, laser-cut Pacific cedar marine plywood, New Guinea blackbean

Commissioned as one project, the brief required two spaces with two identities that would operate independently and be physically linked (the Link is a common stair that can be subdivided with a bamboo gate). One kitchen would service both spaces.

bungalow8's ambience comes from a painterly materiality and interaction with light sources. The warm 'off black-brown' textured and lacquered space, washed with differential low levels of illuminated and reflective light act as a seductive painting. This golden colored light paints the reversed split-faced bamboo and stained-rattan walls.

The long bar runs parallel with the water's edge and buries itself deeply within the cool recesses of the building, a retreat from the light and heat. The open kitchen was planned to have immediate address with the public domain as well as the interior space. This project utilizes quite common materials and has acoustic treatment throughout.

theloft is a lunch and dinner tapas bar and a cocktail bar by night. The space is precious and ornate, rich in color and texture, with oversized couches. Furniture was over-scaled, padded and cigar-like, ►►

soft, and comfortable. Dani Marti, a rope artist, collaborated with the architects to produce a large wall piece.

The placement of the large horseshoe-shaped bar is highlighted by the intensity of the tangerine beaded jelly-like chandeliers above. A screen device ensures a separate function area while remaining visually connected.

4

5

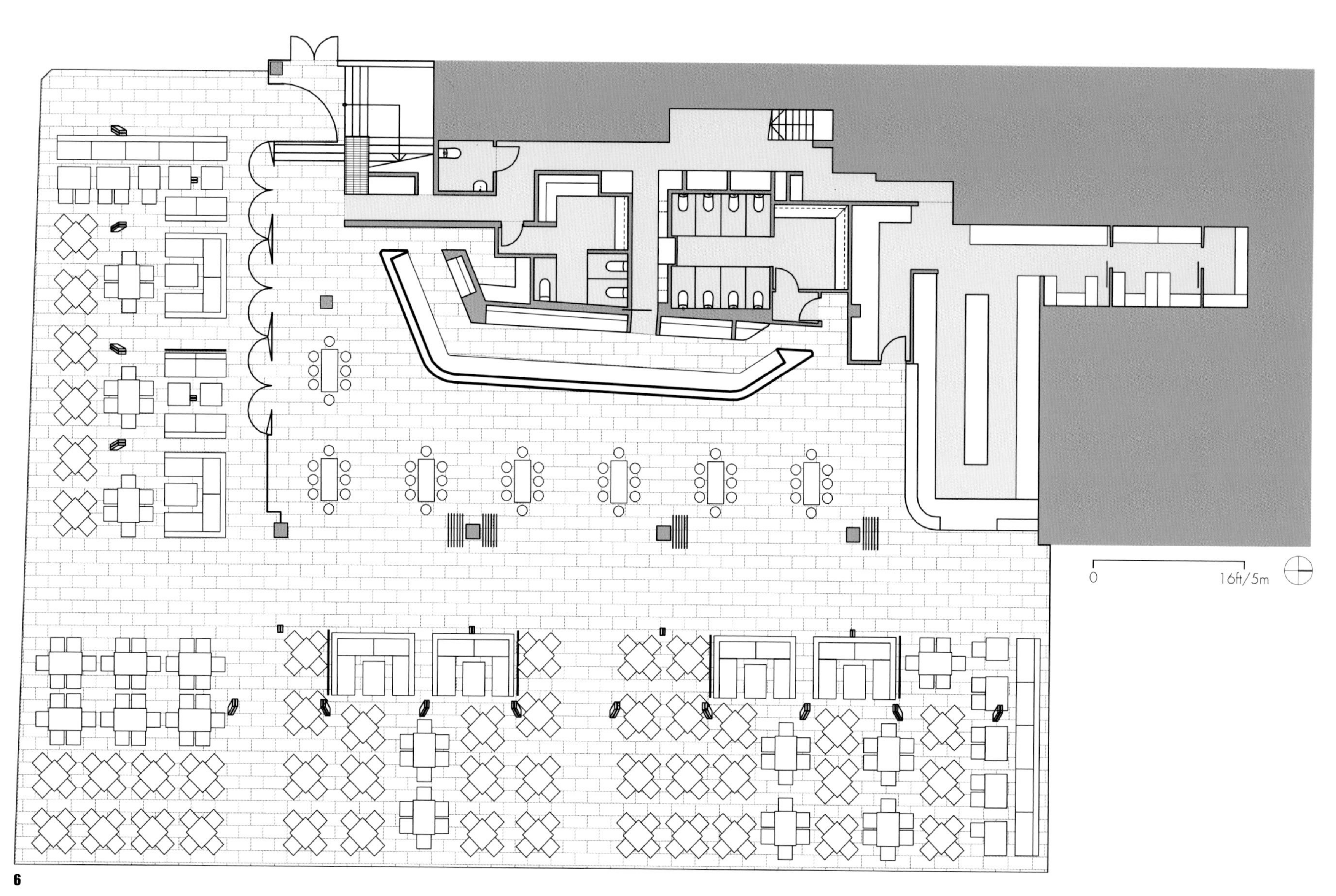

6

7

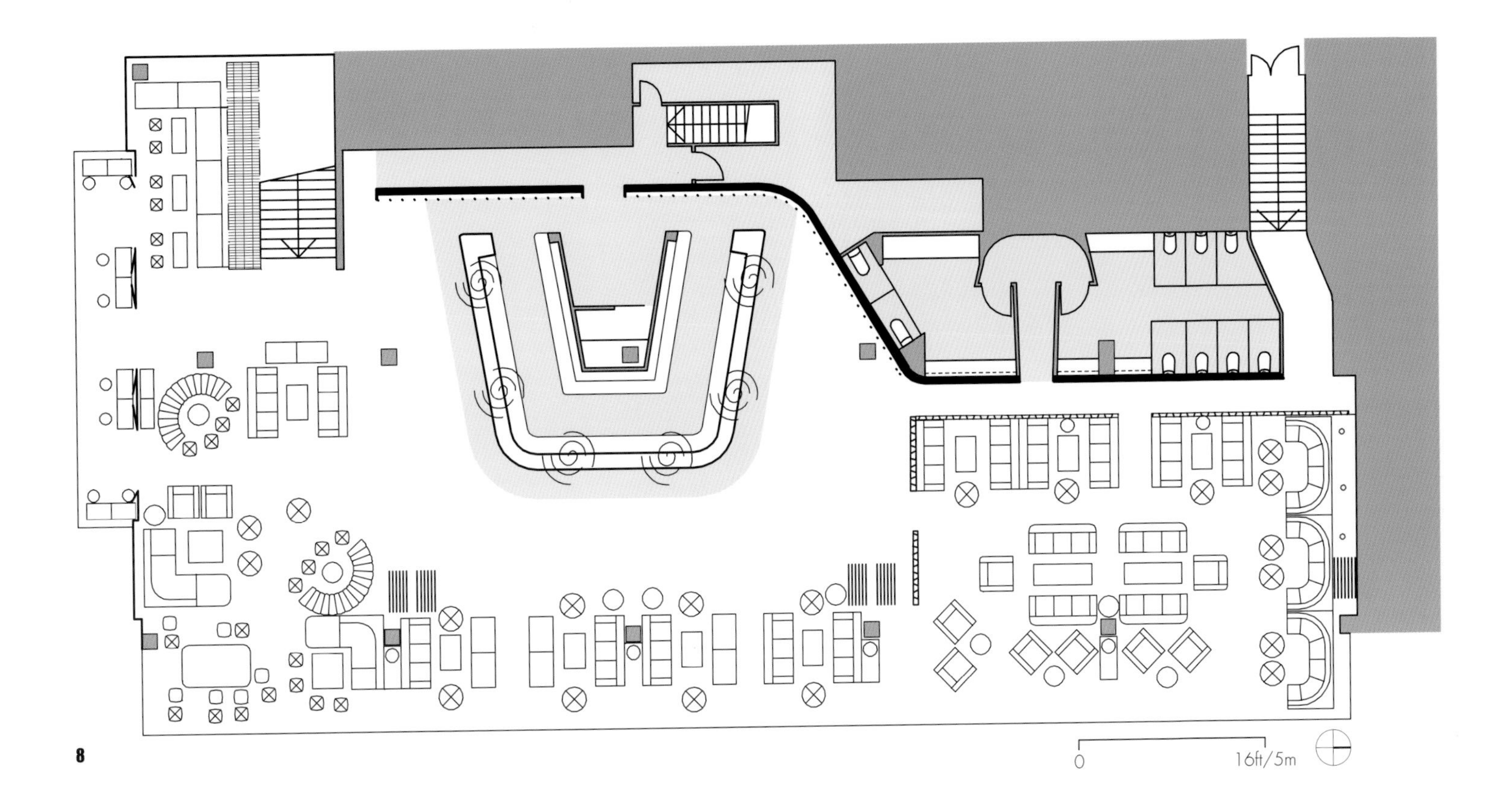

8

4 Lightbox and stairwell, linking two floors

5 Horseshoe-shaped bar

6 Floor plan, bungalow8

7 Chandeliers, bar, lightbox in background

8 Floor plan, theloft

9

10

11

12

9 Laser-cut screens containing lounge area

10 Beaded chandelier detail

11 Lounge area with laser-cut screens

12 Rear-illuminated wall feature

Photography: Paul Gosney

1

HOLLYWOOD, CALIFORNIA, USA
ORANGE COUNTY, CALIFORNIA, USA

Lucky Strike

SFJONES ARCHITECTS

1 Private party area, Hollywood

2 Bar, Hollywood

3 Lanes and sign, Hollywood

4 Bar from seating area, Hollywood

3

2

4

Client: Steven Foster
Usage: Bar/bowling alley
Area: 19,580 square feet/ 1819 square meters (California)
24,790 square feet/ 2303 square meters (Orange County)

Material was salvaged from the interior of a long-running bowling alley before it was torn down and reused for this project. Lane 16 from the old venue formed the new bar top and some of the furniture was designed using various other parts of leftover lanes. The Hollywood sign and the stars, once used as movie props, were also rescued.

The new Hollywood venue is located in a basement space that has its own street entrance. A 9-meter bowling pin hangs from the side of the wall outside the door. Inside, photographed art is projected on large screens at the end of the lanes. These images are synchronized with a DJ stand that plays music and coordinates the art images on the screens.

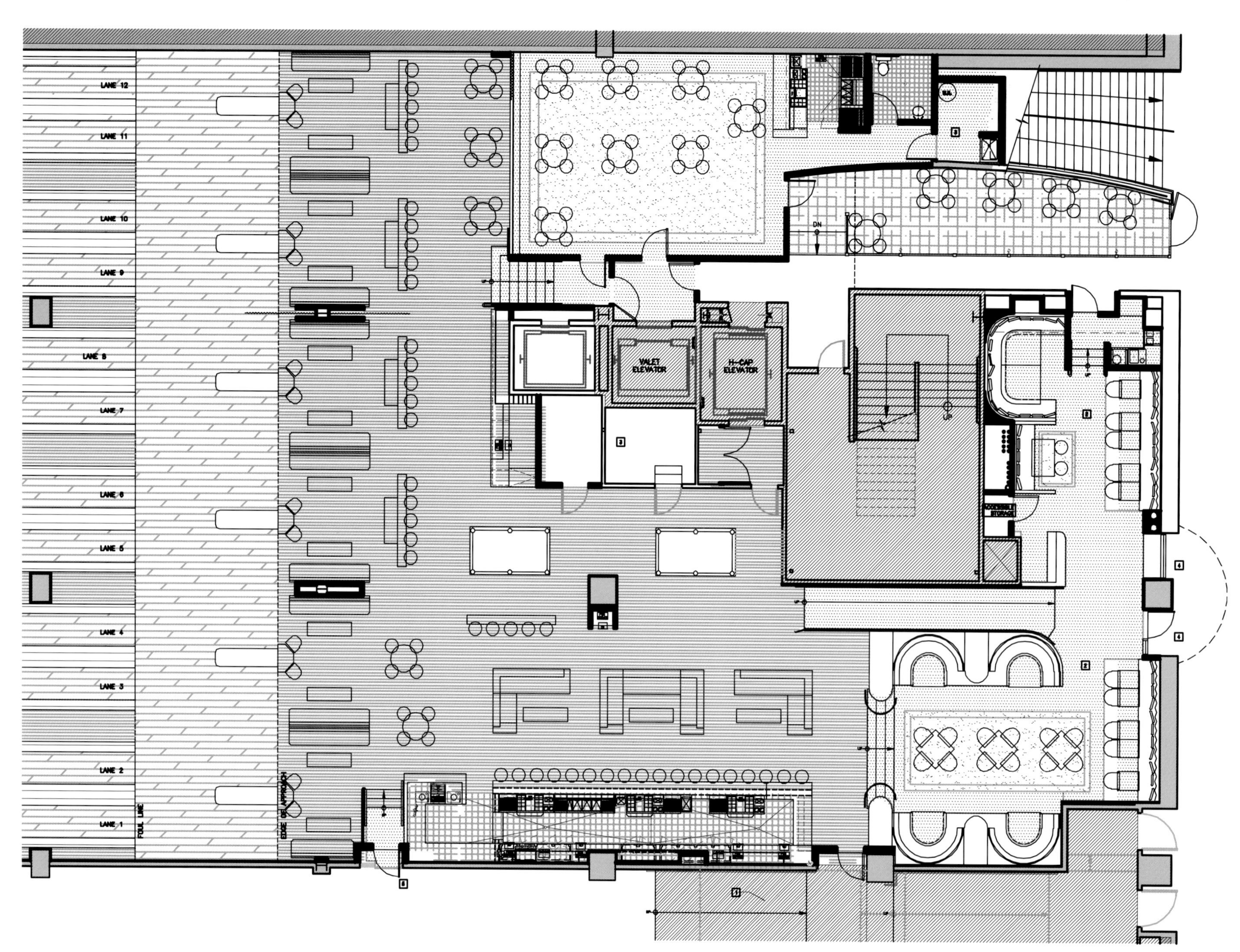
LANE 12
LANE 11
LANE 10
LANE 9
LANE 8
LANE 7
LANE 6
LANE 5
LANE 4
LANE 3
LANE 2
LANE 1
FOUL LINE
VALET ELEVATOR
H-CAP ELEVATOR
UP
DN
ACCESSIBLE STORAGE

5

6

7

8

5 Floor plan, Hollywood

6 Exterior, Orange County

7 Pool area, Orange County

8 Private lounge/lanes, Orange County

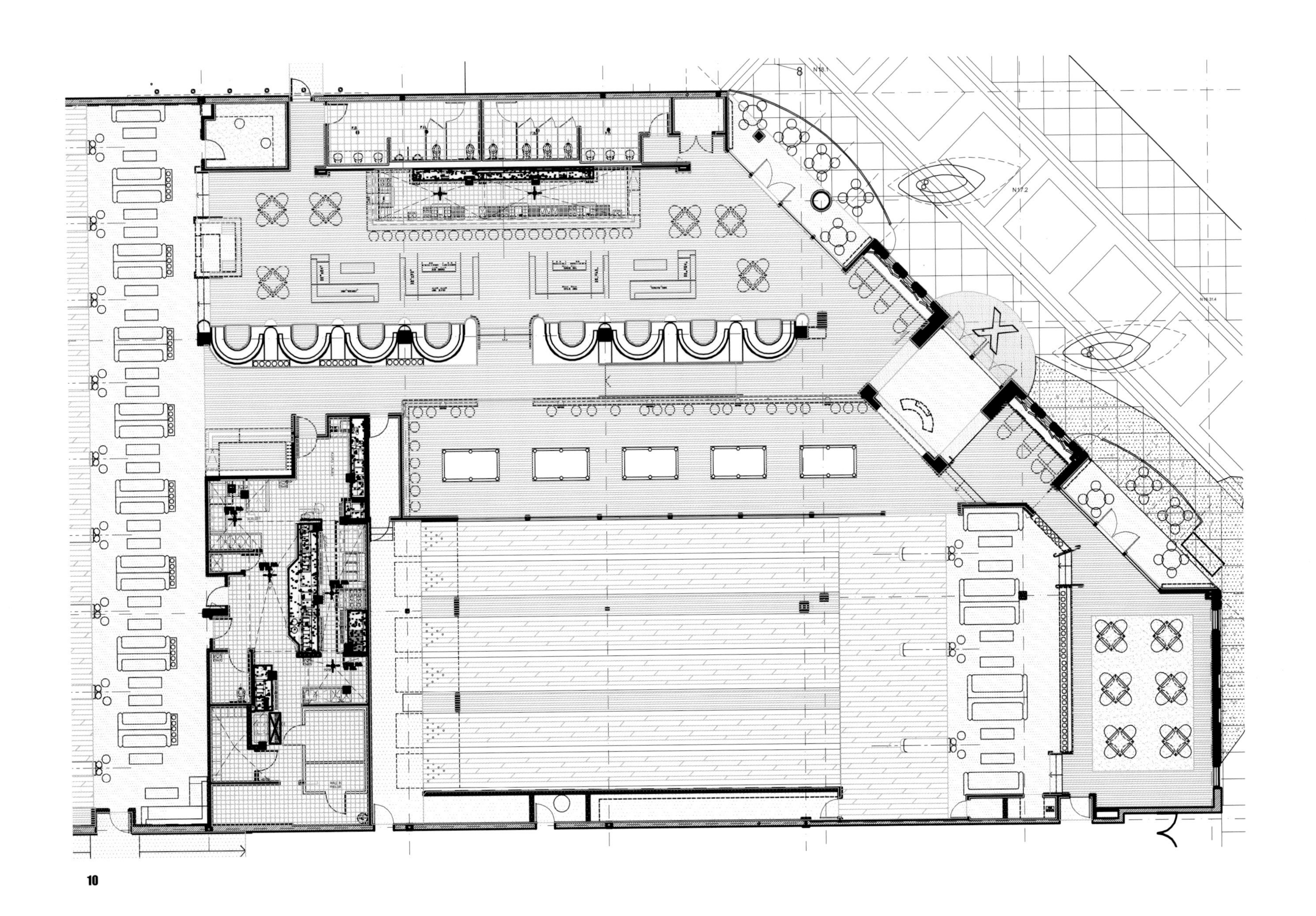

10

Opposite Dining area/bar lounge, Orange County

10 Floor plan, Orange County

Photography: Weldon Brewster

1

2

1 Zinc-topped bar

2 Cosy niche with signature Malmaison sofas

3 Full-height wooden blinds

4 Stair to bar

5 Internal elevation of bar and restaurant

Photography: James Morris

BIRMINGHAM, **UK**

Malmaison **Birmingham Hotel Bar**

JESTICO + WHILES

3

4

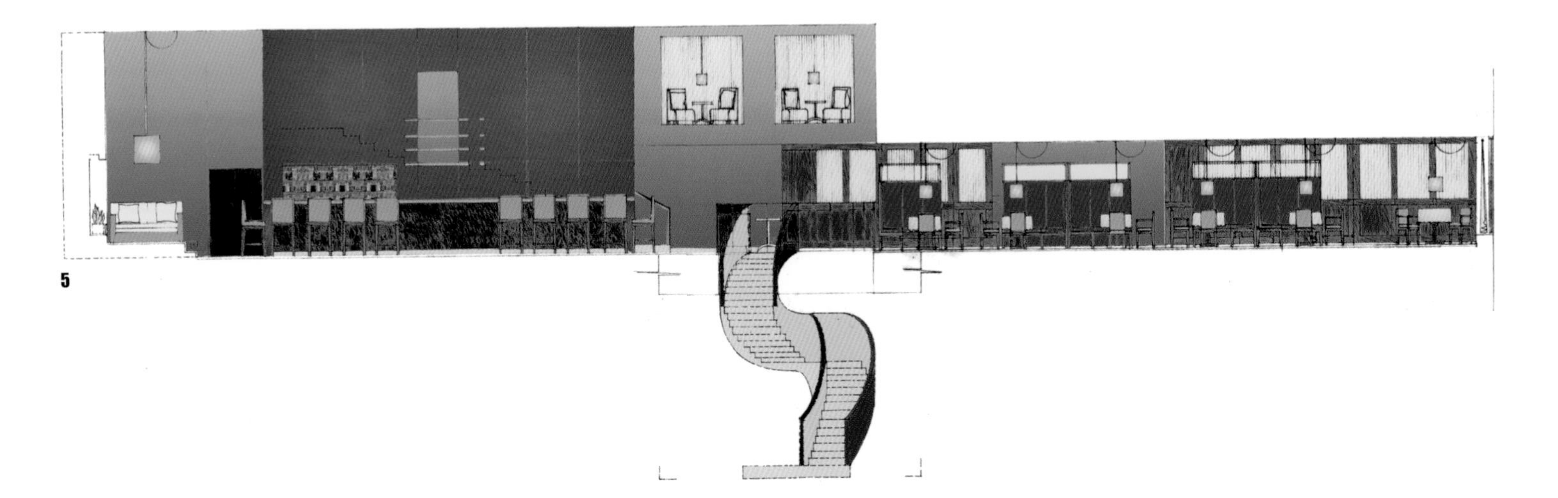

5

Client: Malmaison Ltd

Usage: Bar

Materials: Glass, limestone flooring, wood, zinc

Malmaison is a boutique hotel brand. Its unique character is defined by a blend of Scottish origins and strong continental influences, namely the 19th-century French chateau Malmaison, whose name and image it borrows.

Malmaison is a highly individual and stylish hotel group so it was important that the architects responded to the established core values, but also take them forward to a new chapter.

The Mailbox building's steel structure has allowed for more generous spaces, particularly in the front of house areas. Jestico + Whiles embraced this opportunity to open the space and created a magnificent double-height bar with a large raspberry-red backlit glass backdrop and soaring double-height bar and brasserie that become the heart of the hotel. In contrast, the soft niches have a real fire at one end, and by the window at the opposite end, high-back signature chairs. The window in the bar area is dressed with full-height wooden blinds which feel both welcoming and impressive. The bar offers a modern, yet relaxing, urban drinking spot.

1 Exterior
2 Upper bar
3 Seating
4 Entrance box
5 Ground floor plan
6 Candle bulb wall
7 Bench seating

Photography: Leon Chew

2

1

3

LONDON, UK

Market Place Bar

BLOCK ARCHITECTURE

4

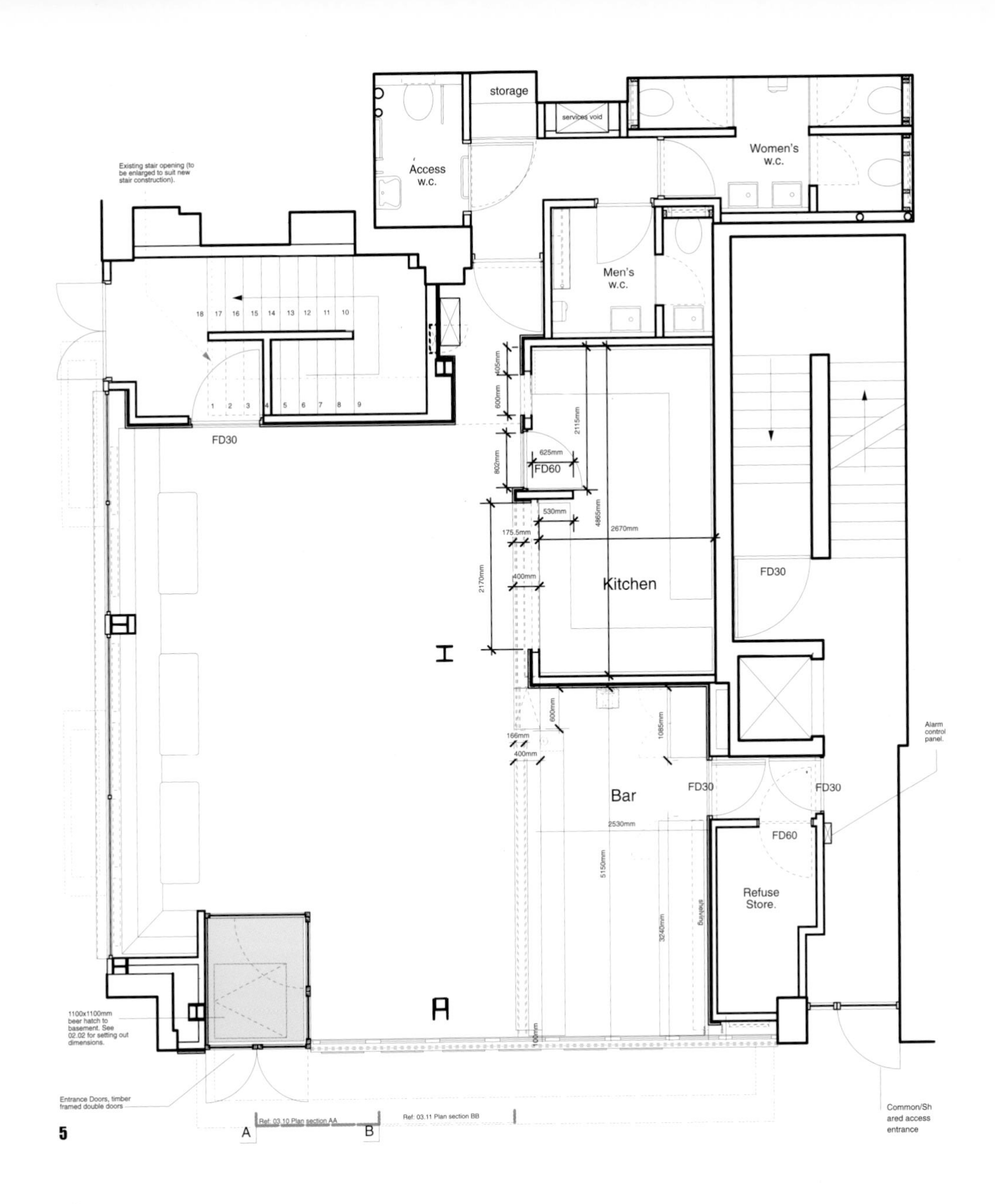

5

Usage: Pub

Area: 2583 square feet/ 240 square meters

Market Place was essentially a modern take on the traditional pub—an environment that is exclusively unexclusive. To recreate this, the architects took their influence from the aesthetics of the traditional Swiss chalet, incorporating the use of rough-sawn Douglas fir boarding. The idea of the Swiss chalet is used to give a sense of escapism, a rural environment in an urban setting and a welcome retreat from the bustle of central London. In contrast to the warmth of the timber, the restrooms, stairwell, and entrance are lush and green, drawing from the natural environment of a hilltop hideaway. To generate a sense of visual warmth, flickering candle bulbs on a rear wall were used. The bar furniture is also made from solid Douglas fir and was designed loosely around the classic picnic table.

6

7

1

SYDNEY, **NEW SOUTH WALES, AUSTRALIA**

Mars Lounge

DAVID HICKS PTY LTD

1&3 Bar

2 Bench seating

2

3

Client: Peter O'Brien, George Hatzis, Natalie Keon

Usage: Bar

Area: 3875 square feet/ 360 square meters

Materials: Aluminum, black terrazzo, stainless steel

Located at the end of Oxford Street and the edge of Surry Hills, the existing building had many intriguing features. Timber ceiling beams, existing timber flooring, and feature brickwork walls were maintained and incorporated into the scheme. This gave the area a lofty warehouse feel that provides a project contrast with streamlined insertions of silver and black glitter bar boxes, a drinking bench, and circular 'Vivid White' gloss and red-lined seating pods. The red links the space back to the Mars theme and makes it exciting, vibrant, and contemporary.

The venue's warehouse feel was further emphasized with a glamorous undertone highlighted with slick detailing. Conflicting materials were used to bring warmth to the space while still maintaining a high level of design resolution. Materials and paint colors were chosen to highlight the venue's modernism—metal mixed with timber mixed with stone, and shiny mixed with matt mixed with rough. This was achieved with the 'Burmese Beige' wall render and slick insertions of 'Vivid White', 'Deep Onyx', and punches of 'Cherry Red'.

This blend provides a stimulating environment to be in, both on a visual and tactile level. The various seating arrangements allow patrons to stand and have a beer, lounge and sip a cocktail, or sit and dine. For those who get itchy feet, dancing is encouraged on top of the drinking bench.

5

6

Opposite Red-lined seating pod

5 Seating creates lounge atmosphere

6 Seating

Photography: Kyle Ford

1

2

BEVERLY HILLS, **CALIFORNIA, USA**

Mastro's

GABBAY ARCHITECTS WITH DON CARSTENS ASSOCIATES

3

4

Usage: Bar/restaurant

Mastro's, the steakhouse with a personality, offers an unparalleled experience featuring a cutting-edge menu accompanied by live music seven nights a week in the piano bar.

These features are wrapped in an elegant atmosphere with the cosmopolitan feel of Manhattan's finest establishments. The dining experience at Mastro's is completed with a masterful wine list and outstanding service and personal attention.

Walnut furniture with rich high-backed over-stuffed chairs, gold Bendheim glass windows, lamps, and accents of bronze and marble add sophistication, warmth and comfort throughout the venue and the live entertainment adds the right festive ambience.

1 Bar and dining

2 Piano area

3 Stair

4 Dining

Photography: Weldon Brewster

1 Exterior

2 Patrons using street interface at night

3 Timber-paneled wall

4 Numerous reclaimed materials

5 Gattic drain in bar

Photography: John Gollings

1

2

MELBOURNE, VICTORIA, AUSTRALIA

Meyers Place

SIX DEGREES ARCHITECTS

3

4

5

Usage: Bar

Area: 807 square feet/ 75 square meters

Materials: Various reclaimed objects

Situated down a little-used laneway in the central business district, Meyers Place was the first small bar in Melbourne, and the first in a wave of more than a hundred bars now operating in the city center. Six Degrees Architects set out to design and construct the bar as resourcefully as possible, selecting found objects and materials. Budget, recycling, and conservation were only some of the issues predetermining the use of this palette, resulting in a layering of histories and textures that could not be achieved using new products.

A timber-paneled wall is composed of cupboard doors from an old departmental building. Two of these doors fold down during quieter times to form tables, the hinges of which are old train arm rests from demolished local railway maintenance buildings. The cupboard above the bar also came from this demolished building and the timber paneling under the concrete bar was once the stage front of the Melbourne Town Hall. Timber and shag-pile carpet were used for sound attenuation, and a square recessed into the paneled wall forms a wallpaper-style art wall, which is plastered over by a new artist each month.

Meyers Place has won numerous design awards and was recognized by the City of Melbourne for its 'outstanding contribution to the city'.

1 Perforated panels provide sound attenuation

2 Gaming bar

3 Gaming bar with mosaic tiling

4 Buffet restaurant

5 View of lounge bar and entrance to Ming bar

6 Ming bar entrance

7 Walkway

1

2

3

4

TUMBI UMBI, NEW SOUTH WALES, AUSTRALIA

Mingara

PDT ARCHITECTS

6

5

7

Usage: Bar/club/lounge

Area: 48,437 square feet/ 4500 square meters

Materials: River pebbles, tiles, Perspex, timber veneer

The brief for Mingara was to create a timeless and individual interior, with a tropical yet sophisticated feel that would appeal to a patron demographic ranging from 18 through to 80 years old.

The design concept combines the color palette of the local NSW central coast and the simple and elegant design detailing found in a tropical resort or hotel. A natural coastal palette of blues, greens and aqua colors complements more earthy browns and burnt oranges. Color has been used sparingly to create the most impact and to contrast against a refreshing clean white backdrop.

The club consists of a series of large barrel-vaulted spaces that have an inherent commercial aesthetic. Ambient lighting, soft furnishings, and warm tactile finishes have been used to visually soften the existing structure. To create a more intimate feel, suspended ceiling elements hang within the barrel vaults, bringing ceilings down to a human scale as well as accentuating the unusual height and volume of the spaces. To add a sense of theater and entertainment to the patron's journey through the club, Pdt superimposed a more organic pathway that meandered through the building.

►►

Part-height partitions were used throughout the fitout, allowing patrons to make a visual connection between spaces, while still allowing each area to have an individual look. Because of the huge variety of different people that visit the club, it was important that there was a certain level of visual transparency between areas.

Simplistic design was exploited to accentuate and focus attention on carefully planned feature elements within the design. This has given the space a sense of integrity and refreshing visual clarity that gives the club its own unique experience.

8

9

10

11

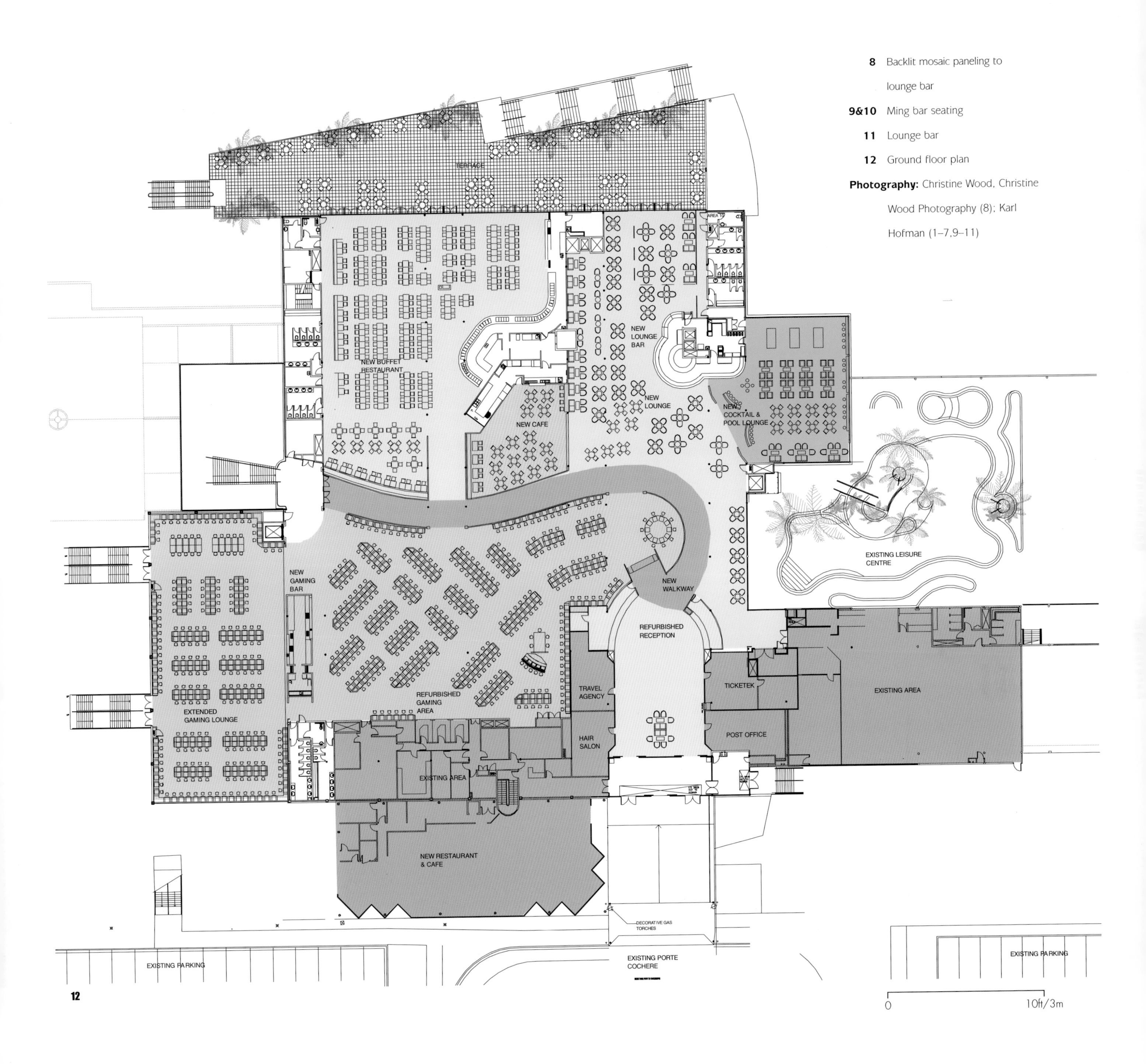

8 Backlit mosaic paneling to lounge bar

9&10 Ming bar seating

11 Lounge bar

12 Ground floor plan

Photography: Christine Wood, Christine Wood Photography (8); Karl Hofman (1–7,9–11)

1

2

1&3 Main bar

2 View to x-ray houseclub

4 Cocktail bar

3

COPENHAGEN, DENMARK

Nasa

JOHANNES TORPE STUDIOS

4

Usage: Nightclub

Area: 4628 square feet/ 430 square meters

Materials: Acrylic, epoxy, foam, car paint, fiberglass

The owners of two of Copenhagen's most successful clubs desired a true 'members only' venue with a small but well-chosen audience, and a quality and level of service that would please the royals, the models, and the popstars: a pearl of design never seen before.

Science-fiction films of the 1960s inspired the outstanding original design. Although the interior is reminiscent of the past, Nasa established a new standard in nightclub design in the late 1990s. Everything from the ashtrays to the toilet doors is customized to Nasa.

Nasa is the only completely white nightclub in the world, or as the English lifestyle magazine *Wallpaper* says, 'Nasa is a hermetic obsessively white club with a glass lift to beam up in – it makes London's Pharmacy (a bar/club) look like Boots – the chemist.'

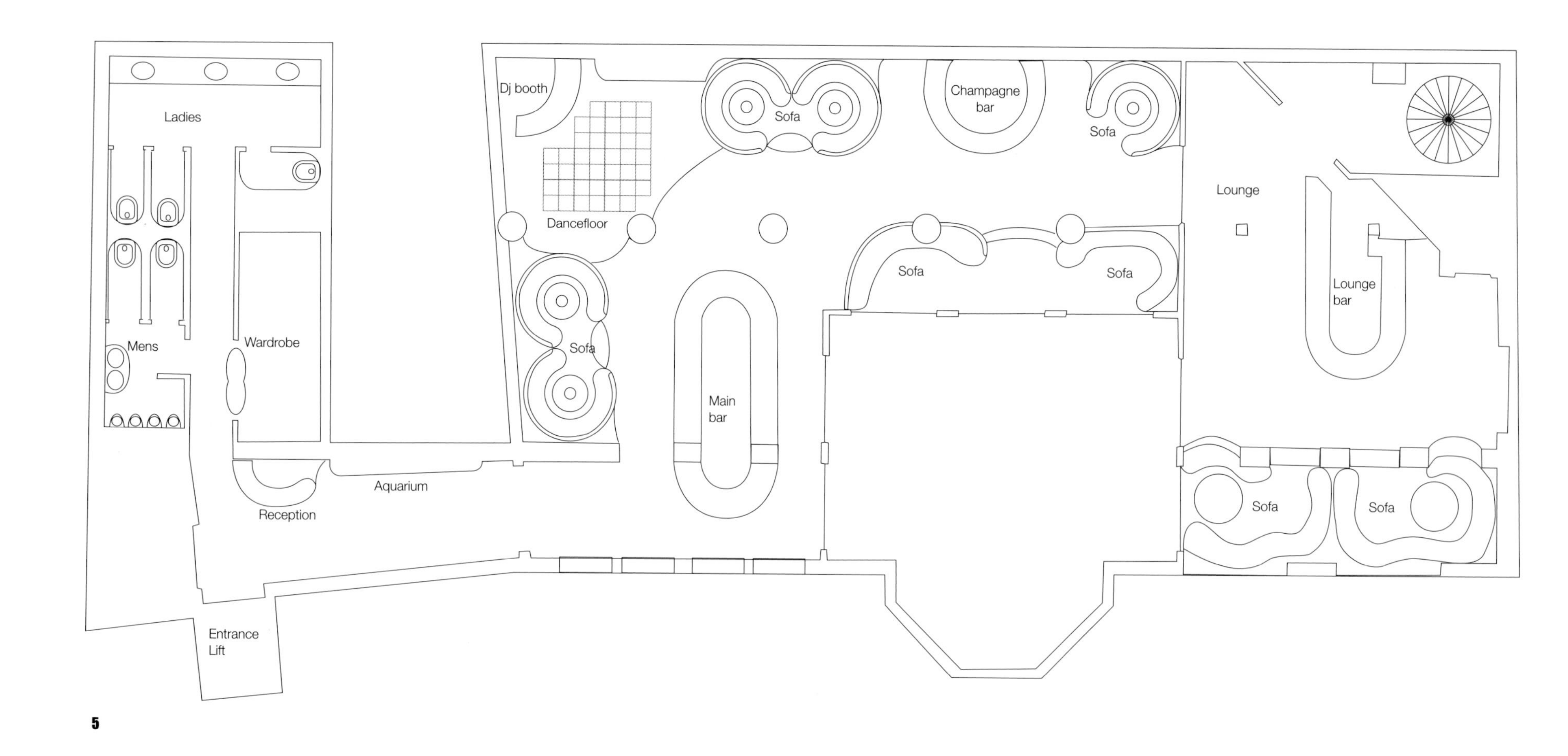

Ladies
Dj booth
Sofa
Champagne bar
Sofa
Lounge
Dancefloor
Sofa
Sofa
Lounge bar
Mens
Wardrobe
Sofa
Main bar
Aquarium
Reception
Sofa
Sofa
Entrance Lift

5

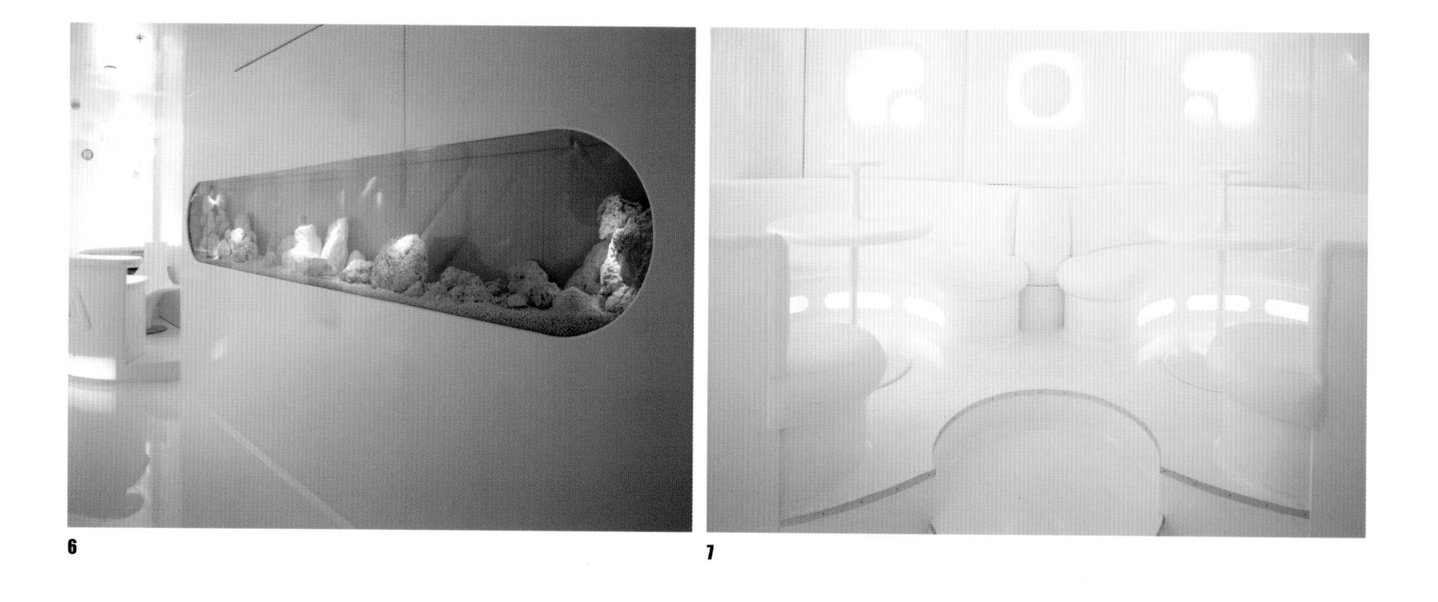

6

7

8

9

10

5 Floor plan

6 4000-liter aquarium

7 VIP seating with latex walls

8 Restroom

9 Restroom mirror

10 Dance floor

Photography: Jens Stoltze

1

1 Main bar

2 Partial floor plan

3 Bar, toward restaurant entry and seafood display

4 View from restaurant

5 Custom two-tier ice-bin

Photography: Doug Snower

LAS VEGAS, NEVADA, USA

Nectar

JORDAN MOZER AND ASSOCIATES, LIMITED

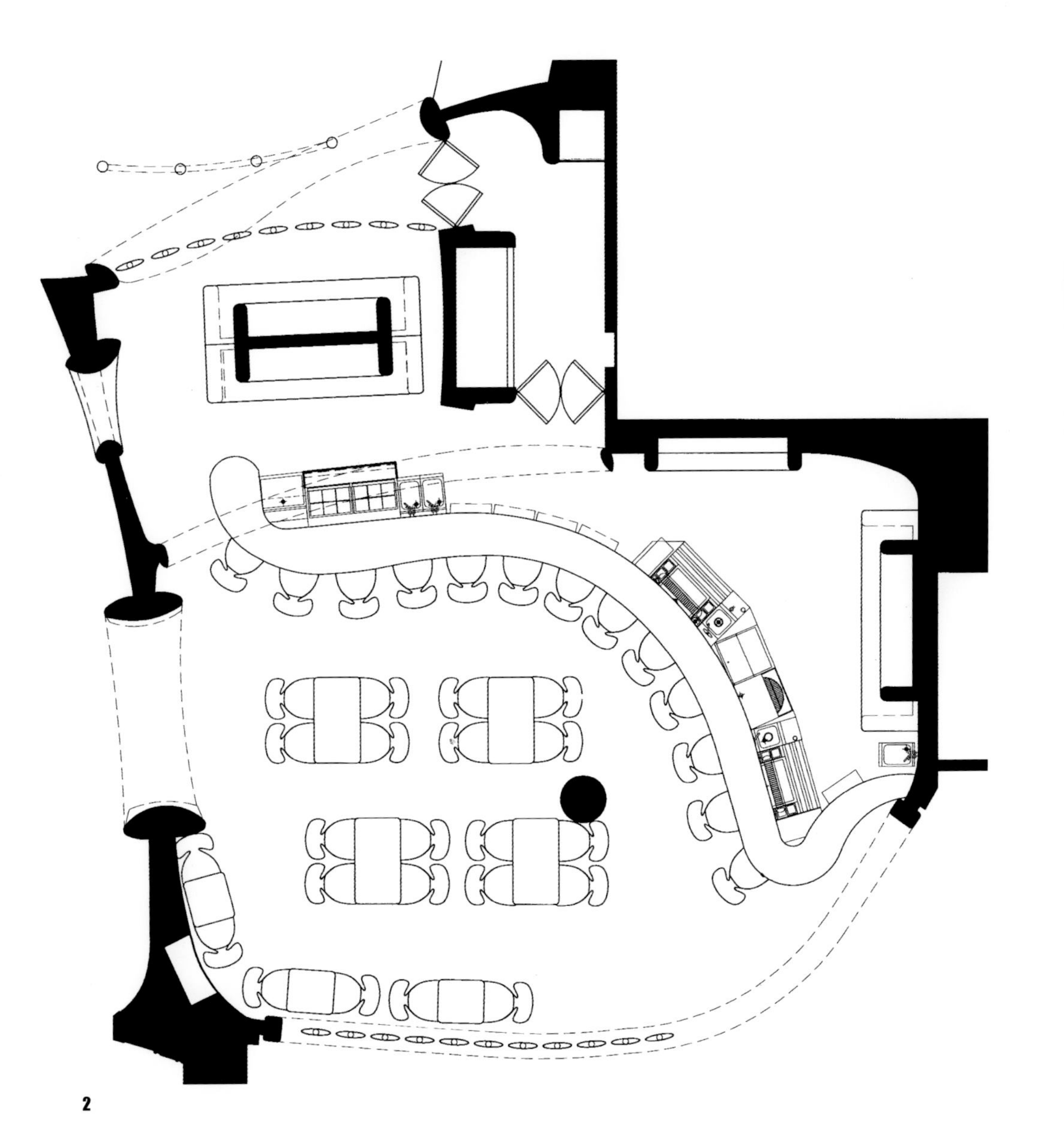

2

3 4

5

Usage: Bar/restaurant

Area: 8500 square feet/ 790 square meters

When asked to develop a bar in the Nevada desert, the design team came up with an image of melting forms. They created a single food and beverage facility for simple, fresh seasonal food with two distinct parts to balance one another: a yin-yang idea—a contrast between the two halves making a complete whole.

A German team that usually restores old European churches manually plastered CAD-CAM sculpted framing for the walls and ceiling. Hand-sculpted, seamless terrazzo bar die melts down to create a floor, while the terrazzo is infused with blue glass shards. The barstools were also CAD-CAM sculpted and cast in Kevlar-reinforced non-combustible resin, and with cast aluminum–magnesium foot rests. The tabletops are composed of hand-polished glass mosaics set into cast-aluminum, magnesium-alloy frames, with a base of the same metal. The back bar cabinets are also CAD-CAM sculpted, with inset panels of poured art glass.

1

2

3

LONDON, UK

Neighbourhood

POWELL TUCK ASSOCIATES

1 View of bar through hole

2 Bar

3 Staircase to mezzanine

4 Mezzanine booth seating

Usage: Bar/nightclub

Area: 8428 square feet/ 783 square meters

Materials: Galvanized steel, painted plaster, plywood

As Subterania, this club in West London had been a cult venue for many years. The previous design had worked well and had been a great success. The owners now wanted to do something new with the space by removing the 'post modern' language of the original design and improving circulation and visual relationships between key elements.

Previously, the bar had been the focal point. The aim was to make visitors become immediately involved with the venue's atmosphere: its people, sound, and light, rather than its architecture. The upper mezzanine level was remodeled to produce a more useable space with an intimate relationship between the ground floor and stage. The bars, stage, DJ position, and stairs were repositioned to allow patrons to see movement throughout the club.

Once the spaces were reorganized, the architects relied on the quality of the new sound system and the projected light graphics to convey the atmosphere. Key areas were painted in strong colors and intensified by adding matching colored lighting.

5

5 View of dance floor through hole

6 Mezzanine bar

7 Floor plan

Photography: Edmund Sumner

6

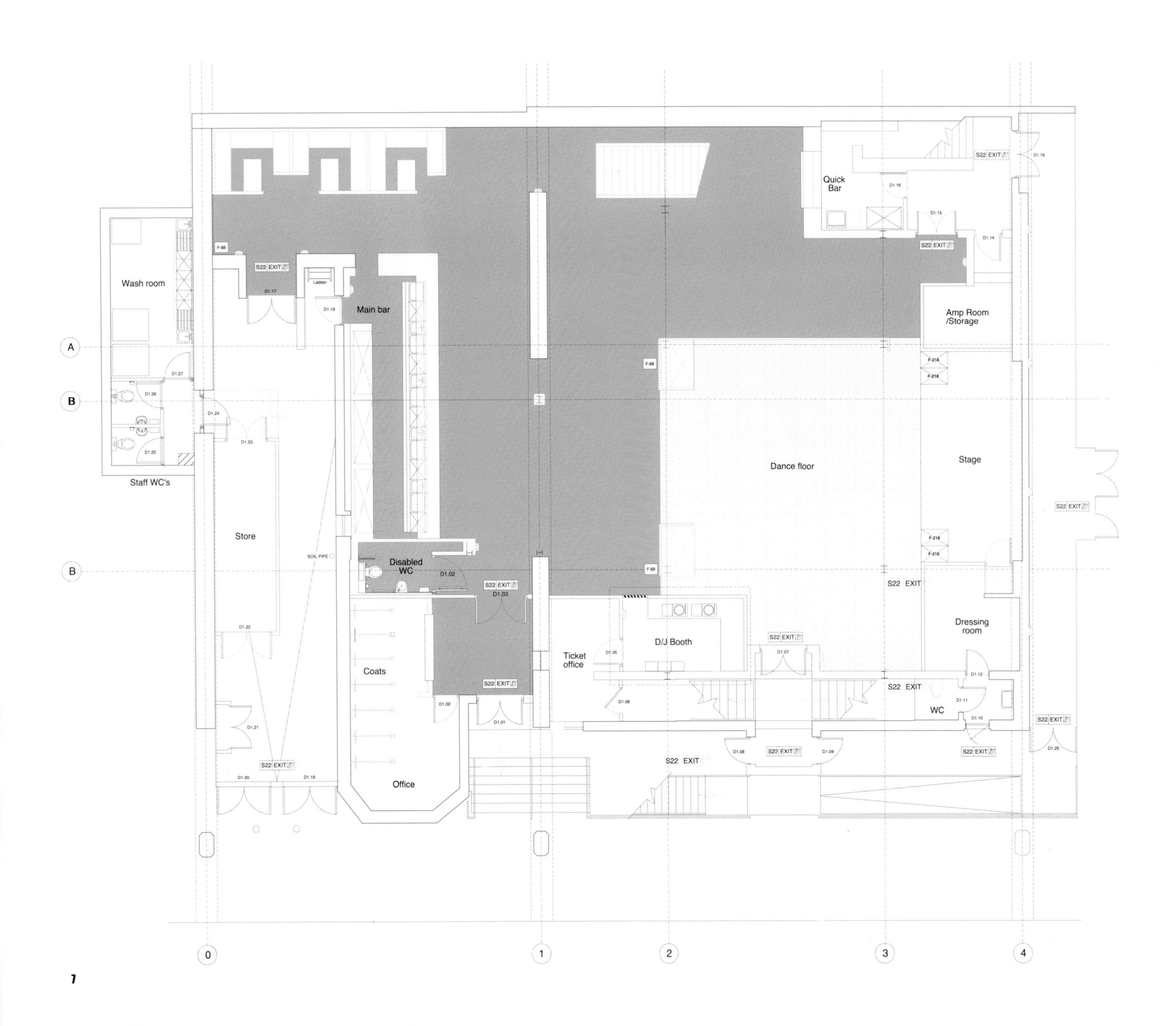
Wash room
Staff WC's
Main bar
Store
Disabled WC
Coats
Office
Ticket office
D/J Booth
Dance floor
Quick Bar
Amp Room /Storage
Stage
Dressing room
WC
S22 EXIT

7

1

3

2

4

MUNICH, GERMANY

NEKTAR

FERRIER INTERIOR WITH JULIA HÖLZEL

1 Main dining room

2 Orange salon

3 Rouge bar

4 Main dining room, different light setting

5 Dining room and art performance stage

6 Floor plan

Photography: Martin Saumweber and Benny Monn (2,3); Derek Henthorne (1,4,5)

5

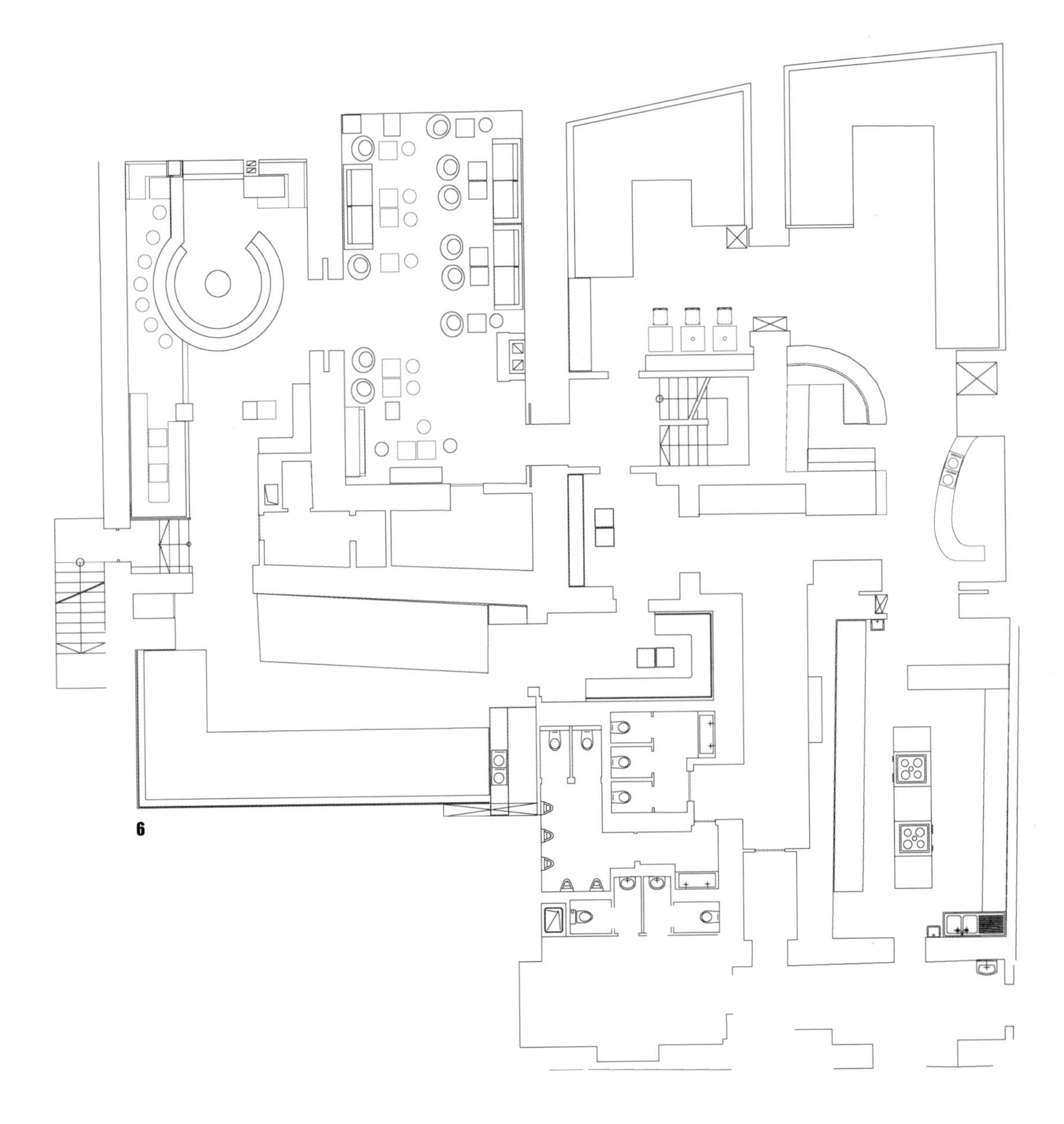

6

Usage: Bar/ lounge/restaurant

Area: 4305 square feet/ 400 square meters

Materials: Wood, fabric

NEKTAR was designed and built with two distinct bar areas, the 'bar rouge' and 'salon orange' separating the dining rooms, offering patrons contrasting spaces for exclusive evenings. Wood and fabric, together with classic 19th-century ceiling ornaments give these areas a warm and cozy atmosphere.

The dining rooms feature a reductionist approach: decorated in white, a complex lighting and projection system allows for constantly changing atmospheres and moods. Combined with selected music from top DJs and daily changing art performances, the dining rooms constantly morph in design and style, offering guests a rich and unique experience throughout the first-class four-course menu, served while they recline on the central coachbed landscape.

This design contrast between the two main areas is also key to a successful 'tuning in' to the virtual, spectacular world at NEKTAR, located underground in the remains of century-old royal beer storage cellars. As guests automatically enter the 'bar rouge' from the outside, they find a warm and welcoming spot to unwind and cool down from the day's business, and move on to drink in the 'salon orange'.

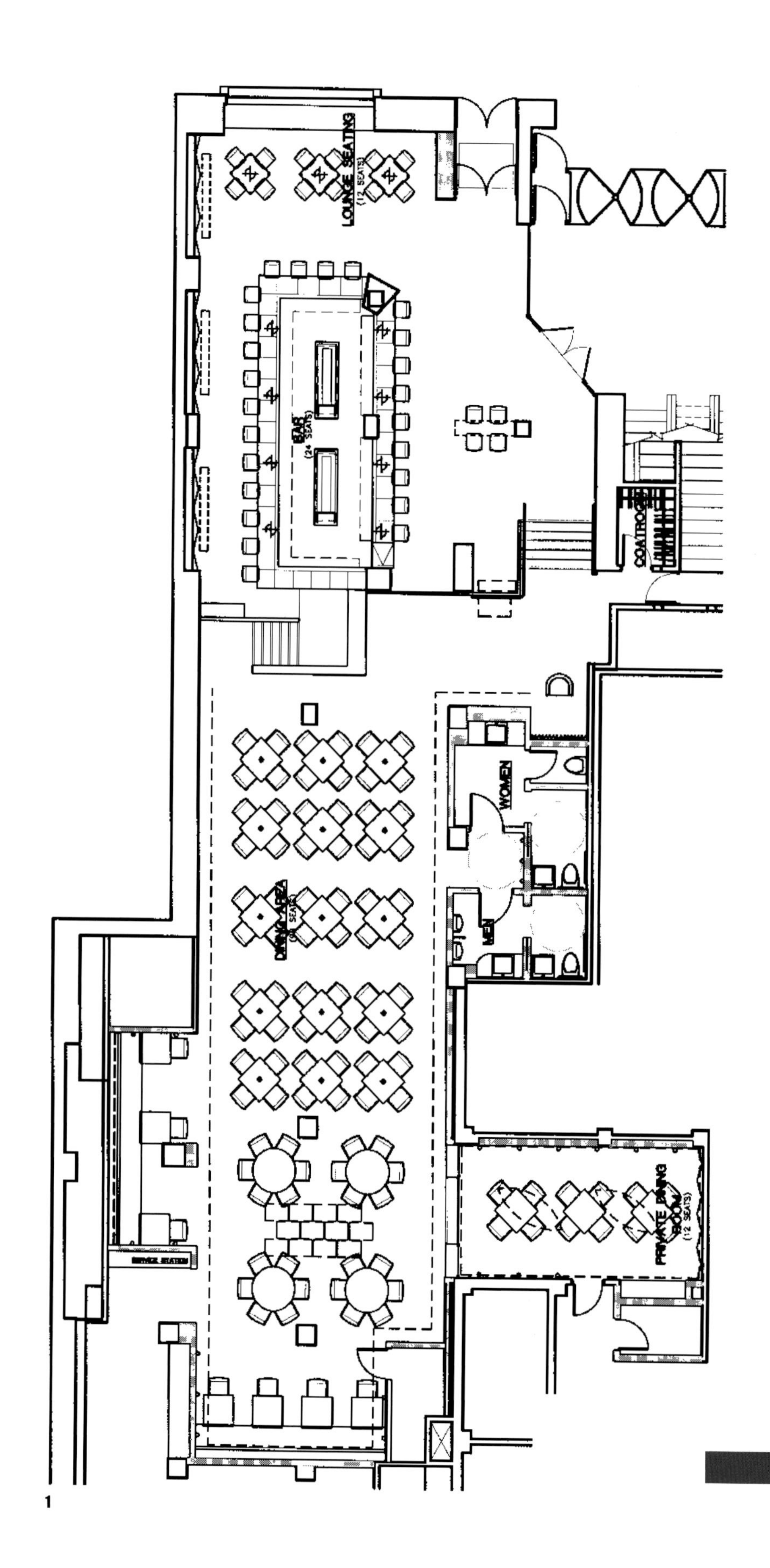

1

2

NEW YORK, NEW YORK, USA

Niles Restaurant and Bar

DILEONARDO INTERNATIONAL, INC.

3

Usage: Bar/restaurant

Area: 5000 square feet/ 465 square meters

Niles is a fresh, contemporary restaurant and bar, celebrating color and innovation. Established at the ground level of the Affinia Hotel on 7th Avenue, this exciting space engages the streetscape at an unparalleled location across from Madison Square Garden, and will be sure to attract native New Yorkers as well as first-time visitors to the Big Apple.

Clean iridescent finishes accentuate an oversized bar, anchored by a lit-glass decorative column that greets visitors upon entering. The use of metal and other reflective surfaces explodes the visual perimeter of space that surrounds the bar area. Colorful finger-like light fixtures give this lounge a fresh sense of elegance. In the dining area there is a rhythmic play of color that has been orchestrated with the use of art and lighting. This sophisticated dining room has been softened with the playful art of James Rizzi showing comical renditions of city events and everyday tasks. Primary colors set against a white backdrop make this an exciting space for an early start or a very late evening. Once seated, patrons will experience the exciting presentation of dishes prepared by Alex Aubry, while subconsciously witnessing a light display that continually changes the surrounding environment.

1 Floor plan

2 Reflections in lounge

3 Main bar with backlit glass panels

4

5

6

7

4 Main dining room with custom artwork

5 View into private dining room

6 Detail of private dining

7 Detail of main dining

Photography: Michael Wilson Photography

1

MILAN, ITALY

Nobu

GABELLINI ASSOCIATES

1 Sushi bar in luminous onyx panels

2 Ground-level lounge

3 Bronze and walnut stair

4 Walk-in sake cooler

5 Custom bar seating

Photography: courtesy Gabellini Associates (1–4); Bruna Ginammi (5)

2

3

4

5

Usage: Sushi bar/restaurant

Area: 7500 square feet/ 696 square meters

Materials: Walnut, translucent onyx, bronze

Nobu opened in conjunction with the 100,000-square-foot Armani Center in Milan. It involved an interesting collaboration between the two business partners, Giorgio Armani and Nobu Matsuhisa, and Gabellini Associates. The venue includes a large lounge and sake bar, a sushi bar, and a 130-seat dining area. Occupying a discreet corner of the Center primarily dedicated to service activities, Nobu's public façade is on the interior overlooking the Galleria Rotonda. Its corner location occupies both the ground and first levels, allowing its interior façade of taut clear glass panels and stacked stone piers to conceptually penetrate the floor.

The ground level features a large lounge area with a communal bar table, built-in bench seating with flexible cushions, and custom tables and chairs. The chairs and cushions were designed in collaboration with Vladimir Kagan. Natural materials and various subtle lighting techniques bathe the area in warm ambient light. A floor of closely spaced pietra serena stone slats folding onto stone piers, American walnut wall panels and furniture, natural plaster walls and ceilings, and bronze details provide a rich palette of materials.

The main restaurant, located on the first level, is accessible through a double-height atrium lined in walnut panels enclosing a floating walnut stair. The main focus of the restaurant is the sushi bar, constructed of walnut, bronze, clear glass and translucent onyx panels that emit a welcoming glow. Sliding translucent panels offer the option to subdivide the space for private dining.

1

2

BARCELONA, SPAIN

Noti

ESTUDI FRANCESC PONS

3

1 Façade
2 Entrance
3 Bar
4&5 Dining area

4

5

Usage: Bar/restaurant

Area: 3444 square feet/ 320 square meters

Materials: Brass, Formica, glass, linoleum, Japanese silk wallpaper

Housed in the former Barcelona offices of the now-defunct newspaper, *El Noticiero Universal*, the venue is already establishing a reputation for unusual cuisine and an ambience to match. The existing situation was fraught with problems: unclear circulation, a single entrance for both deliveries and diners, and an unusually dark basement.

The designer made a virtue of necessity by transforming the service area with its dumbwaiters into a major feature. He inserted a 5-meter-long stretch of brass paneling set against a background of shocking pink Formica, an element that screens secondary spaces. Pons readily admits the risk involved in such an intervention, but reiterates how vital a sense of drama is to his designs. One diner compared eating here to walking on set and waiting for filming to start.

The ground level is split in two by a sassy black cocktail bar. Red velvet sofas skirt the eating area, while three circular seating arrangements create more intimate dining settings. A private room for business dinners on the floor below offers direct views into the kitchen.

Dressing spaces in this manner have become part of the architect's repertoire. At Noti, Pons layers fabrics and other materials like pieces of clothing, taking snippets of inspiration from other eras to concoct his particular brand of glamour.

6

7

6 General view

7 Private room for business diners

8 Restroom waiting area

9 Bar detail

10 Shelving detail

11 Dining area

Photography: Raimon Solà

8

9

10

11

1

4

2

3

PRAHRAN, VICTORIA, AUSTRALIA

Onesixone

GRANT AMON ARCHITECTS PTY, LTD.

1 Uplit shelf in restroom cubicle

2 Women's restroom

3 Women's restroom, washbasins

4,6&7 Lower-level bar seating

5 Dance floor

Photography: Jules Smith

5

6

7

Usage: Nightclub

Area: 3444 square feet/ 320 square meters

Materials: Timber paneling, wallpaper, patterned carpet, retro lights

Onesixone is an established Melbourne nightclub that has recently been transformed and extended to cater for a growing but discerning clientele. Located in the thick of Chapel Street's hectic commercial zone, the operators set out to create a sensual plush venue, offering exceptional service with a friendly and intimate ambience.

A narrow stair lit by an original 1960's glass chandelier greets patrons as they enter the venue. Flocked wallpaper adorns the club's walls and fluted timber paneling lines the bar front and the many seating alcoves. Toward the dance area, light, movement, and volume build up to the appearance of one of Australia's first flashing dance floors since the death of disco. Recycled basketball court flooring has been used to line the walls, padded panels, and seating. Fish tanks are located above lounge areas, in washrooms, and over corridors, and specialist neon lighting is used throughout.

The new lower-level bar reflects the same tongue-in-cheek design elements, with the use of black acid-etched mirrors, and retro light fittings and wallpaper.

1

3

4

2

EDINBURGH, UK

Opal Lounge

MALCOLM FRASER ARCHITECTS

5

1&3 Sunken seating area

2 Dining area detail

4 Dining alcove in main bar

5 Entrance from George Street

6 Main bar showing leather-upholstered front

7 Burr oak tables in sunken seating area

Photography: Peter Iain Campbell (1–6); Brendan Macneill (7)

6

7

Client: Montpeliers Edinburgh Ltd
Usage: Bar/ restaurant/nightclub
Area: 8611 square feet/ 800 square meters

The design brief was for a 'luxury club' with membership (much like a typical gentlemen's club), but later became a bar/restaurant and late nightclub with limited membership. The site, two adjoining but unconnected basements on Edinburgh's George Street, presented considerable design problems. Both had low ceilings, little natural daylight, and a steep flight of steps at the entrance that discouraged passersby from entering.

New openings were made to connect the three adjoining spaces. Consequently, the finished design is a sequence of rooms at varying levels. The three main spaces, bar, dance-floor, and dining room, are sufficiently separate to feel like contained spaces, but the new openings allow for views into spaces beyond, and encourage people to explore the interior.

The idea of a 'gentlemen's club' was never completely abandoned by the client and many of the materials used in the finished design were chosen to evoke the qualities of that environment, in particular, extensive use of leather upholstery, dark wood floors and furniture, and natural limestone.

The padding and leather upholstery, as well as the depth and configuration of the timber slats that clad the wall in the main bar, help to absorb sound. Elsewhere in the interior, specially commissioned fabric panels conceal acoustic insulation.

1

2

PRAGUE, **CZECH REPUBLIC**

Oscar's Bar at Andel's Hotel

JESTICO + WHILES

1 Polished stone bar

2 Bar detail

3 Bar, beneath glowing spiral copper light

Photography: Ales Jungmann

3

Client: UBM and WARIMPEX

Usage: Bar/café

Materials: Polished stone, coursed slate, copper voile

Following the success of its internationally acclaimed One Aldwych and The Hempel in London, Vienna International appointed Jestico + Whiles as interior designer of its new-build hotel at Andel City.

The 280-bedroom hotel is designed to be the social heart of Andel City, and will bring hotel 'lobby culture' to Prague for the first time.

The ground floor café bar at Andel's has become Prague's most fashionable new venue. Both guests and city dwellers alike gather to experience the cool atmospheric space in the established tradition of the hotel lobby.

Studded with glowing white glass cubes and with slots lined with blood-red glass, a wall of random coursed slate stands in contrast to the polished stone bar counter. Against this eye-catching and theatrical backdrop, the most talented of barmen serve extravagant cocktails and the best coffee in town.

An elliptical shell, partially enclosed with shimmering metallic voile offers an intimate and sheltered atmosphere. For those who want to be seen, high glass tables are placed in the windows, beneath a huge, glowing spiral copper light.

1

2

3

1 A 1924 bank building is reused as the vibrant nightclub

2 Spotlit cocktail tables

3 Curved niches echo building's exterior arches

4 Rough historic and new industrial elements

5 Bar with perforated metal panels and frosted glass sheets

6 Open dance floor surrounded by bars, viewing areas, and seating nooks

Photography: Laszlo Regos

DETROIT, **MICHIGAN, USA**

Panacea Nightclub

MCINTOSH PORIS ASSOCIATES

4

6

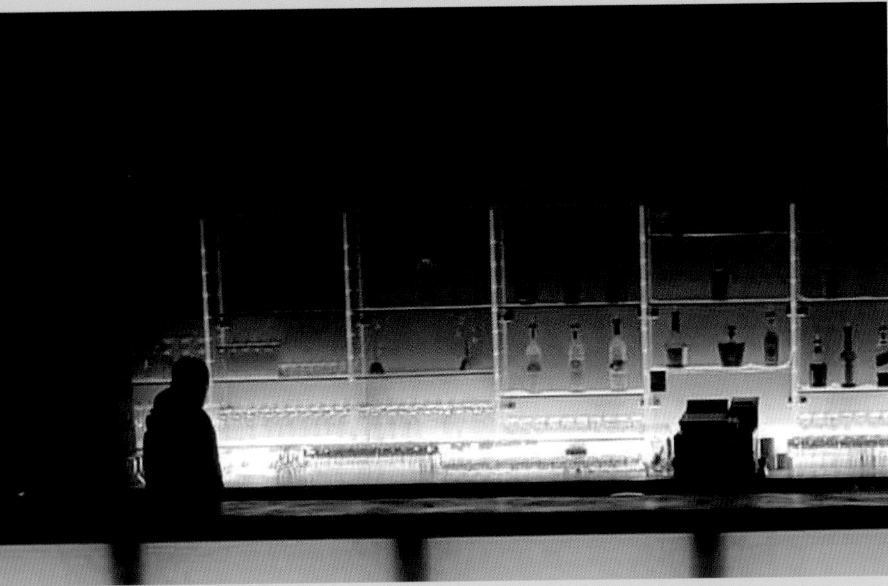

5

Usage: Nightclub

Area: 9000 square feet/ 836 square meters

This corner building at West Congress and Shelby was in a dilapidated state prior to renovation. Originally a bank when completed in 1924, there were repeated, ill-advised renovations and many tenants from the 1970s onward, including fast food restaurants, delis, and cafés.

The architect's solution embraced the existing original elements, including an outstanding Moorish Revival terra cotta and limestone exterior with a second-floor perimeter arcade, a curved sliding bronze entry door, concrete structural columns, and a mezzanine-level bank manager's office. What was not readily apparent was uncovered through careful archeology. The most prized find was the building's original suspended plaster ceiling with its hand-stenciled detailing that covers two-thirds of the space.

The architects retained and restored these elements, accentuating the contrast between the historic and the contemporary. The sand-blasted exterior is representative of its original, exotic, and elaborate façade, which now looks refreshed during the day. During club hours, the windows are lit, throwing the façade into silhouette. Clubbers enter to find an intimate space consisting of a dance floor, bars, lounge areas, entry stair, and service areas.

Patrons interact with the selected finishes of wood, metal, and concrete, and with various elements, such as leather benches, plastic sofas, cloth pod seating, and high bar chairs. In a more ephemeral way, they dance in the spotlight or converse in the shadows. Through careful restoration and sensitive addition of material, provocative new life is brought to the site. Archeology meets techno.

1

2

1 Upper-level bar

2 Abstract relief painting of grassland/cityscape in upper bar

3 A cluster of lights

4 Ground floor bar and suspended staircase

Photography: Trevor Mein

MELBOURNE, **VICTORIA, AUSTRALIA**

The Phoenix Hotel

SIX DEGREES ARCHITECTS

3

4

Usage: Bar/restaurant

Materials: Timber paneling, concrete, vermiculite

The Phoenix Hotel was well known during the 1970s as a pub visited by journalists and football players. A complete refurbishment by Six Degrees incorporated some of this history and maintained a link with this colorful past. The four levels of the hotel include several bars, a dance floor, and a restaurant.

The design challenge was to create distinct environments on each level, yet make it easy for patrons to move through the hotel. A new central circulation stair allowed for this. A composition of amber glass lights accentuates and reinforces the central stair. The imagery is a combination of the detail of the 'Falling Water' river stair with an 'Escheresque' sensibility.

1 Business class service desk

2 Stainless steel long bar

3 Smoking bar

4 First class restaurant 'The Haven'

1

2

HONG KONG SAR, PRC

The Pier, Cathay Pacific First and Business Class Lounge

RICHARDS BASMAJIAN WITH WOODS BAGOT

3

4

Usage: Bar/ passenger lounge

Area: 53,820 square feet/ 5000 square meters

Materials: Black granite, marble, larch wood, etched glass, slate, stainless steel

The Pier is a long rectangular space which originally comprised two separate areas bisected by an arrival corridor. The designers' key challenge was to link these two spaces, relocate the arrival corridor between the First Class section and the single external window wall, and still maintain appropriate levels of privacy for lounge guests. A double-glazed partition, housing electronically controlled roller blinds, was developed to lower discreetly when the arrival corridor is in use, and to quietly rise again to maintain daylight and views for passengers in the First Class Lounge.

In Business Class, the Long Bar overlooks the runway and is offset by the self-serve Noodle Bar. Both of these facilities were first established in The Wing, also at Hong Kong International Airport, and were successfully reinterpreted for The Pier. Because the Long Bar and Noodle Bar are also available to First Class passengers, the designers needed to create a space that was not only seamless but also retained the distinct character of both the First and Business Class areas. Principal finishes such as wall and floor stone are consistent elements in both spaces, while simple palettes of timber veneers and lush fabrics help differentiate the two lounges yet maintain a connection with The Wing. A 'daylight wall' was created along the major circulation route linking the two lounges to create an illusion of natural light, with pattern, speed, and color changes fully programmable to suit the time of day, season, or festive occasion.

5

7

6

5 Business Class Noodle Bar

6 Business Class Lounge and work zone

7 First Class work zone

8 Business Class work zone and private partitioned workstations

9 First Class shower suite

10 First Class Lounge

Photography: P.T. Au-Yeung/Polestar

8

9

10

1

SYDNEY, **NEW SOUTH WALES, AUSTRALIA**

Posh

LANDINI ASSOCIATES

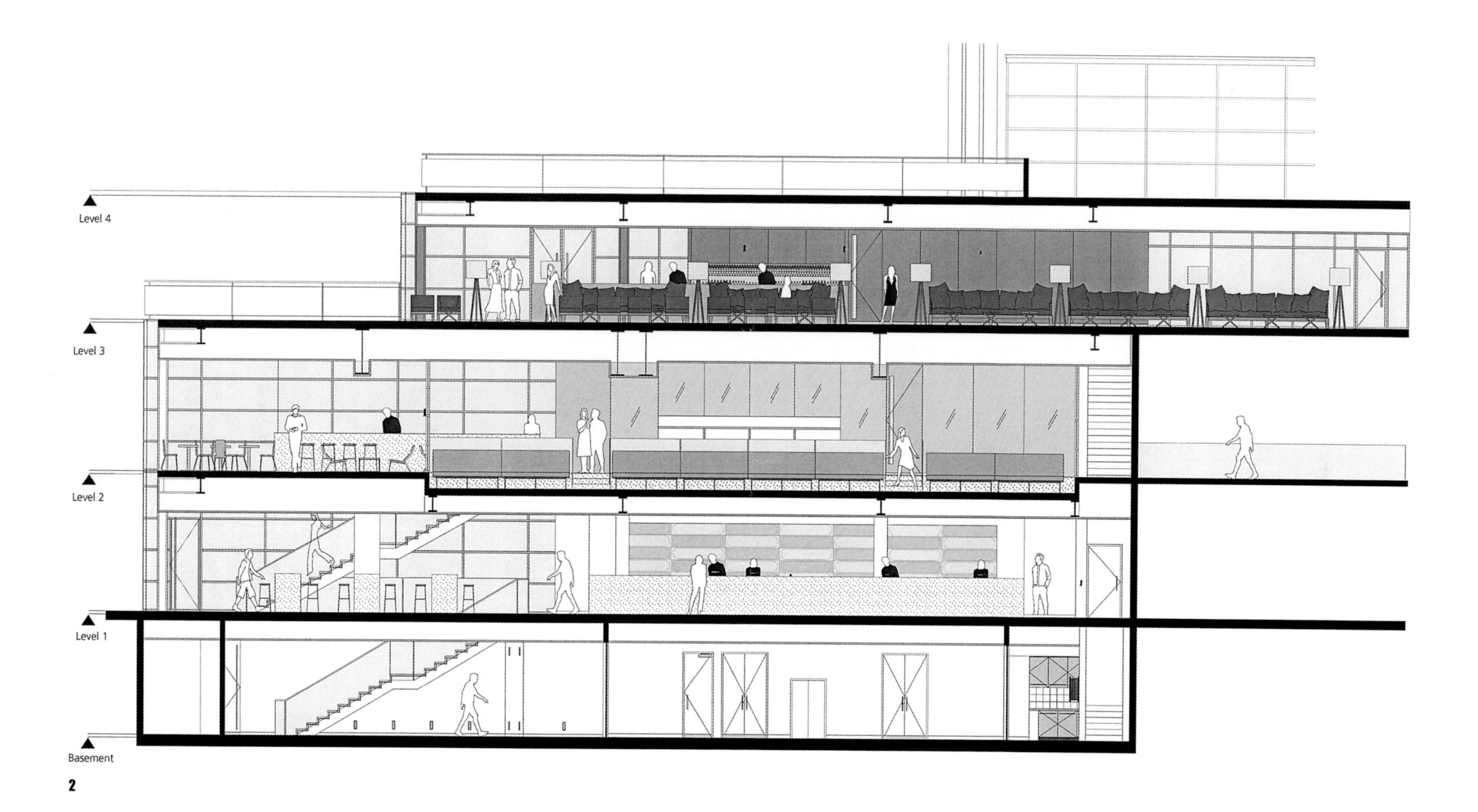

Client: Chris Cheung

Usage: Cocktail bar

Area: 3337 square feet/ 310 square meters

Materials: Silver-gray wall paneling, leather, silk

Landini Associates created a retreat for lovers of fine wines and cigars in one of the world's most enviable locations. The site was originally a viewing deck at the international passenger terminal in the heart of Sydney Harbour. Port Outbound Starboard Home, or 'POSH,' describes the deck given to first-class passengers of Transatlantic voyages on the great cruise ships of yesteryear.

Landini Associates designed a set of sumptuous furniture in a palette of dark chocolate leather, charcoal shot silks, slate needlepoint, and wenge wood to line the perimeter. The lounge bar is softly lit by dark wenge standard lamps with natural parchment shades. The dark gray terrazzo bar proudly displays an enviable list of fine wines, champagnes, and liqueurs for sale by the glass. The envelope of deep charcoal gray finishes ensures a discreet and sultry atmosphere for the bar's premium clientele, as well as maximizing the unsurpassed views of Sydney Opera House.

1 View toward city

2 Section

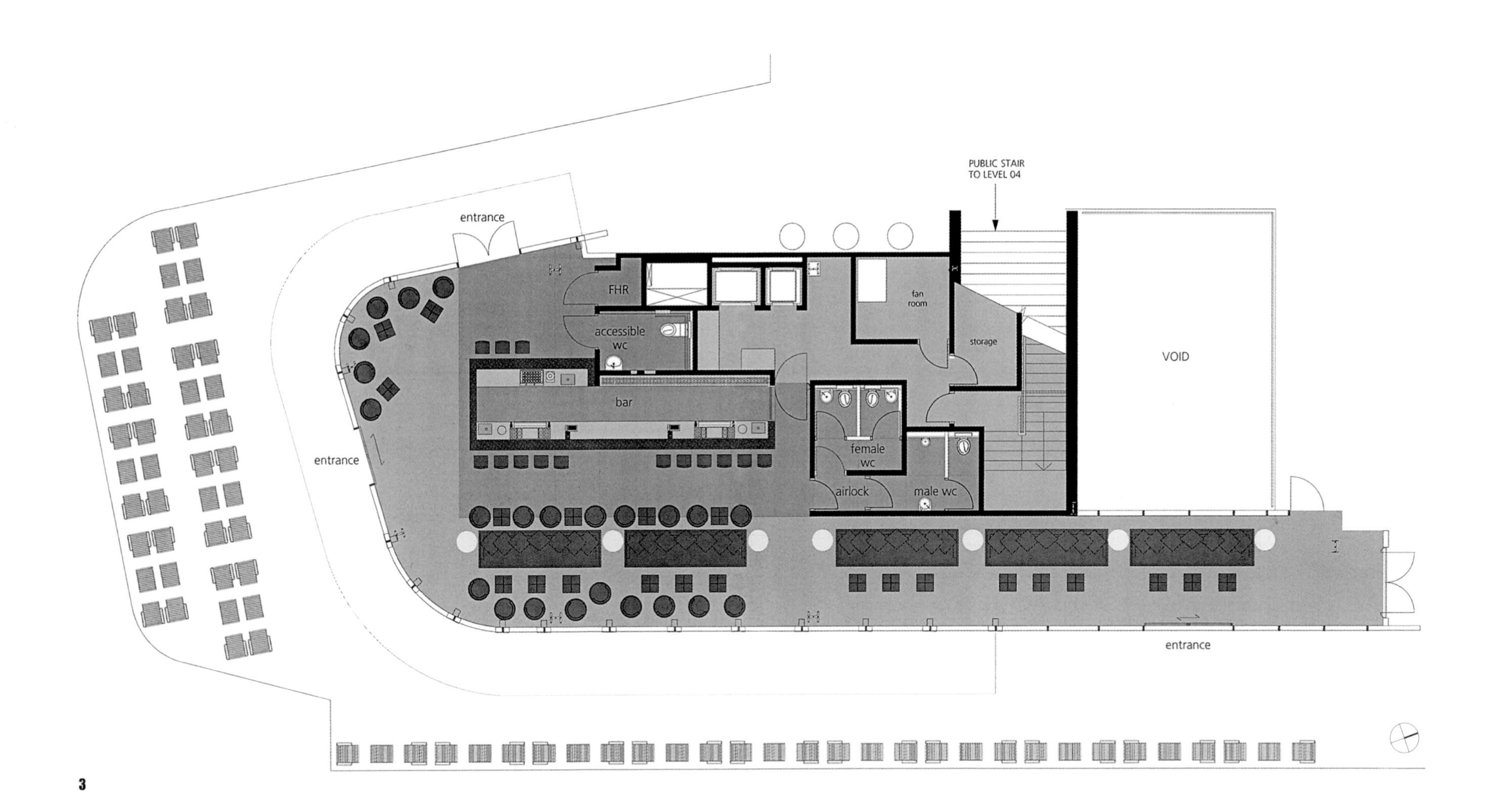
PUBLIC STAIR
TO LEVEL 04
entrance
FHR
fan room
accessible wc
storage
VOID
bar
female wc
entrance
airlock
male wc
entrance
3

4

5

6

3 Floor plan

4 Free-standing light softens textured surrounds

5 Dark natural materials exude comfort, luxury, and style

6 View of Sydney Opera House through external glass walls

7 Gray terrazzo floor merges into bar

Photography: Ross Honeysett

7

1

3

2

BANGKOK, THAILAND

Q Bar

ORBIT DESIGN STUDIO

1 Exterior

2 Restroom

3 Upstairs bar and lounge area

4 Downstairs chill out lounge area

Photography: Marcus Gortz

Usage: Bar/nightclub Located in the undisputed heart of this party city, Q Bar has ushered in a new standard for bars and nightclubs in Thailand. Located on Sukhumvit Road, Q Bar hosts the largest selection of spirits and cocktails in Bangkok and the resident DJs spin the latest house, hip-hop and jazz grooves from around the world.

The visually stunning club, in a minimalist style, features black upholstered walls highlighted by vivid lighting and is accented with retro 50's and 60's swivel chairs and leather sofas. Personalities such as Mick Jagger, Matt Dillon, Oliver Stone, Eric Cantona, Michelle Yeoh, Steven Segal, Colin Farrell and the Black Eyed Peas, have lounged about while soaking up the resident DJ's mix of chillout and club tunes. Billed as the first New York-style cocktail bar in the Thai capital, Q Bar attracts an edgy, cosmopolitan crowd.

1

2

TORONTO, ONTARIO, CANADA

Rain

II BY IV DESIGN ASSOCIATES

1&3 Main bar

2 Entrance

3

Usage: Cocktail bar/ restaurant

Area: 4700 square feet/ 436 square meters

Materials: Frosted glass, concrete, acrylic, pebbles

The clients wanted a sophisticated destination that was ultra-cool and sensually inviting: a glamorous upscale cocktail lounge where the city's chic set would come to be seen.

The lounge area is furnished with small, armless couches, surrounding a central feather pouf covered in transparent vinyl. A top-lit suspended ceiling of stretched plastic adds human scale and reinforces the formal geometric planning below. This room is warmed by the glow of a circular cluster of fat white bulbs suspended through the canopy's central cut-out.

Clear bands in frosted glass partitions reveal the small dining room, which features a long, bar-height communal table, also constructed of stainless steel and frosted glass, and internally lit. Its rear wall comprises divider screens of 3-inch diameter bamboo canes embedded in concrete bases, bringing a touch of natural texture into the sleek surroundings.

Black vinyl seating units and white tables are set against the stunning, theatrically lit brick wall. Frosted glass dividers separate the dining rooms from the large lounge area, which features two bold internally lit white glass structures, a 20-seat service bar, and matching 8-seat drinks bar. A water feature, that seems to trickle among the display bottles, backs the glass panel and glass shelves of the back bar.

With deflected and reflected light as the key design elements, this dramatic interior is simultaneously evocative of a misty lakeside, all softly gleaming shapes and mysterious shadows, and of an utterly urban and sophisticated setting—the perfect backdrop for sparkling conversation.

4

5

6

7

8

4 Entrance to washrooms

5 Feature bar

6 Dining area

7 Communal table

8 Lounge

Photography: David Whittaker

1

2

3

4

1 Booths

2 Entrance to booths

3 Light slots in timber paneling

4 Bar to rear lounge

5 Main bar to front lounge

Photography: Gavin Fraser

READING, UK

Revolution Bar

MALCOLM FRASER ARCHITECTS

5

Client: Inventive Leisure

Usage: Bar

Area: 5382 square feet/ 500 square meters

Materials: Black granite, reclaimed jarrah, red lacquer

The building of this new bar involved the stripping out of an existing pub interior to reveal the shell of an old garage warehouse. It takes advantage of the different nature of existing spaces to provide a range of simple bar and seating areas.

A new façade was inserted within the porch of the existing single-story frontage. Composed of a large area of frameless glazing and black enameled panels and door, it allows for views deep into the interior. A series of ramps negotiate the site level changes, delivering customers into the heart of the space at the main bar area. From this point, the two main spaces of the low front lounge and rear dance area are apparent. The continuous reclaimed jarrah flooring unifies the two spaces.

The walls in the front room were painted white, while the walls in the rear are lined in ribbed timber with a pattern of ceiling panels hung from the revealed steel roof trusses above. In both areas the bars are monolithic forms of black granite. Throughout the venue a variety of lighting methods serve to animate the simple spaces.

1

2

1 Exterior

2 General view

3 Cupola from below

4 View from behind bar

5 View from DJ booth

PITTSBURGH, **PENNSYLVANIA, USA**

Sanctuary Nightclub

FUKUI ARCHITECTS, PC

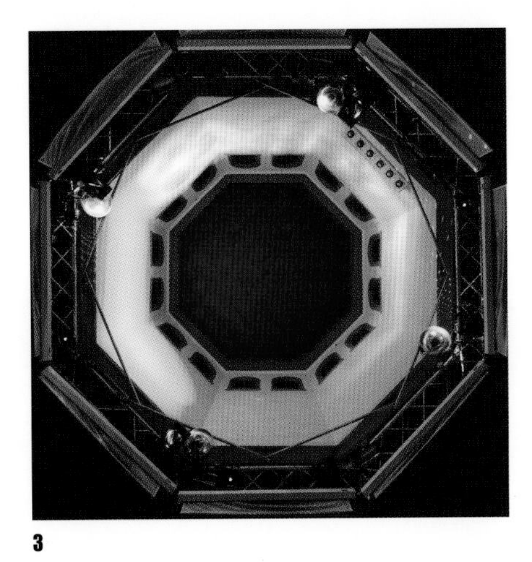

3

4

5

Usage: Nightclub

Area: 10,000 square feet/ 929 square meters

Materials: Steel, translucent glass, fiberglass panels, lycra, translucent avonite

The architect inherited a 10,000-square-foot classical church form and a budget of US$500,000 that precluded any large reconstruction of the form. Fortunately, the parts of the former Catholic church building that remained after formal de-sanctification were intrinsically potent. The design focused on adding new life, as muscle and flesh, over the existing bones.

The architects started with a single large move to soften and refocus the interior church form. The entire floating mezzanine is an ellipse form that, because it has no single center, softens and diffuses the single-point focus of the old church form. It accomplished the architect's goal of capturing a new soft center while diffusing and reorienting the narrow focus on the altar. The processional nave-to-altar axis was eliminated, and the dance floor closed off and contained by the positioning of a large counter and elliptical main stair in front of the main entry, which connects the dance floor to the second floor mezzanine and upper bar. The side of the church facing the most public street was cut open at the mezzanine level. This creates exterior silhouettes of the club activity to draw patrons in.

The original large rose window at the old choir loft was kept and used to strategic advantage by locating the upper mezzanine bar just in front of it. Here it adds color, detail, and illumination to the new translucent back bar. The existing cupola at the top of the church is ►►

the focal center of the dance floor lighting and also serves as a beacon. By pushing the active dance lighting out of the top of the nightclub through the sides of the cupola windows and into the night, it can be seen across the Allegheny River from the far north side of town, and by traffic on both the busy Sixteenth Street Bridge and the busier Veterans Bridge.

6 Bar featuring original rose window

7–9 Main floor

10 Mezzanine floor plan

11 Main floor plan

6

7

8

9

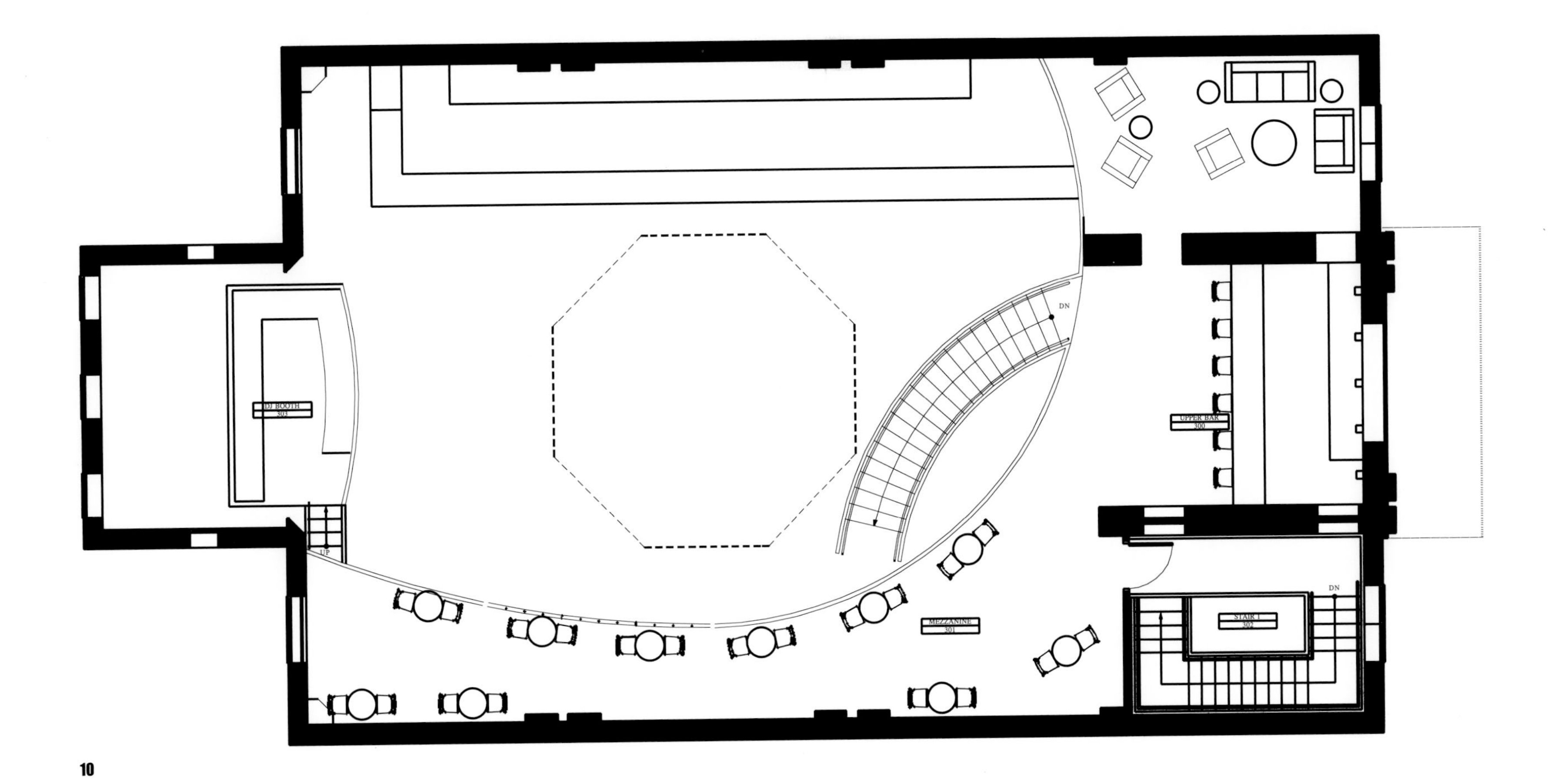
DN
DJ BOOTH
303
UPPER BAR
300
UP
MEZZANINE
301
STAIR 1
302
DN

10

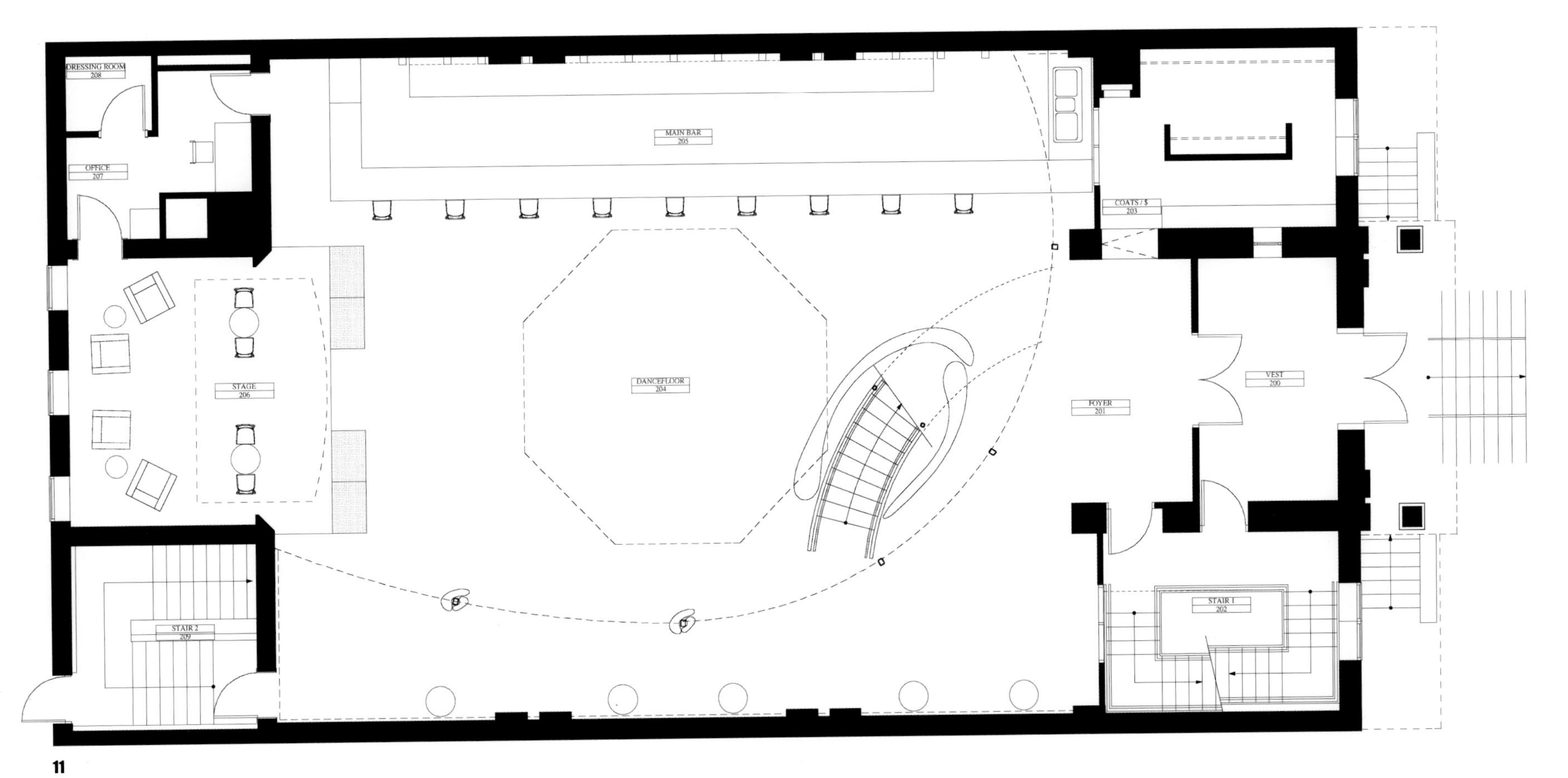
DRESSING ROOM
208
OFFICE
207
MAIN BAR
205
COATS / $
203
STAGE
206
DANCEFLOOR
204
FOYER
201
VEST
200
STAIR 2
209
STAIR 1
202

11

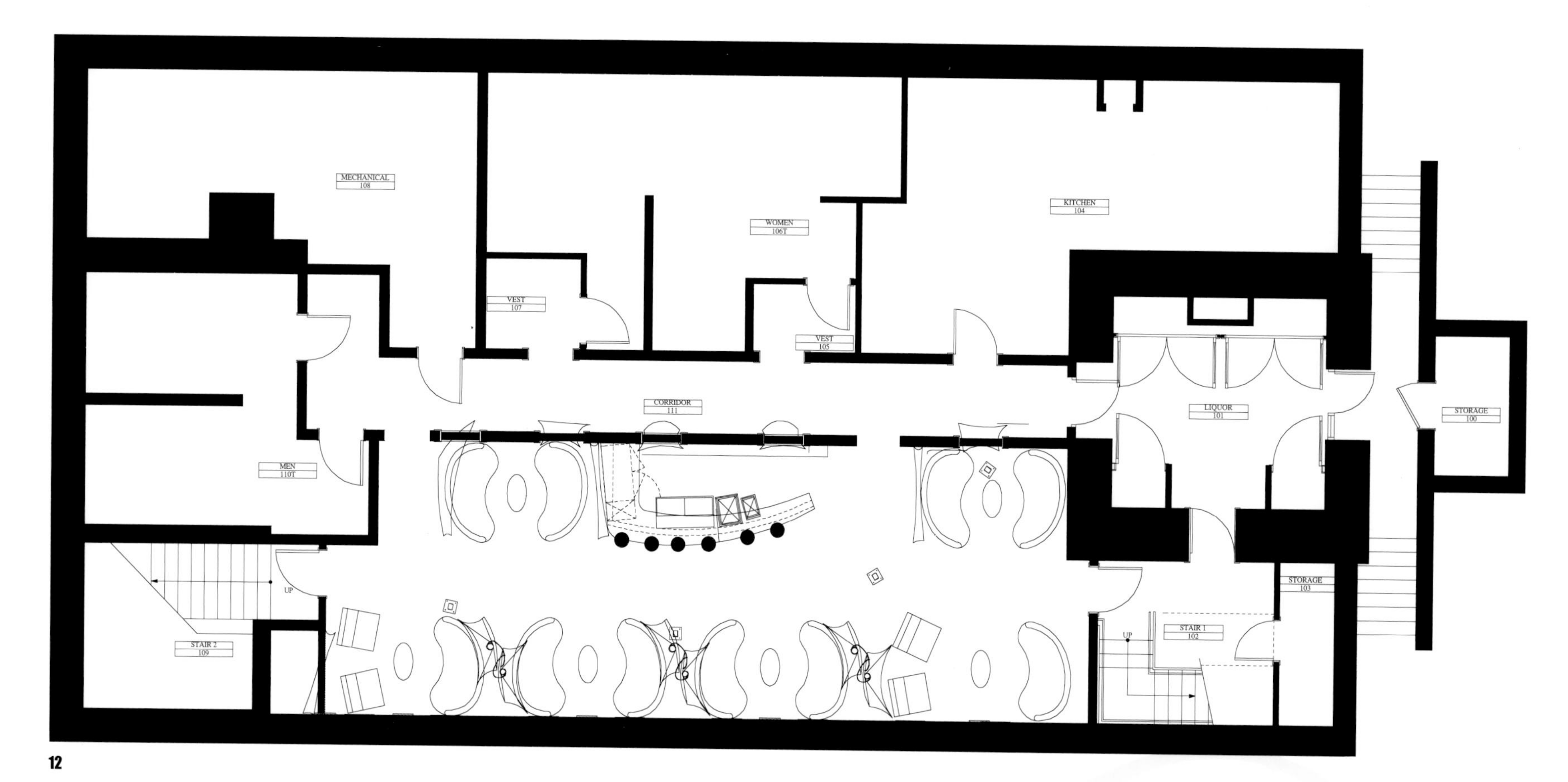
MECHANICAL
108
WOMEN
106T
KITCHEN
104
VEST
107
VEST
105
CORRIDOR
111
LIQUOR
101
STORAGE
100
MEN
110T
UP
STAIR 2
109
STORAGE
103
UP
STAIR 1
102

12

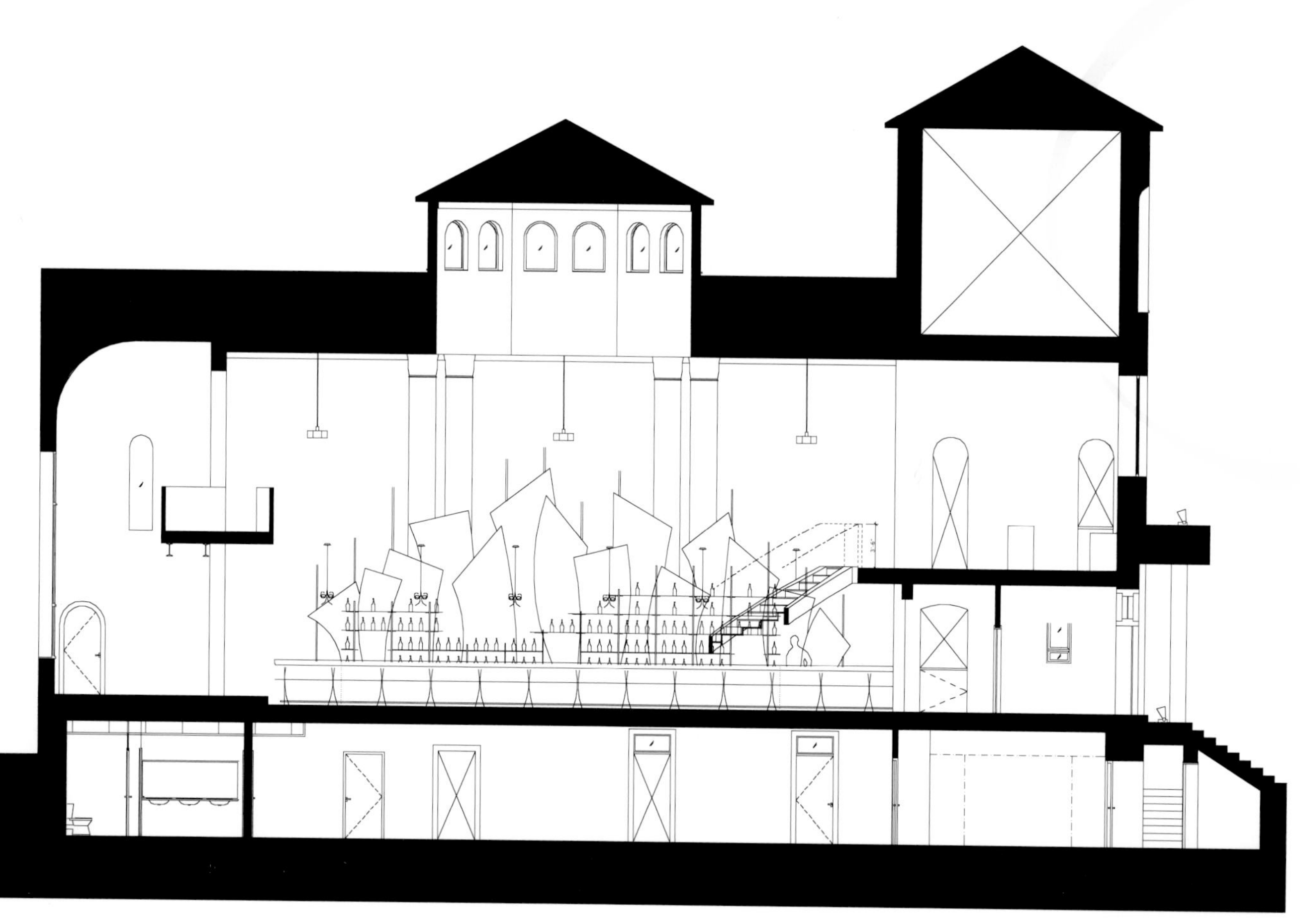

13

12 Lounge floor plan

13 Bar section

14 Lower-level bar

15 Lower-level lounge

16 Section

Photography: Craig Thompson Photography

14

15

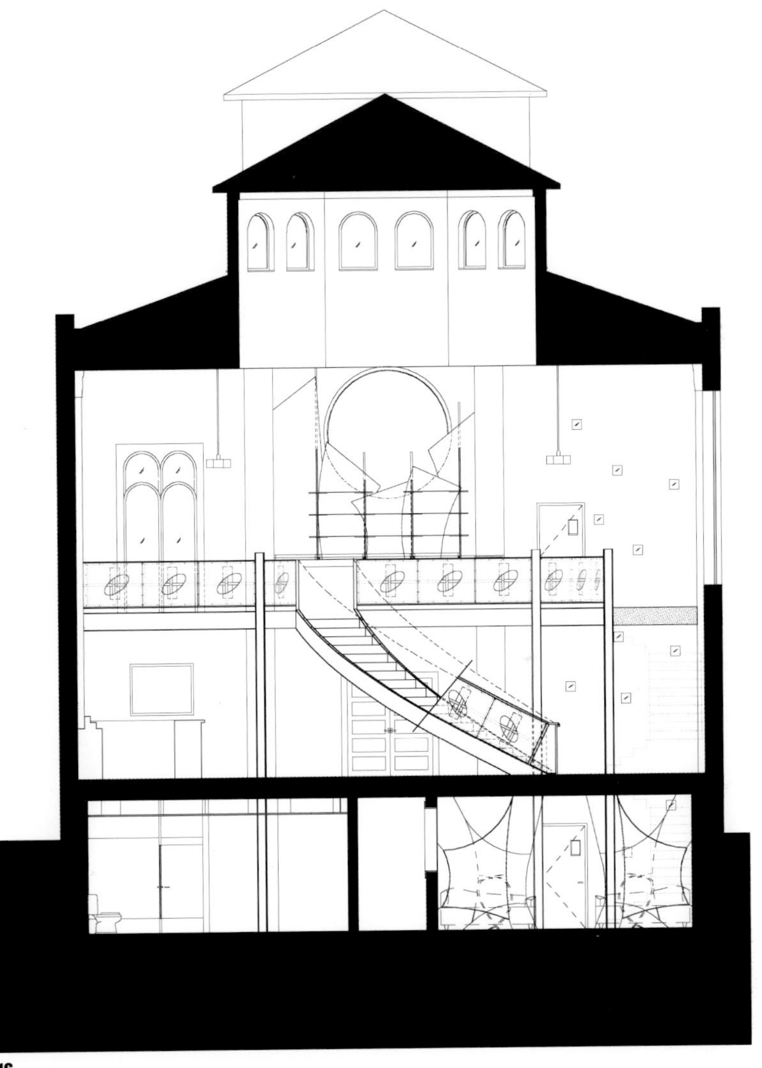

16

1 Exterior

2 Interior façade view

BARCELONA, SPAIN

Sandwich and Friends

ESTUDI FRANCESC PONS

2

Usage: Bar/restaurant

Area: 1496 square feet/ 139 square meters

Materials: Formica, stainless steel, leather, mirrors, linoleum

In the Barcelona Borne, site of the Catalan capital's groovy after-dark scene, sits a bright box of light called Sandwich and Friends. Perhaps the best definition of this party hangout-cum-café is its name. The idea is that on a club tour around the Borne, visitors pop into Sandwich and Friends to fuel up on tasty bocadillo before moving to the next bar or club.

The designer brought in his best friend, illustrator Jordi Labanda, to collaborate in the bar's design. Walls are papered with stylized images of Barcelona's party people. At night chichi murals, combined with the stark aluminum and yellow volumes of the bar's design, attract Barcelona's brightest social butterflies to Sandwich and Friends like moths to a flame.

From the outside, the venue looks like a rectangular box with a long façade, glazed from the waist up. This simple storefront (a combination of glass, canary-yellow planes, and bold graphics) contrasts sharply with the turn-of-the-century sandstone building behind it. Across the threshold, a sunken U-shaped bar in black and chrome claims center stage as it sits rather theatrically against an immense wall mural titled, *People Having Fun*.

The position of the bar determines the establishment's overall layout. Its ceiling height has been adjusted to comply with building regulations and to differentiate its function from the seating areas. ►►

The designer chose four materials that he considers to be modern classics, thanks to their durability and reflective qualities: Formica, mirror glass, chrome, and PVC. Skirting perimeter walls are areas that feature seating in padded black PVC, along with shiny chrome and Formica tables. Keen to create a certain visual chaos, Pons used a series of reflective ceiling and wall panels to conceal fluorescent strips that provide seating areas with added volume and indirect lighting.

3

4

5

3 1950's style bar

4 Bar and dining area

5 Entrance

Photography: Raimon Solà

1

2

SOUTH YARRA, **VICTORIA, AUSTRALIA**

Saratoga

GRANT AMON ARCHITECTS PTY LTD

1 Curved end to main bar

2 Drink display behind main bar

3 Lounge area with sunset poster

4 Dry bar detail with platinum tile and Marblo

3

4

Usage: Nightclub

Area: 2583 square feet/ 240 square meters

Materials: Velvet, gold laminate, Duraloid, Marblo resin

The Saratoga nightclub fitout is a complete reworking of an existing underground bar in Melbourne's South Yarra district. The treatment is lush, employing deep purples and reds with gold highlights throughout the expanded space. The existing main bar has been reclad with a backlit purple Marblo top and vinyl padding front. Behind the bar, the drink display features gold-trimmed shelving units mounted on a black mirror backing.

A smaller bar is located in an opposite corner, expanding service and capacity and providing intimacy. The gold laminate bar sits on red carpet and is surrounded by handmade dimpled tiles and bronzed mirror wall cladding. New chocolate banquette seating has been installed throughout the club in the lounge and booth areas.

The glitz continues, somewhat deliberate and cheesy, with platinum mosaic tiles and gold doors to the unisex bathrooms, the large sunset poster wall, ornate gold mirrors, and other lush tactics all set to swirl deliciously around the central DJ booth. While undeniably tilting its felt hat to the seventies, Saratoga has been reborn for the new millennium to entertain the masses.

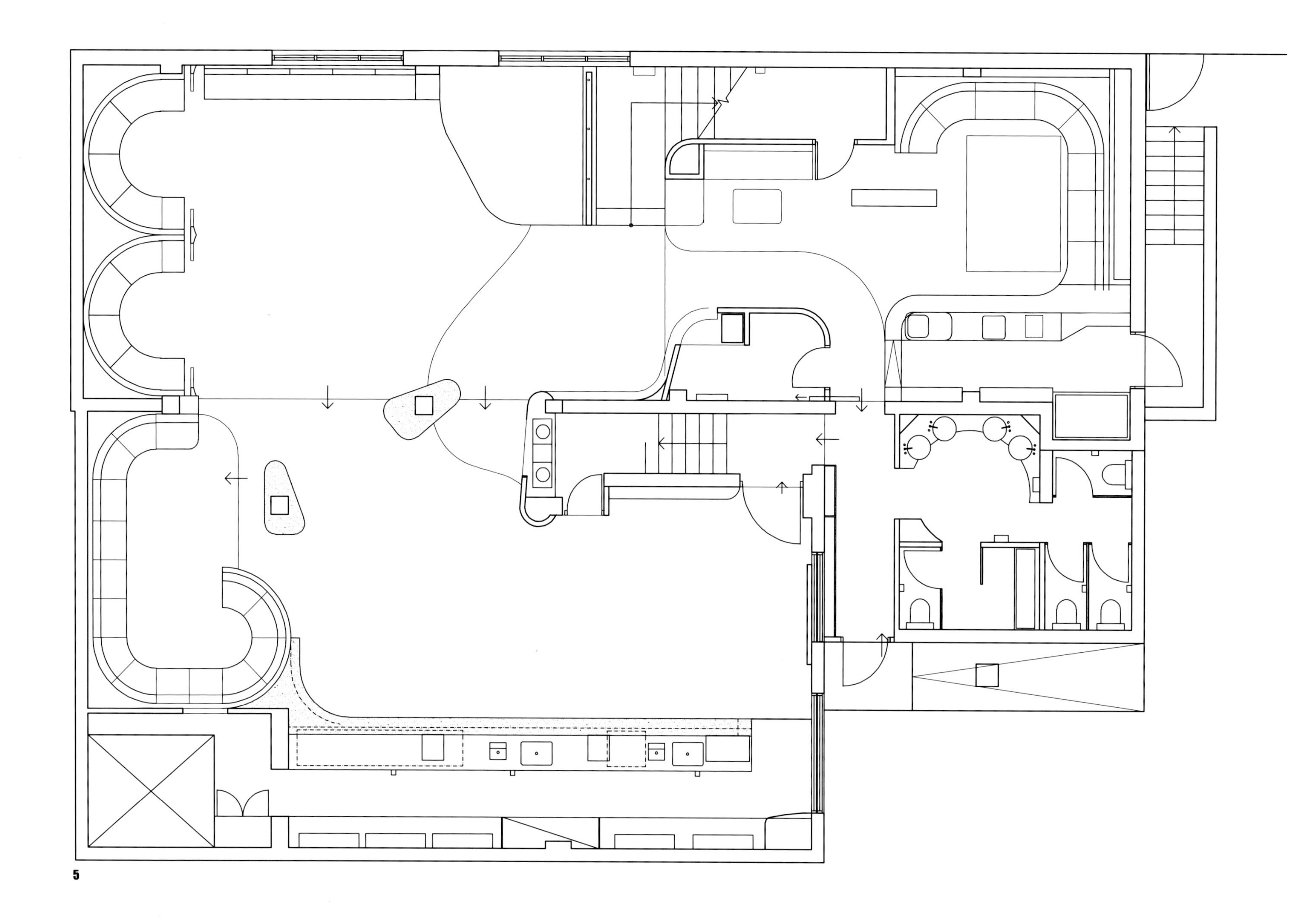

5

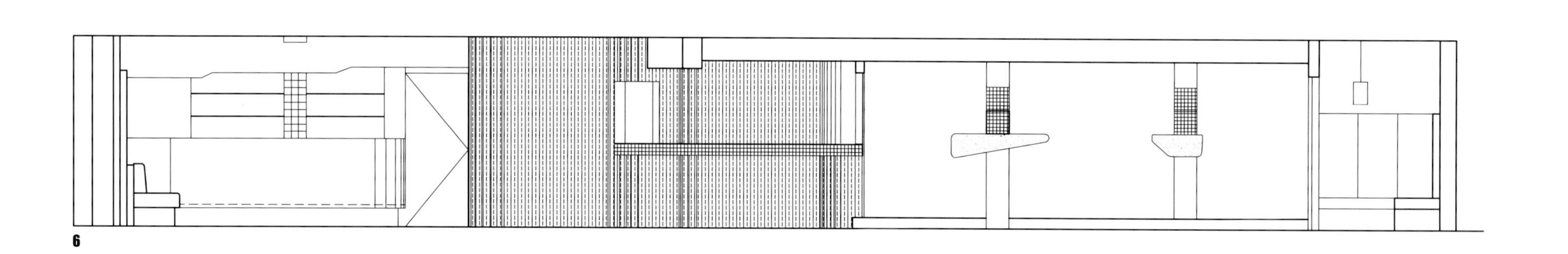

6

7

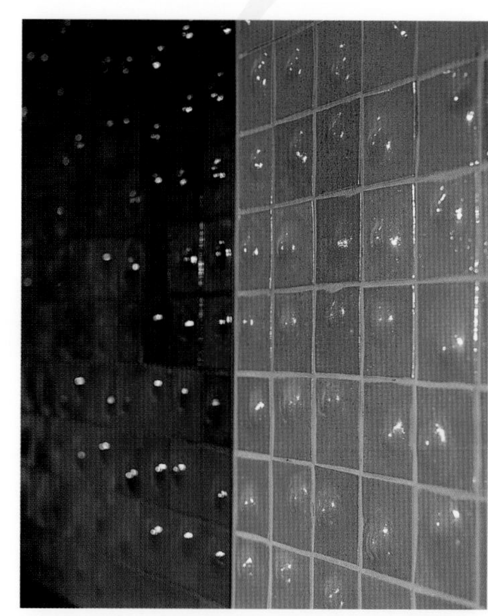

9

10

8

5 Floor plan

6 Section

7 Smaller bar/lounge

8 Handmade tile detail

9 Unisex restroom area

10 Washbasin detail

Photography: Trevor Mein (1–4,7,8,10); Richard Briglia (9)

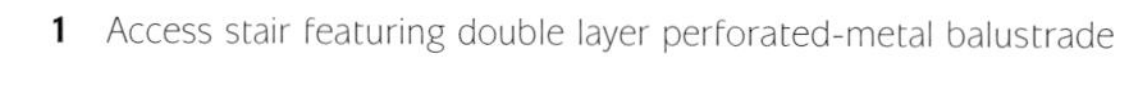

1 Access stair featuring double layer perforated-metal balustrade

2 Bar with pearlescent Marblo top

3 Cocktail bar lounge

4 Main bar/dance area

5 Seating alcoves

1

2

MELBOURNE, **VICTORIA, AUSTRALIA**

GRANT AMON ARCHITECTS PTY LTD

3

5

4

Usage: Nightclub/ events venue

Area: 8396 square feet/ 780 square meters

Materials: Fiberglass, resin, timber paneling, metal mesh

A concrete shell, over two levels buried within a distinctive five-level 1970's office building in South Melbourne became the raw beginnings for Seven. This shell was to house a major contemporary entertainment venue, consisting of ground floor entry, bar, dance zone, stage and service areas with a smaller upper level lounge, intimate bar/dance area and some funky restrooms. A robust steel and concrete stair partially encased in perforated mesh and red glass connects both levels.

The strategy developed along the concept of spatial manipulation of formal objects, where the objects themselves are transformed through material, texture, and light. The liquid flow of surfaces and form yield at times to abstraction and distortion, becoming subtle animated events adding depth and illusion to the other world of club dwellers. Materials such as translucent fiberglass, pearlized resin, and holographic and metallic vinyl rim the space for the main event of DJ, light show, and music.

Upstairs, respite is available in the gold and purple padded-fabric enclosure of the lounge, given a soft glowing depth with a ceiling of stretched Japanese paper panels and dark mirror reflections. The triangular panels are backlit and perform a subtle fold, issuing an origami-like treatment of the surface. The red glass walls of the stairwell produce a backdrop to the bar of deep pink resin and tortoise-shell fiberglass. Beyond, rich timber paneled walls are literally compressed and folded into the main space, punctuated by light slits and pink resin ledges. The room that houses the omnipresent DJ booth is rimmed in a jade metallic-vinyl banquette and framed by gold reflective panels. Behind the panels, a unisex restroom of anonymous cubicles completes the facilities.

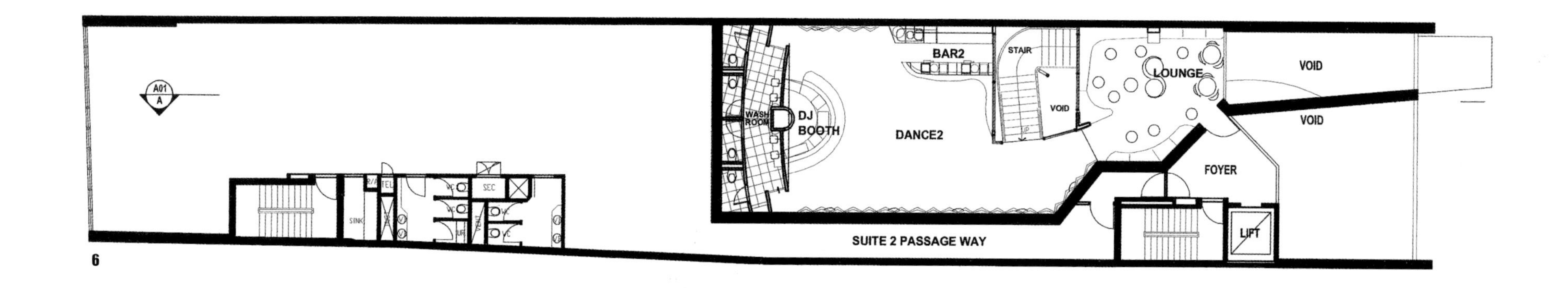
BAR2
STAIR
LOUNGE
VOID
VOID
VOID
WASH ROOM
DJ BOOTH
DANCE2
FOYER
LIFT
SUITE 2 PASSAGE WAY
SINK
SEC
6

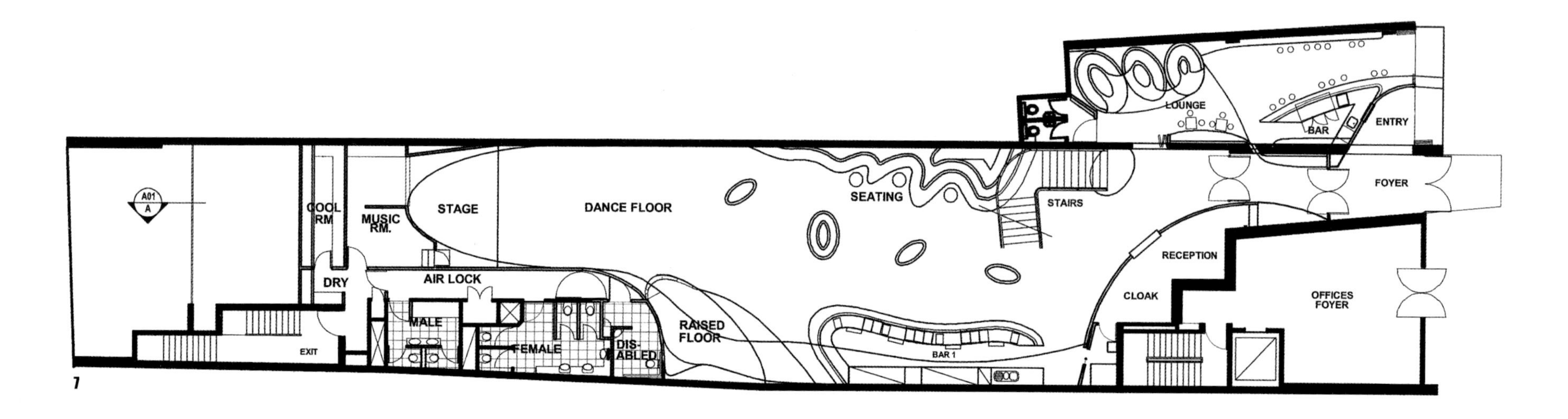
LOUNGE
BAR
ENTRY
FOYER
COOL RM
MUSIC RM.
STAGE
DANCE FLOOR
SEATING
STAIRS
RECEPTION
DRY
AIR LOCK
CLOAK
OFFICES FOYER
MALE
FEMALE
DIS-ABLED
RAISED FLOOR
BAR 1
EXIT
7

8

9

6 First floor plan

7 Ground floor plan

8 Female restrooms with pink bench and black bowls

9 Unisex restrooms

10 Section

11 Curvaceous padded wall, DJ area beyond

12 Folded timber panel wall

Photography: Richard Briglia (1,2,4,12);
Shania Shegedyn (3,5,8,9,11)

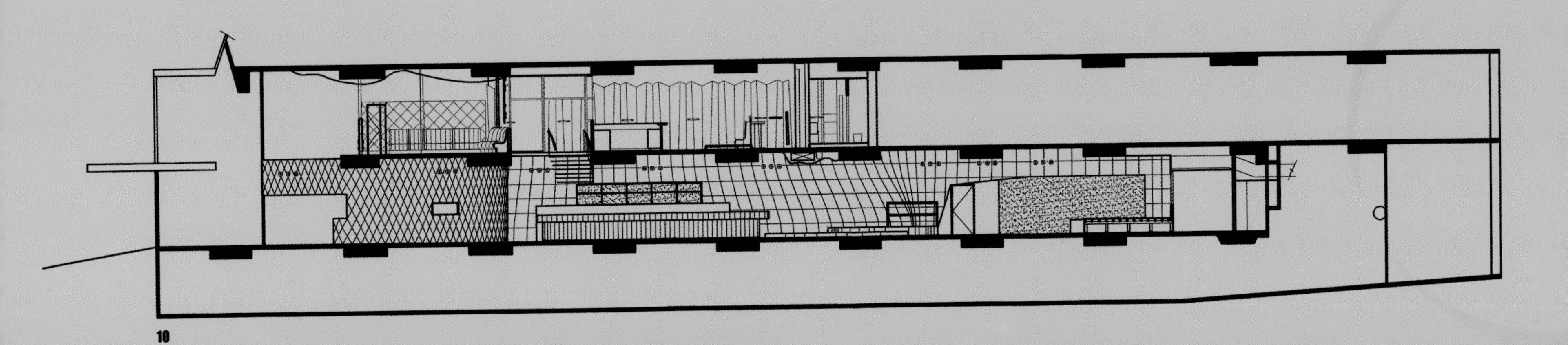

10

11

12

1

TORONTO, **ONTARIO, CANADA**

Seven

II BY IV DESIGN ASSOCIATES

1 Main floor, bar, and mezzanine

2 Illuminated drink pylons

3 Main floor, drink rail, and bumper banquette

2

3

Usage: Nightclub/ events venue

Area: 6000 square feet/ 557 square meters

Materials: Stainless steel, glass, walnut

Asked to create the perfect setting for a high-energy nightclub in a flexible venue, that also generates revenue through corporate and private rentals, II BY IV chose to let the sound and light show—and the guests themselves—animate the space, rather than elaborate design details.

Located in the heart of the entertainment district, the site was an office building already occupied by the owner. To accommodate the new club, a fourth floor was added, connected to the third level by an internal staircase.

The seven deadly sins provide the core interior theme through spectacular lighting effects (lust: blue, pride: violet, envy: green, gluttony: orange, anger: red, greed: yellow, sloth: light blue). These references are repeated throughout the facility.

A 30-foot internally lit bar is backed by a shallow counter in white epoxy lacquer, topped by an integrated stainless drink rail and bottle display surface that curves up to the ceiling to frame the mirrored wall above. Once again, the names of the sins are sandblasted into the mirror surface and backlit in continuously changing color, matched by downlighting on the bottle display.

Whether bathed in periwinkle, fuchsia or sunset-orange light, this remarkably minimalist white interior pulsates with personality, in an intimately scaled, manageable multipurpose venue that invites guests to explore its possibilities.

4

5

4 Mezzanine lounge and bar

5 Mezzanine lounge

6 Digital art at rear and lounge

Photography: David Whittaker

6

1

2

SÃO PAULO, BRAZIL

Shiraz Wine Bar

GUI MATTOS ARQUITETURA WITH ANDREA BRITO AND CRISTIANE MAEDA

1 Façade

2 Main entrance

3 Main floor plan

4 Cellar

5 View from cellar through circular openings

6 Circular openings, cellar in background

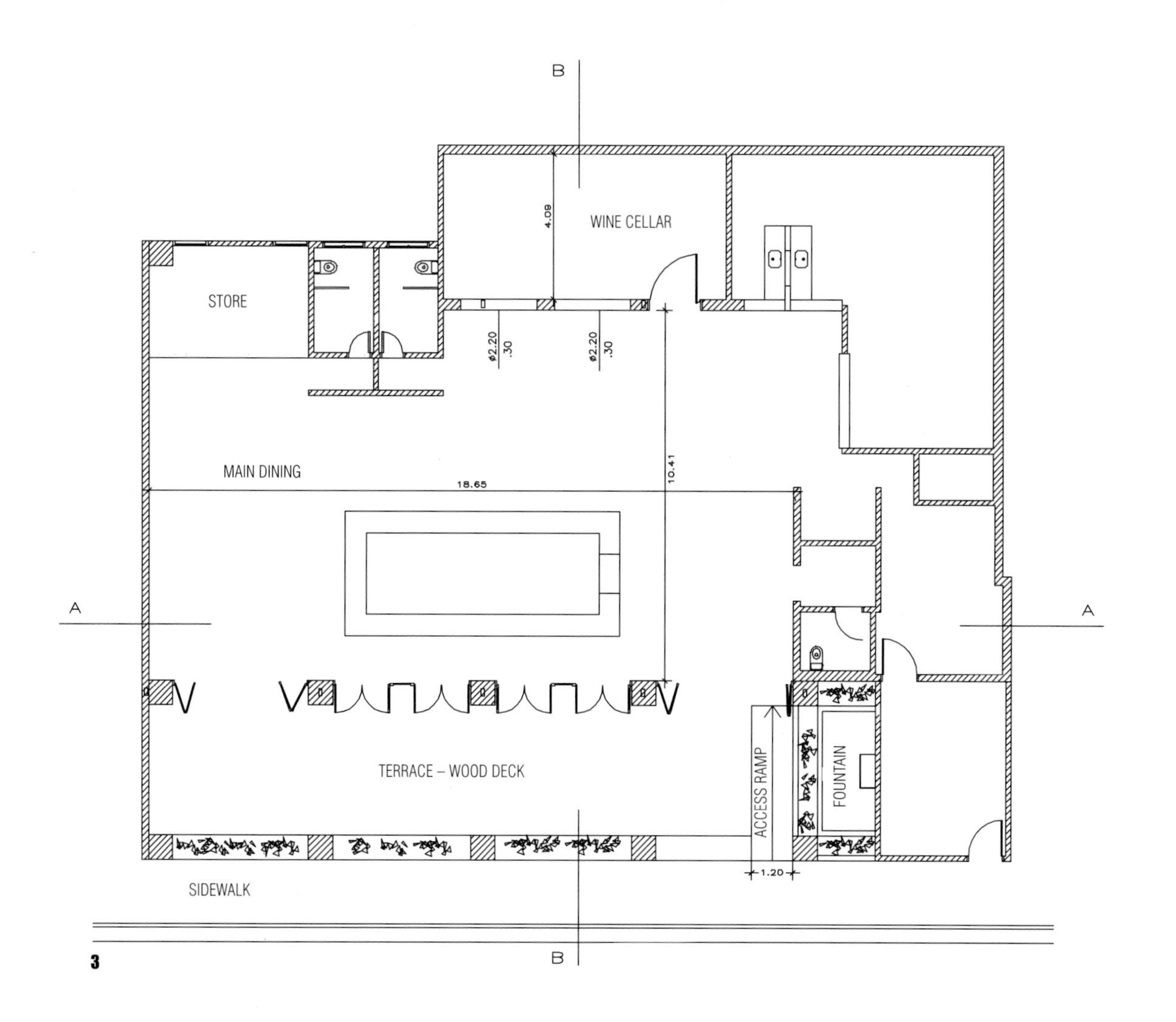

3

4

5

Usage: Wine bar

Area: 3552 square feet/ 330 square meters

The first thing the architect realized while designing the building was the necessity of open areas to create ambience. An existing house with ample walls and small rooms was transformed into a new metallic structure with a big veranda at the entrance that filters natural light and welcomes patrons. Some of the existing materials were re-used to form the frames, and the furniture was remodeled, painted, and sectioned. The cellar can be seen through two circular openings in the waiting area, close to the U-shaped central bar. The atmosphere created by the colors, lighting, coverings, and furniture results in a casual level of comfort.

6

7

8

9

7 Seating

8 Wine bar

9&10 Cellar, seen through the circular openings

Photography: Ary Diesendruck

10

1

MILAN, ITALY

Shu Café

FABIO NOVEMBRE

1 Bar

2&3 Restaurant featuring gold forearms

4 Velvet curtains separate bar and restaurant

Photography: Alberto Ferrero

2

3

4

Usage: Bar/restaurant

Area: 3229 square feet/ 300 square meters

Materials: Resin, velvet, fiberglass, aluminum spray, plaster, wood

The venue is named after the Egyptian God Shu from the *Book of the Dead*. According to the ancient myth, Shu held up the vault of heaven with his arms, separating the earth and sky.

Entry to Shu Café is from the bar area, where a silver counter resembling a spaceship looks like it is taking off from a green, grass-like resin floor. Transparent chairs and mirrored tables assist the event in a triumph of green neon.

Velvet curtains chained to the walls separate the bar from the restaurant. Three steps lead to a black mosaic floor, background walls, curtains, velvet-padded walls, tables, and chairs. A huge electronic ceiling hanging overhead, slightly inclined and separated from the existing walls, gives light through real electronic circuits built as light boxes. The whole architecture of the ceiling allows for the air-conditioning system to remain hidden.

On one end of the room, directly under the lower edge of the ceiling, another bar is covered with rough-edged glass sheets lit up from the back with fiber optics, and framed in stainless steel. On both sides of the room, bulletproof glass walls have been shot at and lit up from the edges. Mirrored walls surround the area, multiplying the dazzling effects, and from the center, two peaceful golden forearms inside a crown of spotlights emerge from the black floor, holding up the ceiling for the patrons of today.

1–4 Bar counter

Photography: Nacása & Partners Inc.

1

2

TOKYO, **JAPAN**

Shu!

CLAUDIO COLUCCI DESIGN

3

4

Usage: Champagne bar

Area: 33 square feet/ 3 square meters

Shu! was created inside an existing small restaurant in a popular district of Tokyo. The designer was confined to a small budget and very difficult conditions. The building's concrete structure meant that walls could be neither added nor removed so the focus is on the unusually shaped bar. Shu! is an intimate members-only champagne bar that seats 10 people, with a delightful interior bathed in red, orange, and fuchsia.

1

2

1 Exterior, Queens

2 S-curve bar, Queens

3 Pool hall, Queens

4 Pool-ball shaped fireplace, Queens

5 Wine rack along window, Queens

QUEENS, **NEW YORK, USA**
CHELSEA, **NEW YORK, USA**

Slate Bar and Billiards

WEISZ + YOES ARCHITECTURE

3

4

5

Usage: Bar/ restaurant/billiards

Area: 20,000 square feet/ 1858 square meters

Named after the slate beneath the green felt on a pool table, the materials and architecture forms are derived from the geometric forms that feature in the game. The two former pool halls have been transformed into unique venues that combine billiards with fine dining and cocktails. They are large spaces that were gut renovated in order to provide a new design for each location.

Slate Queens features a 50-foot, custom-designed serpentine crackle glass bar with fiber optics, and a pool-ball shaped fireplace. The bars were developed out of special layers of laminated cracked glass above a hollow light table that held skeins of fiber optic cable.

Slate Chelsea also has this signature bar. A structural glass staircase in the shape of a pool triangle connects its two floors.

Both venues feature DJ booths and provide ambience for lounging, eating, and playing pool. Metal fabric curtains and a tensile fabric ceiling separate the eating and playing areas. Full commercial kitchens were added to enable these venues to have full menus and cater for special events.

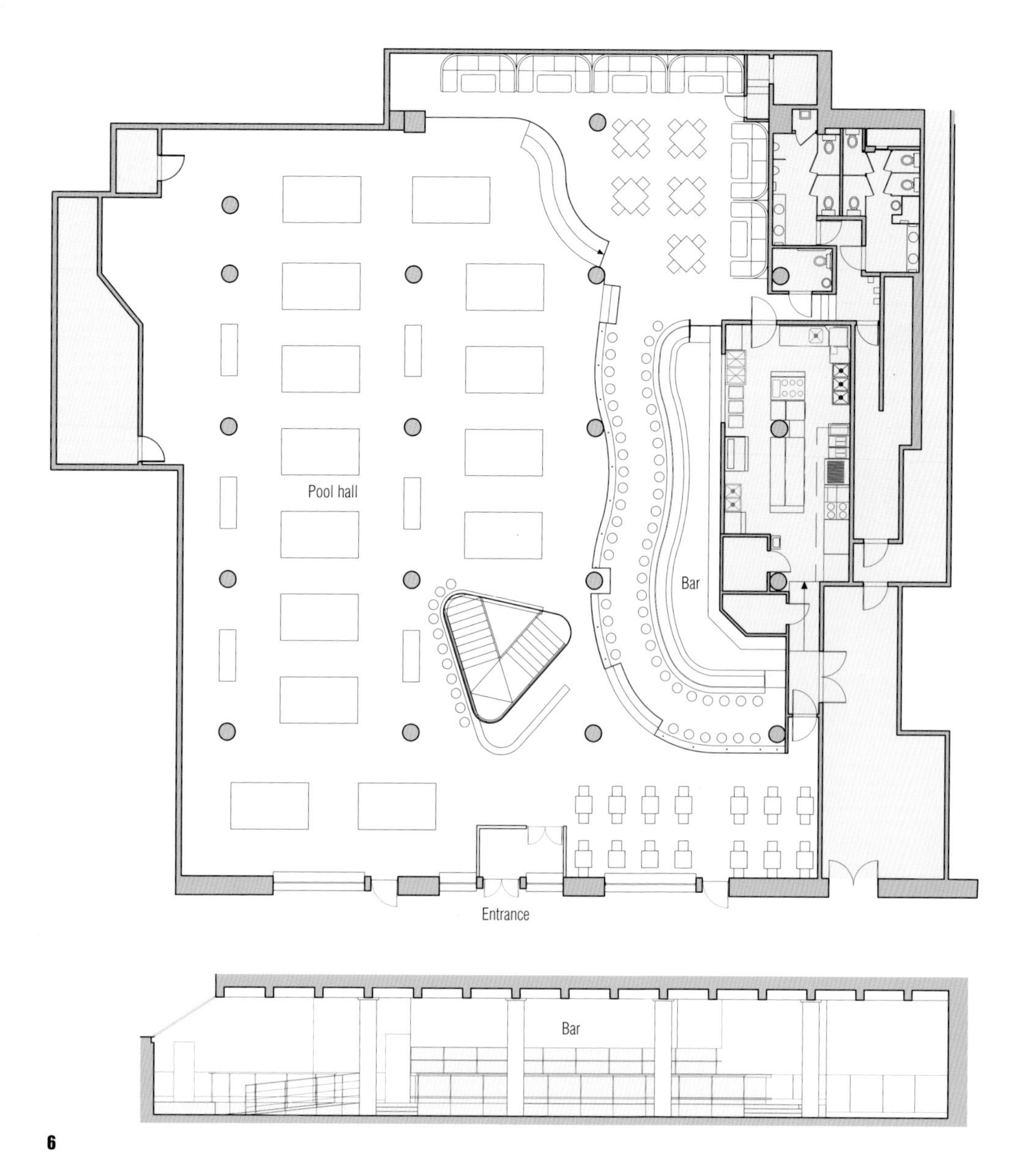

6

7

6 Floor plan and section, Chelsea

7 Tables, Chelsea

8 Glass stair, Chelsea

9 Bar, Chelsea

Photography: Paul Warchol Photography

8

9

1

3

2

1 Main entrance

2 Wardrobe between two free-standing walls

3 Wardrobe

4 Floor plan

5 Small round bar, close to main entrance

6&7 Dance floor with ring of 3-meter-long white threads

MUNICH, GERMANY

Stars

STUDIOACHT.

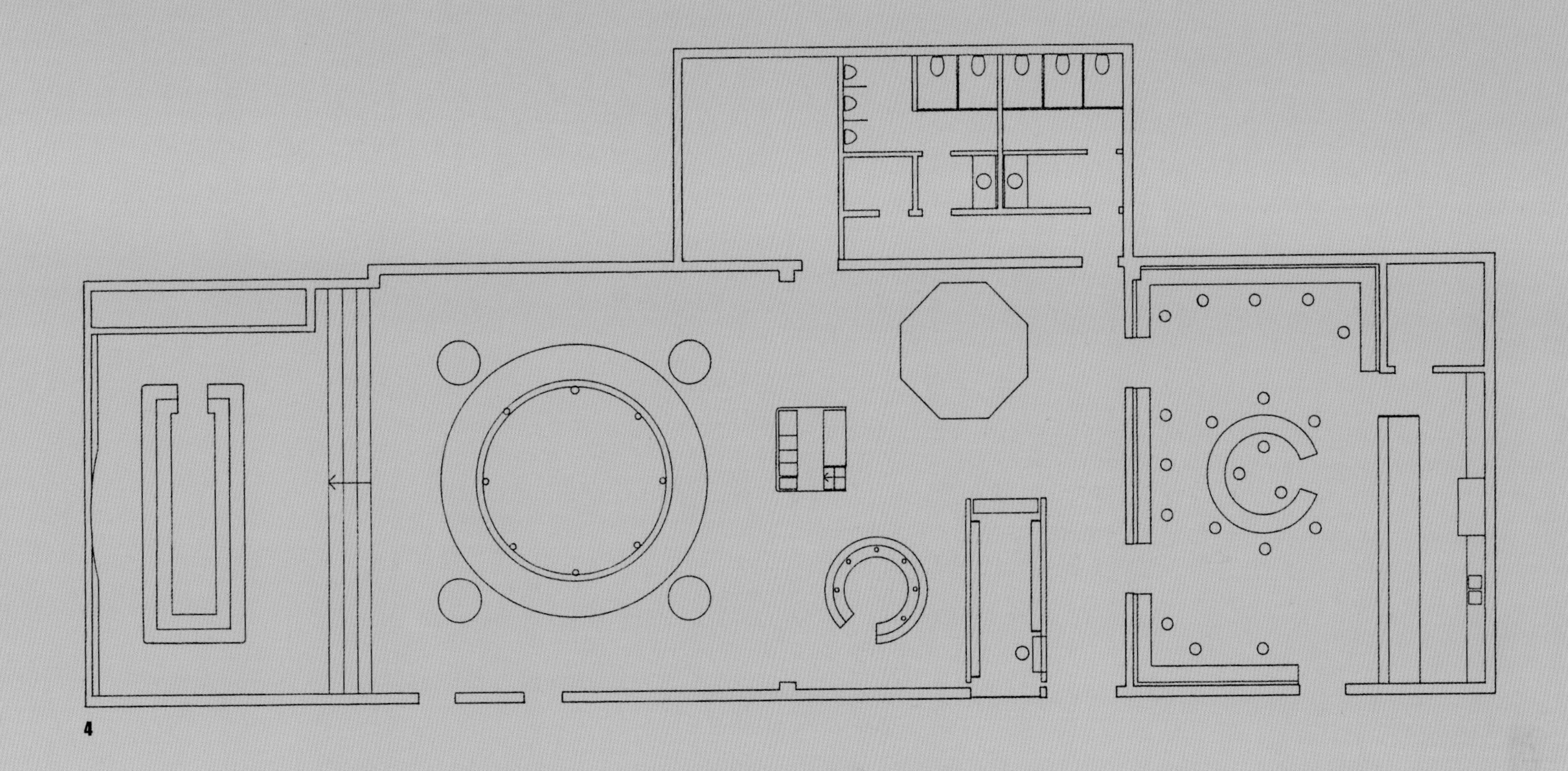

4

5 6 7

Client: Freude am Leben GmbH

Usage: Bar/ lounge/nightclub

Area: 8611 square feet/ 800 square meters

A circular bench and small high-grade steel tables invite the visitor to relax in the lounge area. The walls and ceiling, bar, and shelves are painted white and appear to visually melt together. Silver metal wall-lights can be dimmed, turning the room's atmosphere from cool to warm as desired.

The hall shifts to smoky charcoal-colored walls, ceilings, and floor. The room's furnishing elements create a contrast and their unified white colors emphasize their transformation into sculptural bodies designed with rounded off edges. On the dance floor, the colors change again through the use of orange lights.

The rear wall has a circular depression, 3.6 meters in diameter, with a surface that subtly curves to the inside. Different planets, with their surfaces changed through computer animation, spin around their own axes. The concave wall design emphasizes the three-dimensional perception of the animation of the different planets and seduces into a world of imagination.

8 Lounge area

9 Lounge and bar

10&11 Main bar with animated wall

12 Circular bench and small high-grade steel tables

Photography: Maximilian Mutzhas

9

8

10

11

12

1 Chimney wall with yellow light gleaming from its shaft

2 Round seats in front of chimney and dance floor

3 Tables and chairs in second-floor bar area

4 Curtains with circular hole design

5 Stairs with glass partition and bar rack on ground level

6 Main bar

7 Seating opposite main bar

8 Circular high-grade steel rings above seating

Photography: Rudolf Schnellbach

1

3

4

2

SONTHOFEN, GERMANY

Sudhaus

STUDIOACHT.

5

6

7

Client: Christian and Roman Haltmayr
Usage: Bar
Area: 2475 square feet/ 230 square meters

Sudhaus is located in a popular summer holiday resort. Its first room features a sculptured bar that winds itself around the central staircase. Machined parts were pulled over specifically designed templates and the material was welded together on site, while the vertical elements of the bar are made of walnut. Rays of light fall through the wooden blinds hanging from the high windows facing the street throughout the day and night.

The first-floor lounge is furnished with soft brown leather sofas, varnished side tables, and leather stools. The second-floor bar is painted dark brown, and contains a smaller cubic bar, made of highly polished high-grade steel, combined with walnut.

8

1 Front façade, with dot matrix sign

2 View from rear

3&7 Main dining area

4–6 Basement lounge

2

1

3

COPENHAGEN, DENMARK

SuperGeil

JOHANNES TORPE STUDIOS

4

5

6

Usage: Bar/café

Area: 5263 square feet/ 489 square meters

Materials: Acrylic, epoxy, wool, foam, stainless steel, aluminum

Designed to be developed as a future café chain with international locations, SuperGeil is currently one of Copenhagen's most unusual and eye-catching cafés. Design, lifestyle, and leisure industry magazines from all over the world have reviewed it. In addition to its good-looking interior, it is simply a pleasant place to eat, drink, and play.

The development of the SuperGeil chain was stalled by a troubled economy after the September 11 attacks in the United States. Investors are optimistic and plan to start the chain up again by opening new cafés throughout the European Union.

7

8 Entrance

9 Large group seating

10 Main bar, made from fiberglass painted with gold Maserati car finish

11 Cocktail bar in basement

12 Floor plans

Photography: Jens Stolze

9

8

10

11

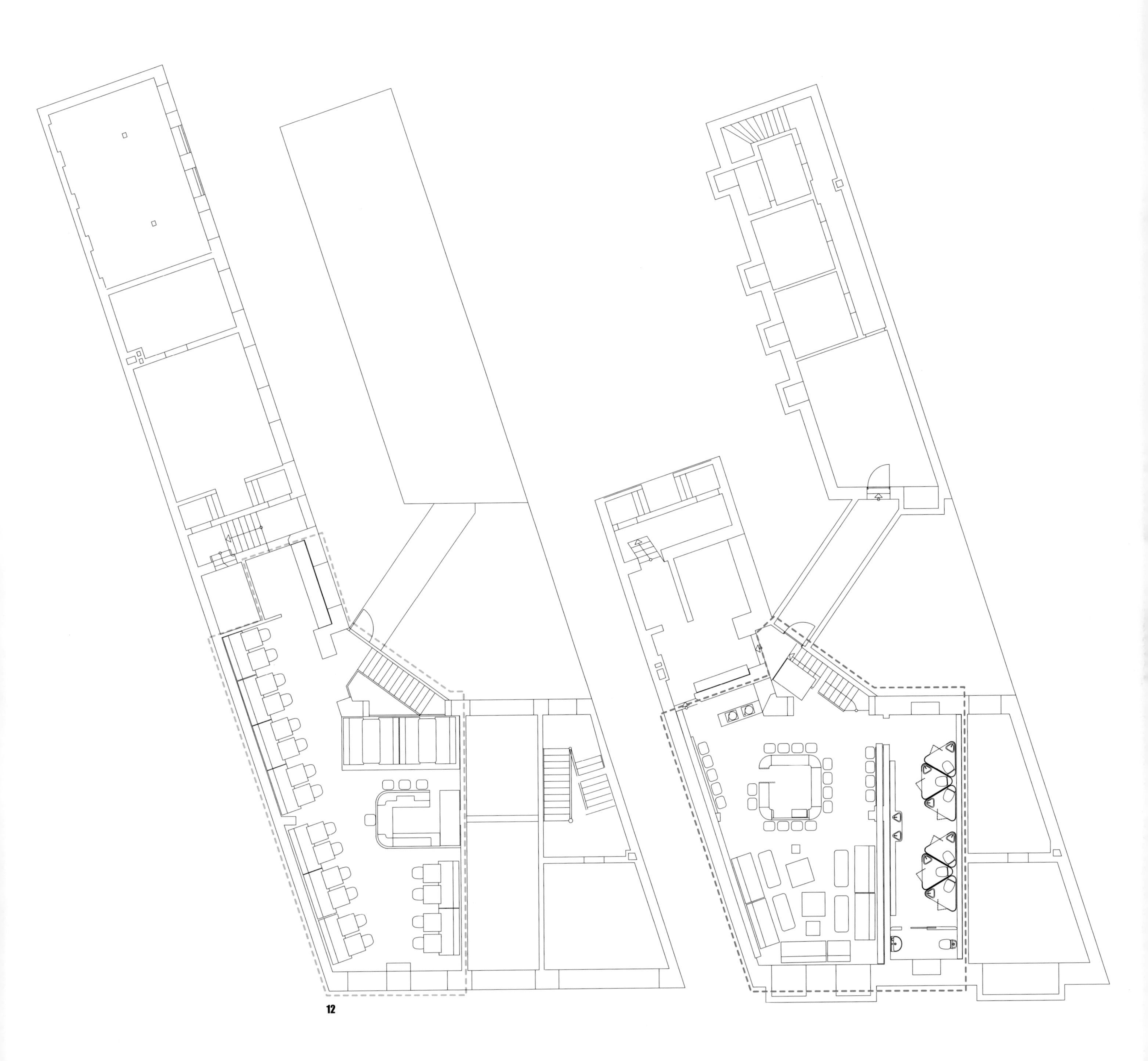
12

1,3&4 La Salle Neige

2&6 Les Toilettes Noir

5 Le Bar Rouge

7 Restaurant

Photography: courtesy Concrete Architectural Associates

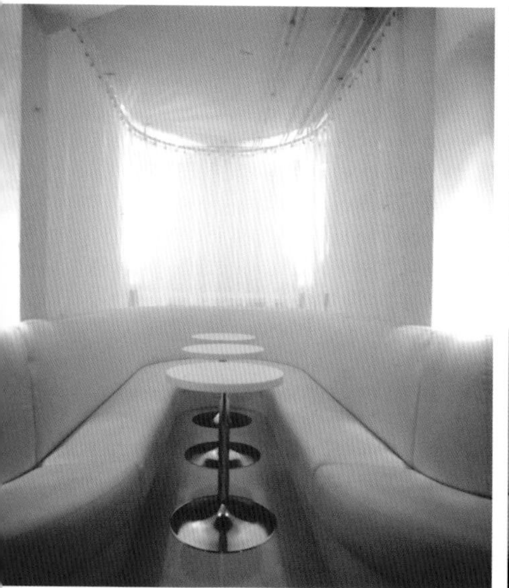

1

3

4

2

AMSTERDAM, THE NETHERLANDS

SupperClub

CONCRETE ARCHITECTURAL ASSOCIATES

5

6

7

Client: IQ Creative

Usage: Bar/ lounge/restaurant

Area: 4305 square feet/ 400 square meters

Materials: Tiles, stucco, stainless steel

Amsterdam's Supperclub is divided into four different rooms; la Salle Neige, le Bar Rouge, le Salon Colore and les Toilettes Noir.

The main restaurant is located in la Salle Neige, an all-white two-level space in which colored lights change the appearance of the room, and video projections decorate the walls. Visitors dine from silver metal trays while resting on huge white mattresses that run along the two main walls. In the center of the room there is the option of more conventional table dining on Verner Panton chairs at round tables. An open kitchen is located at the back where waiters serve the five-course set meal.

The retro-style le Bar Rouge holds up to 60 people and features red curtains and a big neon 'bar' sign. Les Toilettes Noir, the restrooms, feature giant rubber cubes in the center where people can sit and chat. Finally, le Salon Colore can be found in the basement for those who like to just lounge and relax.

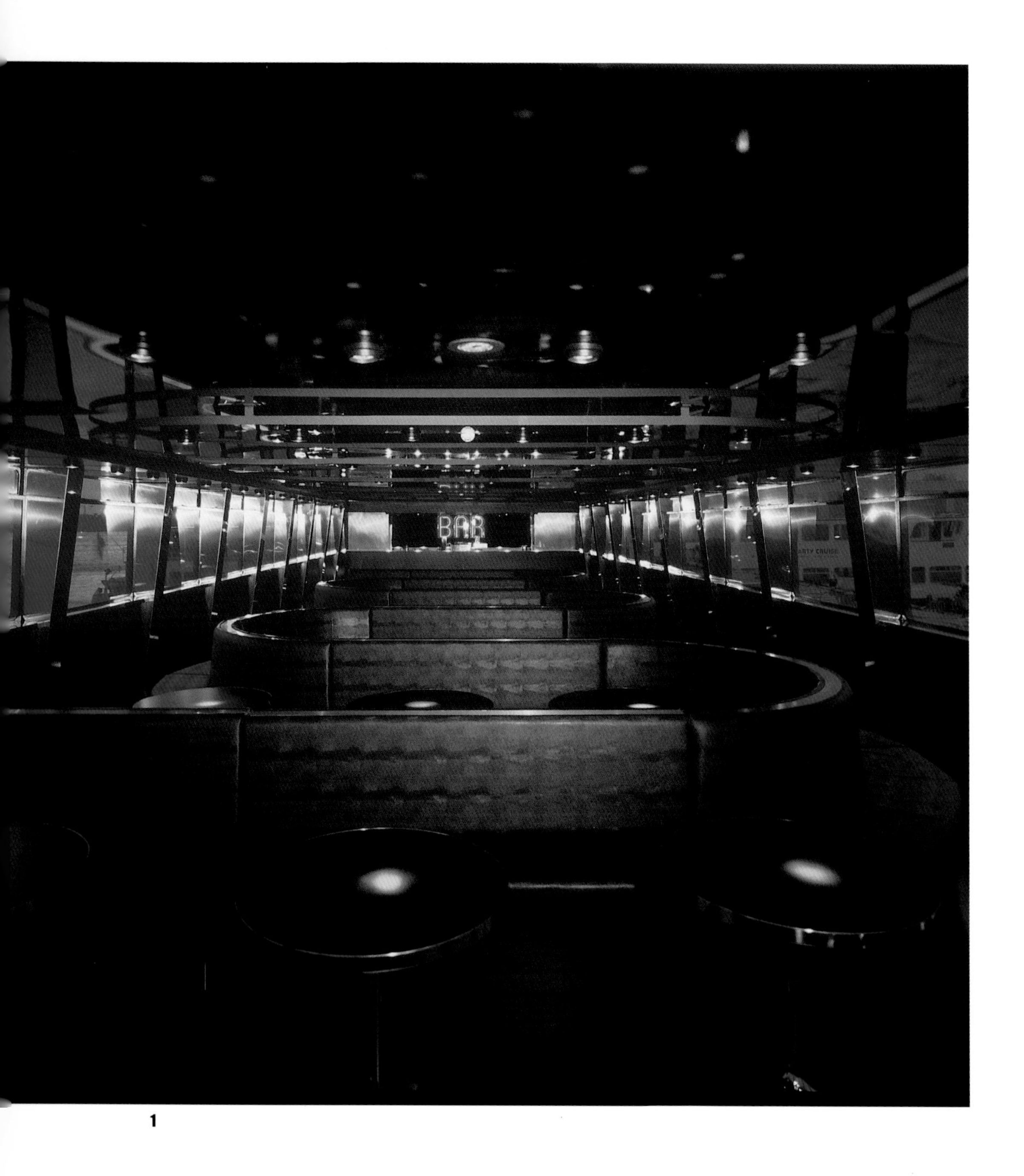

1

2

AMSTERDAM, THE NETHERLANDS

Supper Club Cruise

CONCRETE ARCHITECTURAL ASSOCIATES

1 Le Bar Rouge

2&3 La Salle Neige

4 Le Bar Noir

Photography: courtesy Concrete Architectural Associates

3

4

Client: IQ Creative and Healers & Beads

Usage: Bar/lounge

Area: 3767 square feet/ 350 square meters

The creators of Amsterdam's Supperclub have taken the original concept and transported it to the water: a floating nightclub that can either travel on the waterways to pick up its patrons, or stay docked.

The ship can be divided into three main areas: entrance and restrooms, La Salle Neige, and Le Bar Noir. Each has a different feel and color, as their names suggest.

1

2

3

LAS VEGAS, **NEVADA, USA**

Tabu Ultra Lounge

JEFFREY BEERS INTERNATIONAL

1 Lounge area featuring flowing imagery mural

2 Main bar against main lounge backdrop

3 Main lounge area with interactive video projection tables

4 Revolving liquor towers with holographic glass at main bar

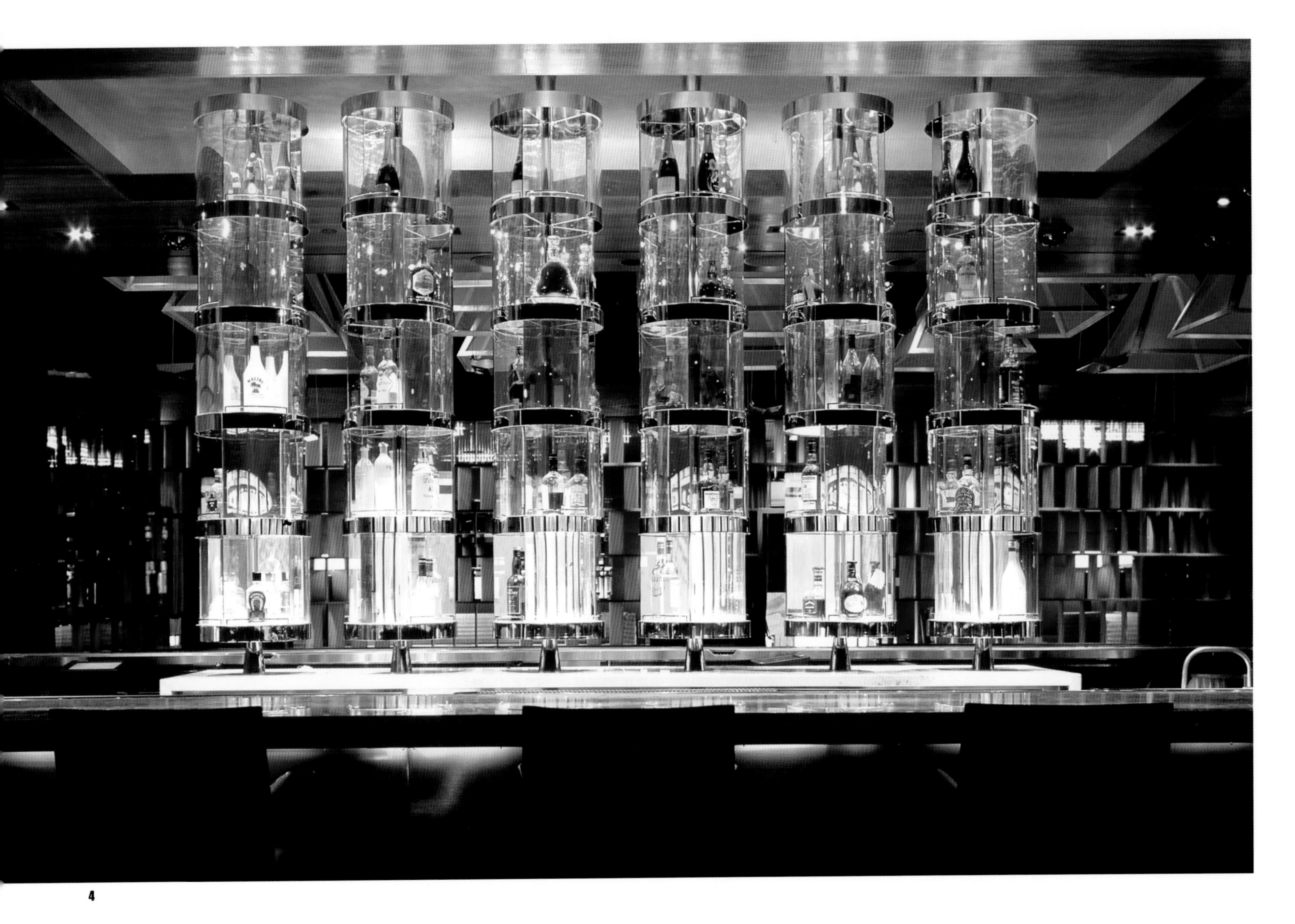

4

Usage: Bar/ lounge/nightclub

Area: 7000 square feet/ 650 square meters

Materials: Marble, wood

Located in the MGM Grand Casino, Tabu features three very diverse rooms, all designed by Jeffrey Beers International. The main room features interactive tables, private guest booths, the main spirits bar, and DJ booth. Revolving liquor towers are behind the main bar. Along the outside wall are private booths, which are slightly inset from the rest of the room and separated from the casino environment by thick frosted glass. These booths are available for bottle service reservations.

The circular 'Tantra' room is complete with its own private bar made entirely of ice. A hand-blown glass and metal pendant hangs overhead while the walls are covered in a beautiful shimmering fabric. From numerous carved niches, tiny candles flicker, reflecting from the black marble floor.

At the rear is the Champagne bar separated by a wood frame boasting hundreds of amber resin panels. With purple fabric walls and crystal lighting fixtures, this room features its own private entrance and restroom facility, for those who desire maximum privacy.

A stunning visual element that captures the attention is an animated mural by Roger Parent, running the full length of one of the walls. The mural is a desertscape featuring faces, images, objects and colored light. Each admirer of the mural will have a different perception of it, depending on lighting of the room and what images are being focused on at that specific time.

Opposite Cylindrical VIP 'Tantra' room

6 Floor plan

7 Entrance—mirrored illumination column flanking reception area

8 View from DJ booth overlooking VIP and lounge area

Photography: Eric Laignel

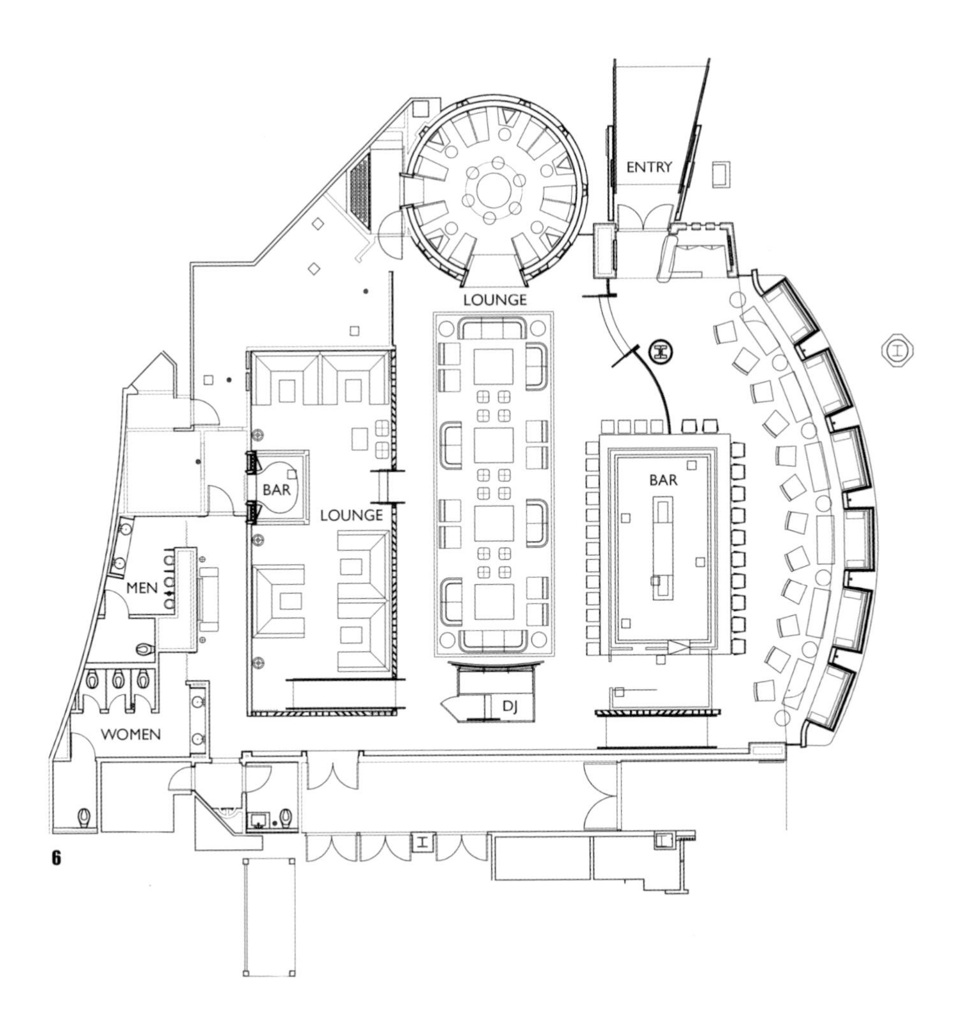

6

7

8

1

1 End of main bar looking toward render wall

2 Restaurant area

3 Render wall with inset felt panels

4 Raised area across dance floor to bar

2

LIVERPOOL, UK

Tea Factory Bar and Kitchen

WELLS MACKERETH

3

4

Client: R+R Bars ltd
Usage: Bar/restaurant
Area: 7000 square feet/ 650 square meters

The site occupies the ground floor of a steel-framed brick warehouse. The client required a bar large enough for a maximum of 600 people with DJ area, seating, and restaurant space as well as associated back-of-house and service areas. The aim was to attract an urban crowd that would dress *down* to go out rather than 'smarten up'. This lent itself to the feel of the vacant site, with its concrete and brick finishes and grand-scaled exposed steel-riveted structure.

The architects organized the main bar along the center of one side wall, making the most of the linear nature of the interior, and using the existing brick finish as a backdrop to the activity of the bar and bottle display. Wells Mackereth exploited the use of materials in a raw form to suit the 'warehouse feel' of the project: galvanized ductwork, 'gunmetal' finish to the steel structure, natural render wall, and the asphalt floor finish. The latter has been highly polished to give a 'just-poured' appearance, almost like an oil slick. The steel-framed modules of the light boxes have inset twin-wall polycarbonate sheeting, a material more commonly used in factory roofing.

Carefully inserted warm materials contrast with hard finishes, seen in the use of natural walnut for the bar cladding, stairs and restaurant seating area, the felt-clad panels, the large leather sofas, and the dark brown coir matting which runs the full width of the seating area.

6

7

8

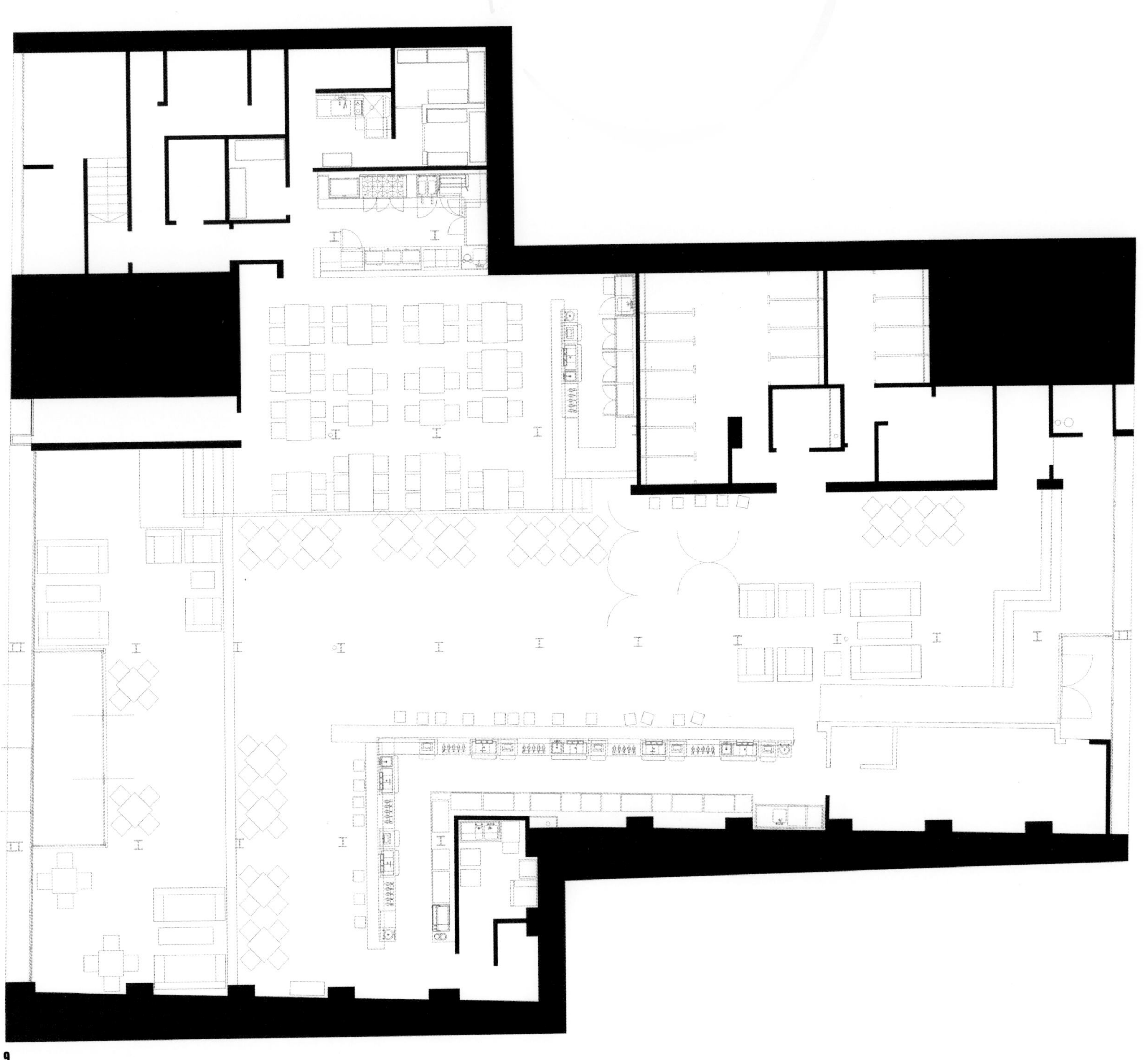

9

Opposite Light boxes over main bar with painted text on brick backdrop

6 Graphic wall

7 Timber cladding to cellar screen wall

8 Raised restaurant area

9 Floor plan

Photography: Chris Tubbs

1 Tables, lighting, seating, and railing, level two

2 View from second sub-level

3 Staircase to roof

4 Stair rail paneling

5&6 Bar

Photography: Rockstar Design (1–5); Todd Dacquisto (6)

1

2

MILWAUKEE, WISCONSIN, USA

Terrace Bar

FLUX DESIGN

3

4

5

6

Usage: Bar

Area: 5800 square feet/ 538 square meters

Materials: Steel, concrete, plastics

Owners David Larson and Nick Howell were looking for a distinctive way to employ minimal materials in a location that demanded a careful and intelligent integration of form and function. The crisp contemporary building rises out of a row of Irish pubs on Milwaukee's Water Street strip.

The site is physically narrow (less than 20 feet across) but the space feels much larger than it actually is. The steel and concrete tables seem to slip right out of the walls and pulsate with the same lighting effect as the building's façade. The bars rise from the floor, beneath dramatic canopies of faux-finished plastic, while the liquor shelves pop out of the concrete block walls. The stairs and two sub-level balconies are lined with steel mesh cast in textured translucent plastic that transmits the changing lights and passing figures.

Three garage-style doors slide open and add to the openness of the space and a breathtaking view of the Milwaukee skyline can be taken in from the rooftop patio. Terrace is testimony that the cramped locations so often overlooked or dismissed can be dramatic and comfortable venues.

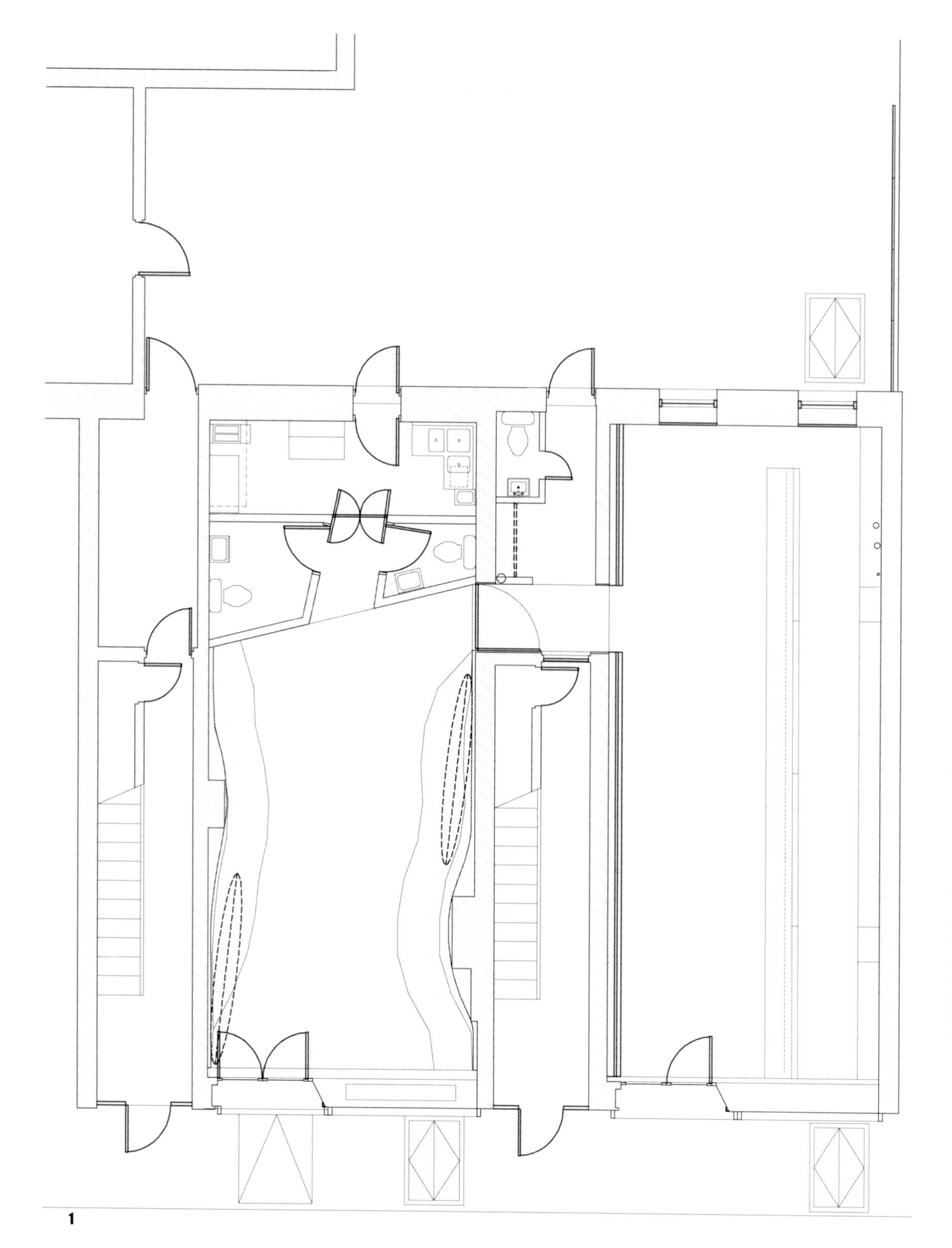

1

1 Floor plan
2 Bar
3 Wall detail
4 Main bar and elk head
5&6 Lounge with passage to bar area
7 Lounge detail

Photography: Jordi Miralles

2

NEW YORK, NEW YORK, USA

Totem Bar

CHO SLADE ARCHITECTURE WITH ANTHONY FONTENOT

3

4

6

7

5

Usage: Bar/ restaurant/lounge

Area: 1614 square feet/ 150 square meters

The architects connected two separate storefronts and created a bar and restaurant/lounge, emphasizing the distinction between the two environments. The client was interested in totems and carved panels, exhibiting them prominently, and building spaces around them. In response, the architects decided that the idea for each room should come from ideas embedded in totems.

For the bar, the focus was on the object quality of totems, as freestanding objects in a landscape. The bar becomes the central focus of the space but each component has a strong separate quality. In the lounge, the architects wanted to explore the idea of carving itself, how a totem is carved out of one tree, one material. This space is formed in felt. The entire space is a container defined by one material that unifies the wall, ceiling, seating, and tables. In contrast to the bar, this space is more like a cave carved out of felt.

Additionally, these spaces offer distinct experiences, with the bar more amenable to mixing and meeting while the restaurant/lounge is closer and fosters a relaxed, intimate setting.

1 View from Transport
2 Typical bar station
3 Northern entry and outdoor court
4 Glazing screen
5 Continuous seating and duct element
6 Main space through to western terrace
7 Main space showing keg room above.

Photography: Rhiannon Slater

2

1

3

MELBOURNE, **VICTORIA, AUSTRALIA**

Transport

MADDISON ARCHITECTS

4

5

6

7

Usage: Pub

Area: 6243 square feet/ 580 square meters

Materials: Glass-reinforced concrete, recycled timber, stainless steel, leather

Located in the hub of transportation, the trams, trains, pedestrians, and automobiles heavily impact on the venue's site. The positioning of the building within a large urban space (Federation Square) allowed for maximum permeability between the pub and the site.

The idea of the main entrance was de-formalized, with each door being presented as a back door. Inside, the form making dominates and dictates the spatiality and spatial interaction. The heavy forms create a continuous element that breaks, encloses, and delineates a notion of intimate spaces within a large volume. Within these nooks and crannies, the clientele are forced into introverted social groups, or they are pressed against the glass for extroverted exposure.

The juncture between hard and soft, and reflective and textured surfaces formalizes a robust language to suit the utilitarian nature of a pub. Elements expressed horizontally emphasize the large footprint and vertical elements used to express the height of the space.

Every element of Transport, including the display keg room, communal inbuilt seating, and leaning rails reinforces the notion of a modern-day pub. The space suggests the notion of 'pub' and embraces its context and site.

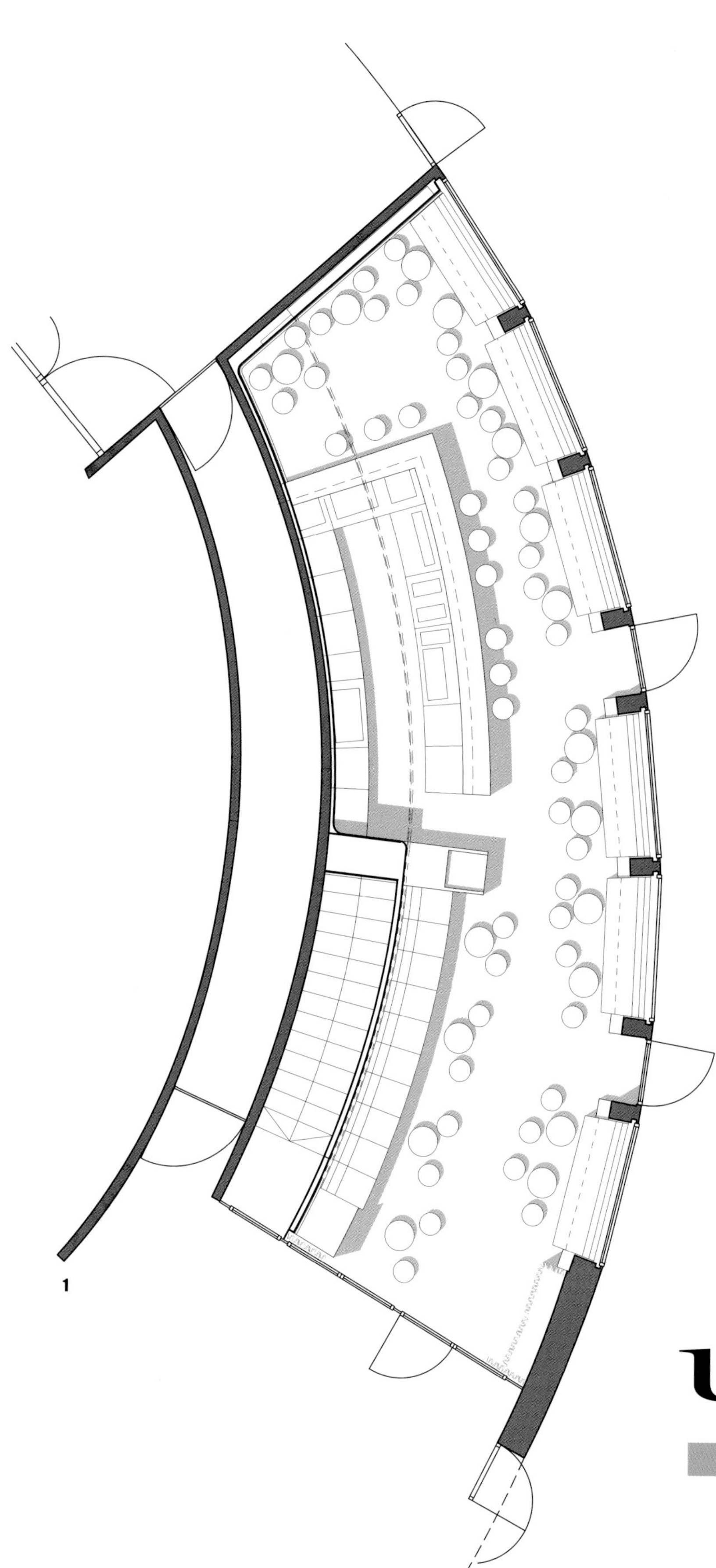

1

2

BERLIN, **GERMANY**

Universum Lounge

PLAJER & FRANZ STUDIO

1 Floor plan

2 View from entry

3 Teak and brass bar

4 Seating

5 Curved light box with images from lunar expeditions

6 Electronic clock in distance shows Houston time

7 Bar front detail, an orthogonal interpretation of a planet surface

Photography: Karl Bongartz

3

4

5

6

7

Usage: Bar/lounge

Area: 936 square feet/ 87 square meters

Materials: Wallpaper, teak, brass, limestone

The Universum lounge is located in what was once the largest movie theater in Berlin, a 1920's German landmark designed by Bauhaus pioneer Erich Mendelsohn. The client had initially requested the creation of an ice-cream parlor but the architects convinced the owner that the venue was too small for ice-cream counters; and that the neighborhood was lacking a bar.

For the architects, the name 'Universum' will always be connected with the most exciting event in space—the day man landed on the moon. Here they took their creative hook, fashioning an interior reminiscent of the loungerooms in which the world watched the event, broadcast from their teak television sets. The architecture is a further development of the dynamic and futuristic modernism of the 1950s and 1960s where Corbusier mixed concrete with wood. It is a South American modernism like that of Oscar Niemeyer's, linked to the present day by its visitors and the use of the materials and the machines that shaped the interior.

MILWAUKEE, **WISCONSIN, USA**

Vucciria

FLUX DESIGN

1

2

3

4

1 Upper-level bar surface

2 Mezzanine railing detail

3 Stairwell and lower-bar wall detail

4 Stair rail detail

5&7 Mezzanine rail and chandeliers

6 Lower-level bar

8 Lower-level back bar

9 Lower level bar, daylight

10 Lower-level front bar

Photography: courtesy Flux Design

5

6

7

9

8

10

Usage: Bar

Area: 5700 square feet/ 530 square meters

Materials: Steel, plastics, woods, granite, LED lighting

This geometric and symmetrical space was drafted and constructed by AE3 [Architects and Engineers]. Flux Design worked closely with Anne Kustner Lighting Design, to integrate virtually every interior fixture with intelligent LED lighting technologies.

By day, the interior is notably achromatic and crisp, characterized by bold contrasts in the tone and texture of the materials and finishes. By night, the entire space transforms into color. More than 200 independently programmable lighting units, capable of 16.7 million colors each, dissolve and pulsate throughout the space.

Specialty lighting elements were integrated into the lower-level bar surface and facing, back bar shelves and canopy structure, as well as the upper-level bar surface, back bar structure, and the entire mezzanine railing system. A thorough understanding of material properties and an innovative method of approaching them enable Flux Design to bridge the gap between designer and builder, without losing sight of the client's wants and needs.

Owners, Joe and Mimma Megna, along with interior designer Jon Schlagenhaft Design, are noted for their insistence on quality and impeccable attention to detail. Each fixture in Vucciria, hand crafted by Flux's team of artists and designers, was constructed from the very best materials, all the way down to the host station and stair rail.

1

2

3

1 West side with Hudson River beyond

2 Slate bar and back bar beyond

3 View facing north

4 Back bar slate wall

5 Raised seating area with moiré column in front

Photography: Michael Moran

NEW YORK, **NEW YORK, USA**

West Bar and Lounge

ENTER ARCHITECTURE

4

5

Client: Patrick Campi and Paul Dektor

Usage: Bar

Area: 1400 square feet/ 130 square meters

The materials used in West's interior play an important part in capturing the exterior elements. The highly reflective black walls suggest permanence and reflect the colors of the sky, from grays, to oranges and blues, as well as the sunsets over the Hudson River.

Chrome-trimmed seating suggests comfortable interiors of low-riding and very plush 1960's classic cars. Building columns have been clad in a military-grade stainless steel mesh that allows transparency and ensures that light is unobstructed, reflecting the industrial nature of the neighborhood.

The completely transparent bar acts as a Hopper-like light from the highway, for a driver to pull in and get a gimlet. Oval in shape, the bar provides a viewing point from every angle as boats sail by, while the clientele strike the perfect New York mix—Lou Reed could sit next to a taxi driver and have a conversation.

1 Late afternoon sun catches curtains

2 Section

3 Evening streetscape

4 Setting sun creates a silhouette through bar shelving and suspended red dot 'logo'

5 Neon backlit shelving unit

1

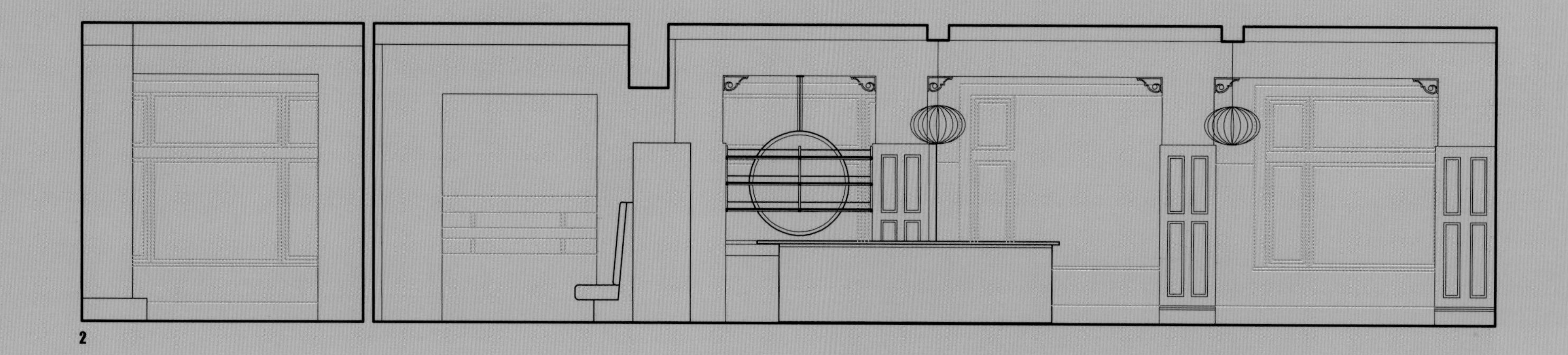

2

ST KILDA, **VICTORIA, AUSTRALIA**

White Bar

GRANT AMON ARCHITECTS PTY LTD

4

3

5

Usage: Bar

Area: 2152 square feet/ 200 square meters

Materials: Stainless steel, existing timber floorboards, rubber, stone

Set within the old George Hotel, a St Kilda landmark since the 1880s, the White Bar and Gallery is a new refit of an existing function room. The bar is centrally located between existing columns with ornate cornicing, and features a backlit circular red Marblo display unit that hovers like a setting sun. The red dot 'logo' is prominent from the streetscape at night providing its own neon signage.

The room is predominantly white, including the bar, acknowledging its gallery function, while the deep reds of the bar top, display shelving, and wall carpeting provide a lush contrast. The entire rear wall has retractable sheer metallic curtains that allow art to be displayed. New George Nelson pendant lights hover over the flexible area that operates as a function room, late-night bar, or gallery space. A separate smaller room is also available for functions or simply an extra lounge area and is notable for its random red tones of striped floor and wall carpet lining.

6

7

8

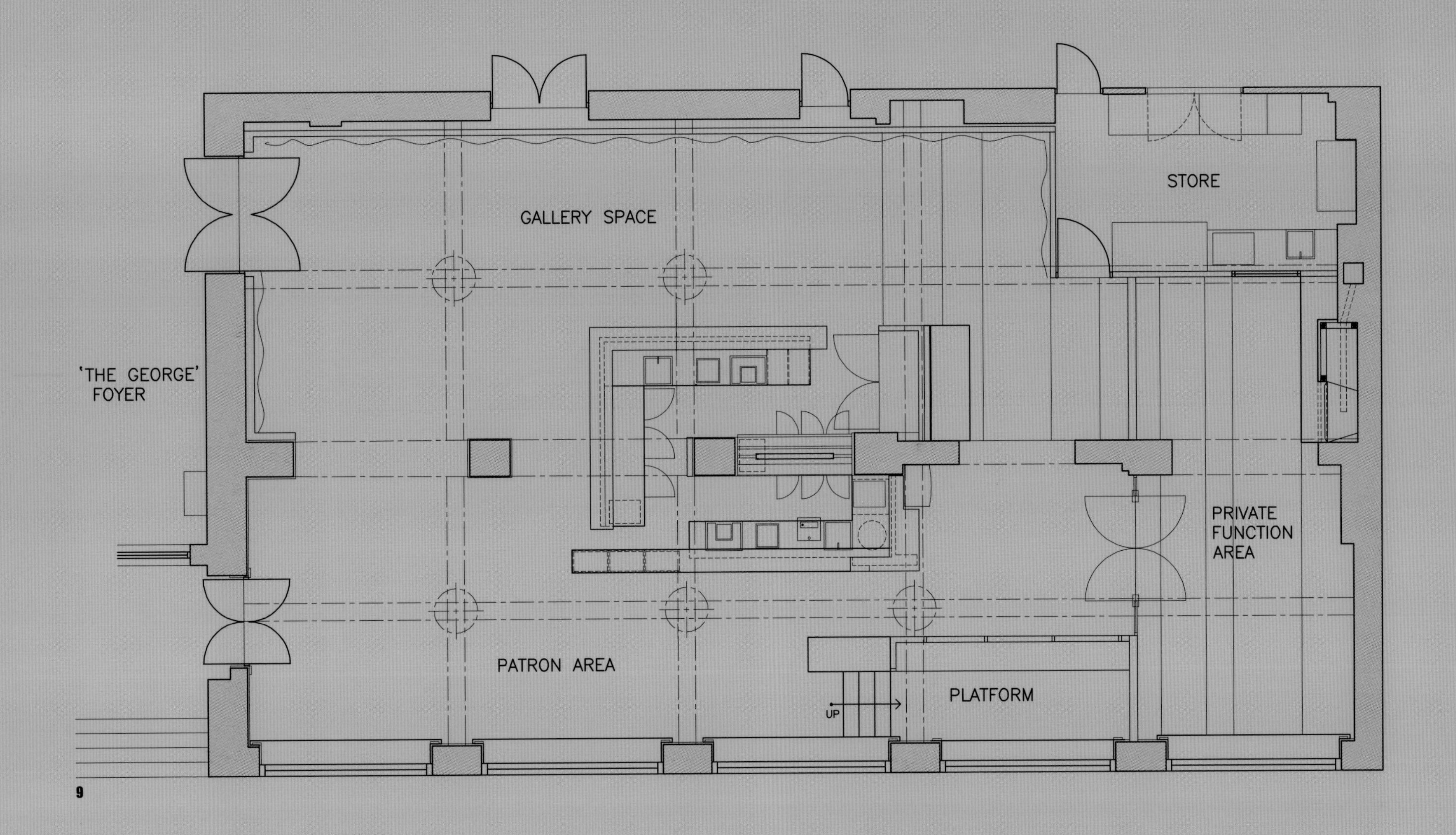

6 Main bar with cantilevered translucent red Marblo bar top and backlit dot

7 Function room

8 Silk thread wall light detail

9 Floor plan

Photography: Trevor Mein

1

2

3

4

TOKYO, **JAPAN**

The Windsor Bar

KISHO KUROKAWA ARCHITECT & ASSOCIATES

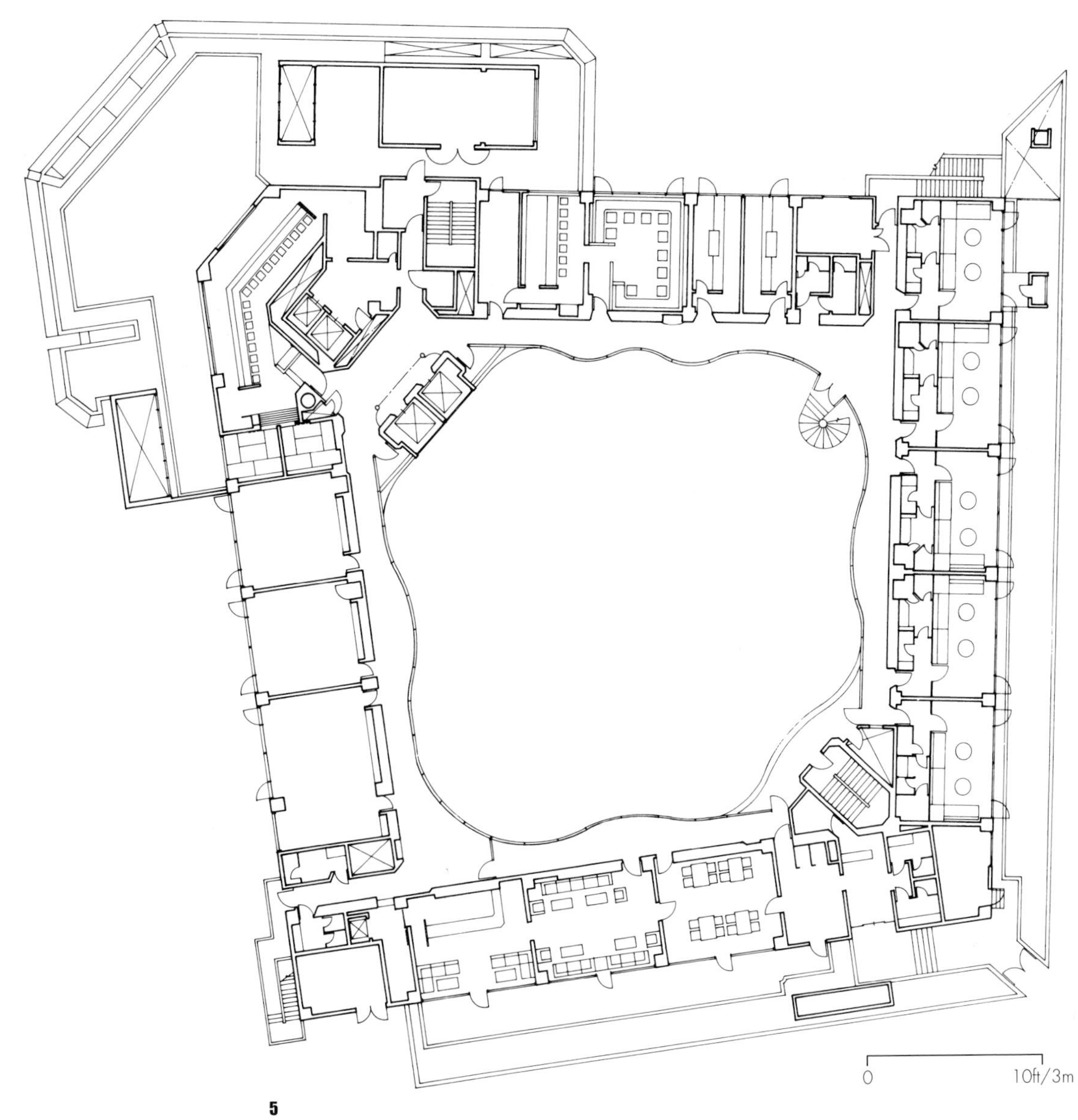

5

Usage: Bar/lounge

Area: 710 square feet/ 66 square meters

The Windsor bar is situated on the third floor of the Roppongi Prince Hotel in Tokyo. The redevelopment of the Roppongi Hills and the construction of the National Art Center (due to be opened in 2006) have contributed to the rise of Roppongi as Tokyo's new cultural center.

The interior space of the Windsor Bar is divided into two areas, the counter bar and lounge bar. The wall of the lounge bar is made up of dark green marble and the area is furnished with a black leather sofa and black tables, finished with traditional Japanese lacquer. In the space between the wall and the ceiling, the architect painted a picture titled *Ruins in the Future*, a homage to M.C. Escher's work, *Other World*.

1 Overall view of hotel

2 Central courtyard pool

3 Undulating wall

4 Approach to entrance

5 Third floor plan

6 Elevator

7,10&11 Ceiling graphic, painted by the architect

8 View from bar

9 Bar

Photography: Tomio Ohashi

6

7

8

9

10

11

1

4

2

3

1 Façade

2 Access to mezzanine

3&4 Bar

5 Main dining area

6 Mezzanine

7 Tables designed by architect

8 Bar detail

9 Mezzanine detail

Photography: João Ribeiro

SÃO PAULO, BRAZIL

Yabany Restaurant

BRUNETE FRACCAROLI

5

6

7

8

9

Usage: Bar/restaurant

Materials: Steel, glass, natural fiber, wood

The architect adopted an amusing play of colors and forms to create a wide, modern, and clean space, resulting in a unique blend of traditional Japanese and contemporary features.

The original building was demolished and a large double-height warehouse was built in its place. Natural lighting enters through the zenithal roof and a glass panel on the façade, creating a warm, and dynamic light that fills the interior. The lighting and color, together with the mix of materials, produce unexpected angles, original forms, and a surprising degree of transparency.

1

2

TORONTO, **ONTARIO, CANADA**

York Event Theatre

II BY IV DESIGN ASSOCIATES

3

4

5

1 Exterior

2 Exterior detail

3 Main lobby

4 Main lobby lounge

5 Stair

Usage: Cocktail bar/events venue

Area: 25,000 square feet/ 2322 square meters

Illumination plays an important role in the exterior and interior aspects of II BY IV's elegant and modish concept for the York renovation. It starts with the use of fiber optics, illuminated signage boxes, and a large video board to add color, light, and movement to the theater's existing monolithic concrete slab face, creating a striking and beacon-like street presence. The large lobby sparkles with white stone flooring, metal wall paneling, illuminated displays filled with glass sculptures, and custom glass drop chandeliers.

Throughout the facility the architects placed illuminated bar features, mirrored walls, ceilings, and display niches, creating a stunning play of light and shadow on unique wood block wall features. Graceful custom furnishings and a palette of taupes and reds add warmth and comfort.

Party organizers find the York Event Theatre an already 'fully-dressed' facility that will demand no additional décor items beyond floral arrangements and the party-goers' own clothing and jewelry. Distinctive, vibrant, and chic, the York Event Theatre will accommodate cocktails for single groups as large as 1800, full banquet service for 800, or smaller combinations across three floors.

6

7

8

9

6 Main floor, main bar

7 Upper-level event bar

8 Main floor, mirror detail

9 Lower-level event bar

10&11 Event level

12 Men's restroom

13 Women's restroom

Photography: David Whittaker

10

12

11

13

Index